Myths of Modernity

Myths of Modernity

Peonage and Patriarchy in Nicaragua

ELIZABETH DORE

DUKE UNIVERSITY PRESS   *Durham and London*   2006

© 2006 Duke University Press

All rights reserved

Printed in the United States

of America on acid-free paper ∞

Designed by Amy Ruth Buchanan

Typeset in Carter & Cone Galliard

by Tseng Information Systems, Inc.

Library of Congress Cataloging-in-

Publication Data appear on the last

printed page of this book.

Frontis: Oscar Prado, *Paisaje de*

Catarina. Pen and ink drawing, 1995.

For Johnny, Matthew, and Rachel

Contents

ix *List of Tables and Illustrations*

xi *Acknowledgments*

1 INTRODUCTION Who Controls the Past Controls the Future

17 ONE Theories of Capitalism, Class, Gender, and Ethnicity

33 TWO Indians under Colonialism and Postcolonialism

53 THREE Patriarchal Power in the Pueblos

69 FOUR The Private Property Revolution

97 FIVE Gendered Contradictions of Liberalism: Ethnicity, Property, and Households

110 SIX Debt Peonage in Diriomo: Forced Labor Revisited

149 SEVEN Patriarchy and Peonage

164 CONCLUSION

172 EPILOGUE History Matters—The Sandinistas' Myth of Modernity

181 *Notes*

213 *Glossary*

217 *Bibliography*

239 *Index*

List of Tables and Illustrations

TABLES

88   1. Distribution of Land in Diriomo, ca. 1900

92   2. Coffee Estates in Department of Granada, 1909–1910

101   3. Distribution of Female Landholding in Diriomo, ca. 1900

173   4. Land Tenure in Nicaragua, 1978–1990

177   5. Changes in Landholding by Small Producer Households,
          Nicaragua, 1978–1990

PHOTOGRAPHS

        All photographs by the author.

90   1. Francisco Salazar, owner of coffee fincas El Amparo and La
          Margarita, ca. 1900.

90   2. Margarita Castillo, wife of Francisco Salazar, ca. 1900.

91   3. Coffee bushes under shade tree, finca on Mombacho Volcano,
          1991.

139   4. Fiesta de la Virgen de la Candelaría, patron saint of Diriomo,
          1995.

139   5. Domingo Dávila, 1993.

140   6. Doroteo Flores Pérez, 1995.

140   7. Teófilo Cano surrounded by his sister and brother, with
          Enrique Rodríguez Ramírez, 1995.

141   8. Carmen Ramírez Pérez, 1991.

141   9. Pedro Pablo Cano and wife, 1991.

142   10. Diriomeña with grandchildren, 1995.

142   11. Teófilo Cano, family, and neighbors in front of his home, 1995.

143   12. Leticia Salazar Castillo, 1995.

157   13. Emilio Vásquez and Orlando Salazar Castillo, 1995.

178   14. La Luz, coffee cooperative on Mombacho Volcano, 1991.

178   15. Rustic choza, 1995.

Acknowledgments

This book is the result of collective efforts. I am indebted to many people in Diriomo, especially Enrique Rodríguez, Margarita Cano, Leticia Salazar, Teófilo Cano, Angela Rodríguez, Gloria Tifer, and the late Carmen Ramírez for their friendship, support, and hospitality. I thank Diriomo's mayors and municipal council not only for permission to use the town archive, but for inviting me to work in the already crowded municipal offices. They demonstrated a degree of trust rare for politicians.

I am very grateful to colleagues at the Instituto de Historia de Nicaragua y Centro América (IHNCA), in particular its director, Margarita Vannini, and Frances Kinloch, who were exceedingly generous with their time, expertise, and research facilities. Alfredo González V., former director of the Archivo Nacional de Nicaragua, first told me about Diriomo's forgotten archive and provided invaluable support over the years, as did Alvaro Argüello of the Instituto Histórico Centroamericano and the staff of the Archivo Municipal in Granada. Many friends and colleagues in Nicaragua helped me in important ways, especially Ivanía Núñez, Alejandro Gutierrez, Malena de Montis, Eduardo Baumeister, Oscar René Vargas, Germán Romero, Judy Butler, and Jimmy Avilés, who early on encouraged my investigation into the hidden history of Granada's coffee barons, including his own ancestors.

I particularly appreciate Steve Topik's enthusiasm for my research; he and Doug Yarrington read the entire manuscript and provided excellent suggestions. Iván Molina did likewise, and the book benefited immensely from his understanding and passion for Central American history. Many other Costa Rican historians, especially Eugenia Rodríguez, Mario Samper, Patricia Alvarenga, Margarita Torres, and Héctor Pérez Brignoli, generously shared their knowledge and research materials. I thank North American scholars Robert Williams, David McCreery, Julie Charlip, Justin Wolfe, Victoria González, Jeffrey Gould, Lowell Gudmundson, Margaret Crahan, and the late great Brad Burns for their insights, generosity, and friendship.

Specialists on gender gave me excellent feedback on earlier incarnations of arguments developed here. I thank Carmen Diana Deere, in particular, as well as Silvia Arrom, Asunción Lavrin, Muriel Nazzari, Carmen Ramos Escandon, Elizabeth Kuznesof, Magdalena León, Maxine Molyneux, Mary Kay Vaughan, Ann Varley, and Fiona Macaulay. My research also benefited from the support of Latin Americanists in Britain, especially John Fisher, Jane Freeland, Alfredo Saad Fihlo, John Lynch, Guy Thomson, Victor Bulmer-Thomas, Rory Miller, Sylvia Chant, David Lehmann, and Rebecca Earle. Tony Campbell, Darren Paffey, and other colleagues at the University of Southampton and the University of Portsmouth provided encouragement and various kinds of material assistance over the years. I thank the Cartographic Unit at the University of Southampton for the map of Nicaragua.

I am deeply grateful to Valerie Millholland, senior editor at Duke University Press, for her excellent advice and ongoing encouragement. She is an editor of the old school whose involvement with authors brings out their best. I also thank Kate Lothman for her excellent work at the copyediting stage.

I thank the Arts and Humanities Research Board (U.K.) and the Fulbright-Hays Fellowship Program (U.S.) for funding this project. I appreciate the smaller grants I received from the British Academy, the American Council of Learned Societies, the American Philosophical Society, the University of Southampton, and the University of Portsmouth.

At crucial points when I got bogged down trying to resolve what seemed an intractable problem, Brooke Larson and Peggy Nelson, two great friends, helped me get on with it.

My husband, John Weeks, and our children, Rachel and Matthew, always encouraged my research and writing. The importance they attributed to this book was invaluable.

Myths of Modernity

N

- cities & municipalities
- △ Mombacho Volcano
- major coffee zones

HONDURAS

Coco River

NICARAGUA

JINOTEGA

CHINANDEGA

LEON

MATAGALPA

Lake
Managua

MANAGUA

Managua

Nindiri   Masaya
Niquinohomo GRANADA
Diria   Granada
Jinotepe   DIRIOMO
CARAZO   Nandaime

Pacific

Lake
Nicaragua

Ocean

San Carlos

El Castillo

Rio San Juan

San Juan
del Norte

0   100 km

COSTA RICA

Nicaragua. Courtesy of the Cartographic Unit, University of Southampton, England.

Who Controls the Past Controls the Future

Who controls the past . . . controls the future; who controls the present, controls the past.
—George Orwell, *Nineteen-Eighty Four*

This book is a metahistory of a small place. It analyzes class, gender, and ethnic upheavals in rural Nicaragua from the colonial period to the twentieth century. My central premise is that class, gender, and ethnicity can be separated theoretically but not experientially.[1] This is a history of Diriomo, a Nicaraguan municipality adjacent to the city of Granada on the plateau of villages known as the Meseta de los Pueblos. The story of Diriomo throws into sharp relief the everyday struggles of ordinary women and men, and it illustrates the Marxist maxim that people's efforts to make history are conditioned by circumstances inherited from the past.[2]

Peasant communities frequently exude an aura of timelessness.[3] Initially, when I proposed to local leaders that I write a history of Diriomo, they told me that nothing had ever happened there. Diriomo was, in their words, a pueblo without history. They suggested that I write about Niquinohomo, Sandino's birthplace, or Masaya, the cradle of the Sandinista Revolution. But, as I suspected, politics and society in the township had changed fundamentally in the previous one hundred years. Before the twentieth century the vast majority of Diriomeños (residents of the township) were Indian, and virtually all land in the pueblo belonged collectively to the men of Diriomo's Indian community (*comunidad indígena*). At that time, class and ethnic differences in Diriomo were modest, but gender differentiation considerable, as Indian women were excluded from the common property regime.

Between 1870 and 1930 Diriomeños' everyday life turned upside down. The state abolished the Indian community. Private property replaced common property. Planters developed large coffee *fincas* (estates) in the township, and a majority of Diriomeños were forced into debt servitude. Unlike the Indians of Matagalpa, who in 1881 took up arms to preserve their way of life, Diriomo's Indians confronted change in a different way; they worked to minimize its disadvantages.[4] Diriomeños accepted ethnic assimilation into the mestizo nation, and they sought to join the private property revolution. By 1930, Diriomo's social order was fundamentally different from before. Out of the indigenous community emerged a society of mestizo peasant proprietors. These upheavals and the ways they transformed class, gender, and ethnic relations in the township is the focus of this study.

Around the turn of the twentieth century, coerced labor laws, landlords' patriarchal power, and growing poverty propelled Diriomeños into debt peonage. Owners of coffee fincas on the Mombacho Volcano, which looms above the township, regularly mobilized the pueblo's women, men, and children to pick coffee. Some Diriomeños were dragged into servitude against their will; others willingly signed up for peonage, their willingness shaped by a labor regime that forced rural men and women to work in plantation agriculture.

The metamorphosis from common to private landed property, from Indian to mestizo, and from freedom to servitude conformed more or less closely to the intentions of Nicaragua's political elite. However, another social transformation was not intentional nor noticed by contemporary observers and historians. Abolition of Indian communities freed females from gendered constraints of customary laws that excluded women from land rights. This change was closely felt in Diriomo; after abolition, many poor women acquired property for the first time. Contrary to the prevailing historical view that females rarely were peasant proprietors in Latin America, at the turn of the twentieth century in Diriomo female land ownership was pronounced in the poorer strata of the peasantry.[5]

This book analyzes changes in the sexual division of land and labor and transformations in the social dynamics of gender. I call planter-peon relations *patriarchy from above* and senior male domination in peasant households *patriarchy from below*.[6] One of my central arguments is that debt peonage persisted in Diriomo because it was part of a patriarchal system that combined coercion and consent. Patriarchy was not simply an aspect of gender culture; planters' power over peons was shored up by laws extending senior male authority from the household domain to the plantation sector. One of the major conclusions of this study is that patriarchal class relations impeded capitalist development.

Although the power of the patriarch is an old trope in Latin American history, until recently its gendered character rarely was examined. Building on the work of others, this book contributes to a rich literature that analyzes the gendered dynamics of patriarchy in Latin America.[7] I demonstrate that gender relations were fundamental to the transformation of Diriomo's social order. Consequently, it is impossible to understand the class character of local society without taking gender into account.

Latin American historians have argued that the rise of coffee production set in motion capitalist development across the region. Many describe the combination of land privatization, liberalism, and economic growth that accompanied the coffee boom as Latin America's capitalist transition.[8] Evidence from Diriomo reveals a different history. There the rise of private property and forced labor was part of a great transformation, but not to capitalism. In the era from 1870 to 1930, class relations between coffee planters and debt peons were regulated directly through the exercise of patriarchal forms of coercion and consent, not indirectly by market mechanisms. It is not that the rise of private property and forced labor had nothing to do with the eventual capitalist transformation of the countryside; privatization and peonage overturned old ways of combining land, labor, and power. But struggles between coffee planters and peons over what would replace the old ways produced power relations, patterns of landholding, and a labor system that hindered more than accelerated the emergence of a bourgeois (i.e., capitalist) order. To inscribe Nicaraguan history between 1870 and 1930 within the framework of capitalist development obscures what took place. Capitalism rests on the mass separation of subsistence producers from the land; its development undermines nonmarket relations, and capitalist class dynamics are defined by the buying and selling of labor power, free wage labor. In Diriomo, the coffee revolution accomplished none of these. It gave birth to individual peasant proprietorship; it institutionalized forced labor and fortified, rather than undermined, nonmarket patriarchal relations. Taken together, these impeded more than promoted capitalist development.

The book's central thesis, its red thread, is that the transformation of Diriomo's social order from 1870 to 1930 impeded capitalist development. One of the central hypotheses of this study is that capitalism represents a unique way of organizing property, labor, and market relations. To underpin my historical argument I examine theories of agrarian capitalist development. Notwithstanding my theoretical proposition that capitalist and noncapitalist societies have fundamentally different social structures, in modern times most societies contain elements of both. The challenge is to understand the dynamics of a particular society, the nature of the prevailing or dominant social relations and how they interact with other social forms. In other words, all social systems are hybrids of one sort or another in which different, sometimes antagonistic, class, gender, and ethnic relations coexist, commingle, and collide. Through this account of Diriomo's historical transformation, I endeavor to illustrate the interplay among forces promoting and retarding capitalist modernization and to explain how these tensions combined to form the fabric of a noncapitalist society.

Capitalism is not a local phenomenon; its development forges national and international markets in commodities and labor power. Consequently, this historical analysis of Diriomo does not pretend to be national history of late capitalist development in Nicaragua. My purpose is to understand the nature of social change in one coffee-producing zone from 1870 to 1930, the era frequently defined as the triumph of Nicaragua's bourgeois revolution.[9] This is a local history, and the micromethod has advantages and disadvantages. Local history facilitates detailed study of how people are drawn into, come to understand, and struggle to alter the matrix of social relations in which they find themselves, but local studies also raise thorny questions about representation. Does micro history provide a window only on a singular place and time, or does it facilitate broader interpretations of historical change? This dilemma festered in my mind from the project's start to its finish. I finally concluded that counterposing micro to macro history is a false dichotomy. Detailed study of one region provides conceptual tools and empirical findings that facilitate interpretations of, and comparisons with, a wider historical landscape.[10] Fortunately, this book is embedded within an extraordinarily rich Central American historiography that analyzes the ways different regions were drawn into the vortex of the international economy by way of coffee production.[11] In the conclusion, I compare my findings with studies of other parts of Central America. Finally, although this local study rarely touches on U.S. imperialism and the country's long neocolonial relationship with Washington, repeated U.S. interventions altered the course of Nicaraguan history.[12]

Social and ideological conflicts in Diriomeños' and Diriomeñas' everyday lives played out against the backdrop of Nicaraguan and Central American politics more broadly. The chronic divide that rent the Nicaraguan elite took the form of party conflicts between Liberals and Conservatives. The rift gave rise to numerous coups d'état and civil wars over the course of the nineteenth and early twentieth centuries, struggles that undermined the country's political stability over the long term. Yet, paradoxically, on a range of fundamental political issues, the warring factions more or less agreed. In the period from 1870 to 1930, with some exceptions at the margins, elite Liberals and Conservatives aspired to replace common property rights with private property. Successive governments of both political persuasions introduced laws aimed at dissolving Indian communities and eliminating communal landholding. Although often at war with one another, the country's elites more or less shared the belief that private property would promote a modern form of agriculture and bring an end to traditional encumbrances that had long constrained investment, commerce, and growth. Somewhat incongruously, the elites' banner was "Freedom of property," though they sought to abolish the majority's free access to land for household production and consumption. In its stead, they advocated the classical liberal concept of freedom: individual freedom to buy and sell private landed property for profit-making purposes.

With the rise of coffee plantations, Nicaraguan landowners regularly complained that peasants preferred idleness and leisure over hard work. But their dichotomy was a false one; rural households tended to devote their energies to household production for consumption instead of to coffee picking on planters' fincas. To resolve this problem, successive governments enacted a mountain of laws designed to make peasants work for commercial planters. With some exceptions, which I discuss later, leading Liberals and Conservatives supported policies designed to draw rural people into the labor force for export agriculture. Their partisan differences centered less on whether the poor should be made to work than on how best to accomplish their aims.

Nicaraguan political leaders' faith in the transformative power of the coffee industry was shared throughout Central and Latin America. From the spread of coffee production across the continent in the mid-nineteenth century to the spectacular crash in world market prices in 1930, coffee cultivation in countries as diverse as Brazil, Venezuela, Colombia, and the Central American republics contributed to export growth, expansion in the size and reach of the nation-state, regularization of a rural labor force, construction of ports, railroads, and telegraphs, and the rise of financial institutions. To Latin politicians and landowners these changes represented the march of progress. To many ordinary people, they represented a threat to their way of life.

Symbols of modernity have tended to go hand in hand with capitalist development, yet the two are not the same thing. The understanding of capitalism that underpins this study, and which I elaborate in chapter 1, is twofold: capitalist societies are regulated by competitive markets, and the sine qua non, the indispensable condition, for capitalism is the predominance of free wage labor.[13] Although capitalist societies contain scores of additional features, market regulation and free wage labor are their defining dynamics. Accordingly, it is possible to have features of modernity without capitalism, but impossible to have capitalism without features of modernity. Powerful examples in our time of modernity without capitalism are Saudi Arabia and the Arab emirates.

The prehistory of this book dates from the 1980s. Soon after the Frente Sandinista de Liberación Nacional (FSLN) swept to power in 1979 on a wave of popular insurrections against the Somoza dictatorship, I went to Nicaragua to work for the new government. I had been invited to direct a research project in the Ministry of Internal Commerce (MICOIN) on the production and distribution of basic foodstuffs, a project meant to address the increasingly fraught relationship between the Sandinista government and peasant producers.[14] Traveling throughout Nicaragua to interview producers of corn, beans, and rice, I was met with hostility, but not because I was a *gringa* from the country whose president was trying to overthrow the Sandinistas. Rural producers distrusted me because I was from MICOIN. They blamed the Sandinistas for depressing producer prices to benefit the urban population, and they referred to MICOIN's staff as "the rural police." In the months I spent criss-crossing the country I interviewed people who were angry at the government, not only because of its pricing policy but also because the FSLN refused to give them land. Under the Agrarian Reform Laws of 1979 and 1981 the government confiscated properties of the Somoza family and its allies, but instead of distributing land directly to peasant households, the Sandinistas created state farms and production cooperatives.[15] Most rural producers opposed the agrarian reform and organized demonstrations calling for land to the tiller; nevertheless, the Sandinistas refused to distribute land to the peasantry.

My work drew me into one of the major debates of the Sandinista Revolution concerning the class nature of Nicaraguan society and its implications for agrarian reform. The Sandinista leadership initially opposed land distribution for pragmatic as well as ideological reasons. On the pragmatic side, they attempted to maintain an alliance with sectors of the landed bourgeoisie who feared empowering the peasantry. On the ideological side, they believed that converting proletarians into peasants through a land distribution program would in effect turn back the historical clock from modernizing agrarian capitalism to traditional peasant production.[16] Leaders of the FSLN maintained that in the nineteenth century coffee planters expropriated the peasantry and forged a rural proletariat (a class of landless laborers), and these events precipitated Nicaragua's bourgeois revolution. Drawing on this vision of the past, the FSLN leadership advocated a state-centered agrarian reform that would create conditions for the development of socialism.

It is frequently said that politicians rewrite history, yet rarely has the connection between history writing and policymaking been as close as in the Sandinista government. Jaime Wheelock Román, the architect of the Sandinistas' agrarian policy, was also the country's preeminent historian. Wheelock's seminal book, *Imperialismo y dictadura: Crisis de una formación social*, is an interpretation of Nicaragua's transition to capitalism. It argues that early coffee planters became agrarian capitalists by violently forcing workers to accept low wages to increase their profits. As a consequence, agrarian capitalism developed rapidly and the coffee bourgeoisie seized state power at the turn of the twentieth century. In Wheelock's account, the government of President José Santos Zelaya (1893–1909) represented the triumph of the bourgeois revolution. After setbacks in the years 1910 to 1940, occasioned by U.S. occupation and the Great Depression, capitalism developed to a mature stage. Its hallmark was the emergence of finance capital out of a fusion between banking and productive capital in the cotton industry. Wheelock concluded that by the 1970s, one hundred years of capitalist development had forged the social and material conditions for socialism in Nicaragua.

Imperialismo y dictadura is a classic text in Central American history and widely read as the authoritative account of Nicaragua's capitalist transition. However, unlike most historical monographs, it was written as a political manifesto, to convince members of the FSLN that Nicaragua was ripe for socialist revolution. In the introduction Wheelock states, "This book . . . was conceived, organized and written as part of a militant political struggle . . . [within the FSLN over the class nature of Nicaraguan society and its implications for revolutionary strategy]."[17] In 1976, the Frente split into three factions: one believed the FSLN should ally with sectors of the upper and middle classes to form a united democratic front against the Somoza dictatorship. The faction headed by Wheelock argued that because capitalism was mature, the FSLN should lead the working classes in a socialist revolution instead of allying with the dominant classes; another group called for a prolonged peasant war.[18] Notwithstanding their differences, *Imperialismo y dictadura* became the Sandinistas' official story. The Sandinista leadership recognized the importance of history, and days after coming to power they created the Instituto de Estudios de Sandinismo, a center of historical research. They shared with George Orwell the conviction that "who controls the past . . . controls the future; who controls the present, controls the past."[19]

Inside the new government, policymakers in the Ministry of Agriculture and Agrarian Reform disagreed about the nature of capitalist development and its implications for rural policy. Wheelock headed the Ministry and drew on historical studies to argue that because Nicaragua had long been polarized into the classes of modern bourgeois society, the rural poor predominantly had a proletarian consciousness. Consequently, they aspired to better wages and working conditions, not individual plots of land, he maintained.[20] Reflecting this interpretation of past and present, the Ministry under Wheelock's command implemented an agrarian reform that favored state farms.

Other specialists in the same Ministry, working at the Centro de Investigaciones y Estudios de la Reforma Agraria, criticized the FSLN's rural policy. In their view, agrarian capitalism had developed from below through social differentiation of the peasantry. This historical process gave rise to an agrarian structure dominated by medium-size capitalists and semiproletarians (a class that straddled the peasantry and the rural working class). Building on this interpretation, they argued that rural people in the main had a peasant consciousness and wanted land for small-scale production and consumption. Accordingly, they advocated a pro-peasant agrarian reform and distribution of land to rural households.

However, events on the ground quickly overtook the policy debate. Increasingly disaffected with government promotion of state farms and a food policy that rested on low prices to producers, many peasants joined the *contras*, a paramilitary force funded by the U.S. government to overthrow the Sandinistas.[21] In 1986, to win the allegiance of the peasantry, the Sandinistas reversed their agrarian policy and began to distribute land to peasant households. But the change came too late. The FSLN never regained peasant support, and as the contra war dragged on, their popularity in the countryside plummeted. In the 1990 presidential elections, a majority of the rural population voted against the FSLN in part because of its agrarian policies, in part because of the economic collapse precipitated by the contra war, and in part because of a widely unpopular military draft.[22]

I left Nicaragua in 1984, planning to return soon to examine the history of class relations in a coffee-producing zone. As it happened, I did not begin research for this book until the 1990s. In the intervening years, persuaded by theoretical debates about gender, race, and ethnicity, I concluded that a focus on class was necessary, but insufficient, to understand social transformations in the countryside. I decided to study Diriomo because in the nineteenth century Granada's oligarchs established large coffee plantations in the municipality, turning the Mombacho Volcano into a small but prized coffee zone. There was another reason to study Diriomo, but I did not know it at first. The pueblo had had an active comunidad indígena, but it ceased to function around 1910. After abolition, Diriomeños never again organized as Indians or called for the reconstitution of their comunidad.[23] Figuring out why Diriomo's comunidad indígena disappeared became an important part of my project. However, when I first visited the township of some twenty-three thousand people, the only inkling I had of Diriomo's indigenous past was a faded billboard outside town that announced *Diriomo: Pueblo de los Brujos* (Pueblo of Witches and Sorcerers).[24]

An additional reason to focus my study on Diriomo was that I had been told there was a large collection of historical documents in the town hall.[25] Following this lead, I found great bundles of papers from the middle of the nineteenth to the middle of the twentieth century stuffed helter-skelter into bags in the municipal storeroom. Later I discovered that Diriomo's municipal archive had survived because successive officials had failed to send their records to the national archive.[26] Other local authorities had complied, and their archives were destroyed when the national archive, el Archivo General de la República, was consumed in the great fire following the Managua earthquake of 1931.

Although at first the disorder of what I call here the Archivo Municipal de Diriomo was a liability, it turned out to be an asset. To make sense of the chaotic documentation, I was drawn into constant dialogue between oral history and the written word. Several Diriomeños helped me organize and transcribe labor contracts, property records, transcripts of court cases, official correspondence, minutes of meetings of Diriomo's *junta municipal*—in short, virtually all the official and much unofficial paperwork generated in the municipality over the course of a century. As we worked at a table in the modest town hall, word spread that I had found long lost land records. Many Diriomeños sought me out to locate old property titles and information about their ancestors. Together we read the relevant documents, prompting people to recount disputes over land and labor and their memories of the past. In addition to these spontaneous, self-selected encounters, I conducted life histories with fifty men and women I chose for their role in Diriomo's history: landowners, politicians, priests, merchants, labor organizers, peasants, peons, artisans, teachers, notaries, feminist activists, midwives, and brujos. In addition, a group of younger Diriomeños organized informal get-togethers where I described my discoveries from the archive and they recounted the stories handed down in the pueblo. This ongoing give-and-take between oral history, memory, and the written word enabled me to understand far more about local history than I could have gleaned from reading documents preserved in an archive at some distance, spatially or spiritually, from Diriomeños' daily lives.

There has been a major shift in scholarly approaches to oral history.[27] In the 1960s, with the intention of writing history from below, historians used oral sources to gather information about people who had been hidden by history. However, the postmodern turn brought a reappraisal of the status of oral sources; many historians held that because memories are highly subjective, they speak only to the realm of consciousness and ideology. At the extreme, some have said that it is naïve realism to think that oral history contributes to understanding what happened in the past. Followers of this approach believe that oral sources should be read primarily for their discursive, textual quality.

Starting from the premise that all historical sources are subjective, and all in different ways, I used life history interviews both to understand why people give different meanings to the past *and* to gain knowledge about what happened in the past. Oral sources are partial and highly subjective interpretations of the past filtered through the present and mediated by the interlocutor. I do not pretend that Diriomeños' testimonies supply facts. My aim was to elicit from the life histories an understanding of the dynamics of social structures and relations in Diriomo, as well as of people's perceptions of the past. In other words, my method seeks to bridge the epistemological divide between oral history as recovery and oral history as a variant on cultural psychology.

Gradually I realized that the apparent disjuncture between oral and documentary sources was not a difficulty to be ironed out, but a cue that alerted me to contradictions I needed to pursue. The oral histories of men and women who had worked as peons on the coffee estates in the early twentieth century altered my initial view of debt peonage. From a reading of debt peonage contracts with onerous terms and conditions, magistrates' descriptions of punishments they meted out to delinquent peons, and texts of successive forced labor laws, I gained the sense that peonage rested singularly on coercion. So, initially, I regarded oral histories with former peons as an opportunity to learn more about the coercive character of the labor regime. In narrating their life histories, Diriomeños described the violence of debt peonage but also their pursuit of a long-term relationship with a good *patrón*. In the beginning, I was deaf to part of their narratives.[28] I focused on the oppressive aspects of debt peonage, but when people's memories turned to patriarchal relations, to the favors and material benefits they hoped to receive from their patrón, often I wondered whether these accounts portrayed false consciousness. At one point, I told Enrique Rodríguez, who accompanied me on my hikes into the *caseríos* (rural hamlets), that I already had enough information about patronage and clientelism. I asked if he knew people whose memories of peonage focused on its coercive side. However, Diriomeños' accounts of peonage gradually altered my interpretation of the labor regime. Many people described how they and their parents attempted to nurture a long-term relationship with a patrón who might help them survive the vicissitudes of peasant life. They talked about *socorro* (succor) and *ayuda* (assistance). With these words ringing in my ears I reread transcripts of court cases between planters and peons and paid closer attention to parts of testimonies that had escaped my attention.

As a result of the interaction between oral history and the written word, my interpretation of peonage changed. Whereas initially I thought that the labor regime was almost exclusively coercive, later I concluded that peonage combined coercion and consent, and that this accounted in part for its resilience. At that time I was reading Steve J. Stern's *The Secret History of Gender*, and his analysis of patriarchal relations in Mexico influenced my thinking. However, in contrast to Stern's emphasis on gender culture, understood primarily as discourses and contested languages of argument, I emphasize, whenever possible, the material and legal foundations of patriarchy.[29]

Over the years, I returned frequently to Diriomo, and in the interim the project changed as the result of a fruitful interaction between what I learned about the pueblo's history and scholarly debates. Although my central objective remained largely the same—to understand transformations in rural society—I expanded my initial focus on class to include analysis of gender and ethnicity.

From early on, Jeffrey Gould's interpretation of the myth of *mestizaje* (assimilation) in Nicaragua influenced my thinking.[30] His emphasis on the resilience of Indian identity and memories of forced mestizaje made me think long and hard about why Diriomo seemed so different from the communities he studied. Following land privatization, I came across few references to Indians in Diriomo. Of course, their absence from the official record in part reflected state policy to assimilate Indians, sometimes called "killing Indians by decree." However, and more enigmatically, few Diriomeños I interviewed knew anything about the comunidad indígena. Furthermore, unlike Gould, I found no evidence, written or oral, that Indian identity inspired struggles over land, labor, political rights, or human dignity in the twentieth century. Consequently, it became clear that the important issues to investigate were why Diriomo's comunidad indígena disappeared and how its memory was suppressed.

This history is told, wherever possible, by men and women of Diriomo. The words of peons, planters, and local officials who lived a century ago have survived in court records, official correspondence, estate papers, and the veritable mountain of paperwork generated by the forced labor regime. Alongside voices from the past, contemporary Diriomeños' life histories contain memories and stories handed down from the epoch of the coffee boom to the present. The diversity of voices, past and present, vividly portrays the dilemmas of everyday life in a community where relations of land and labor, gender and ethnicity were radically transformed in the era when coffee was king.

It is necessary to clarify at the outset several conceptual and terminological issues. The first concerns Diriomeños' ethnicity. Throughout the colonial period and until land privatization altered class, gender, and ethnic relations in the late nineteenth century, the vast majority of Diriomeños were Indian. According to the census of 1883, 74 percent of the population of Diriomo was Indian, and the rest (26 percent) were *mulattos* and *zambos*, people of African and Afro-Indian descent.[31]

But the census obscured the most important ethnic dynamic in the township: the divide between Indians and non-Indians. Although to official eyes, Diriomo's non-Indians were of mixed African descent, that identity played no role in the life of the community. The ethnic identity that counted was Indians' access to common land rights of the comunidad indígena, and non-Indians' exclusion. Within the township, ethnicity was predominantly a signifier of material difference in the form of access to land, not of cultural or biological difference. Diriomo's artisans, traders, and local elite of rich peasants and budding commercial planters were, with few exceptions, not Indian. When these people described themselves in ethnic terms, though they did so rarely, they did not call themselves mulatto but *mestizo*, a category broadly applied to people of mixed Indian and Spanish (or "white") unions. This label represented an aspirational identity, as the Granada oligarchs also tended to describe themselves as mestizo.[32] To emphasize the significance of the Indian/non-Indian divide in Diriomo, and to avoid census categories that played no role in the social life of the community, I use the term *ladino* to refer to the non-Indians, a term widely used in Nicaragua and the rest of Central America to indicate people broadly defined as not Indian.[33] However, after abolition of the comunidad and common land rights, the distinction between Indian and not-Indian gradually lost its significance in Diriomo. Over time, all Diriomeños and Diriomeñas came to think of themselves simply as Nicaraguan.

Following Spanish convention, *ladino*, *indio*, and Diriomeño refer to men, *ladina*, *india*, and Diriomeña to women. To overcome gender discrimination in language and thought, when referring to groups comprising both men and women in the pueblo, I alternate between Diriomeños and Diriomeñas. When I refer to Nicaragua I mean the western or Pacific side of the country, that is, excluding the Atlantic Coast. In many ways, the two parts of the country were and remain separate nations.[34] Finally, I have written this book not only with the broad community of scholars in mind, but for a wider audience interested in Nicaragua and the roots of the Sandinista Revolution. Therefore, whenever possible, I have put the scholarly architecture into footnotes.

Structure of Presentation

Chapter 1, "Theories of Capitalism, Class, Gender, and Ethnicity," elaborates theoretical arguments about the distinguishing features of capitalism, patriarchy, and ethnicity. Following a discussion of what theory is, I survey major Marxist debates about capitalist development and underdevelopment. Drawing on the writings of Karl Polanyi, Robert Brenner, and James C. Scott, I analyze differences between markets in capitalist and noncapitalist societies and the nature of landlord-peasant societies. I then treat theoretical arguments about gender and patriarchy, where I draw on, but modify, Joan Scott's definition of gender and Steve J. Stern's theses about patriarchal authority. Finally, examining theories of ethnicity and mestizaje, including Jeffrey Gould's contributions, I explore pressures within ethnic groups that undermine cohesion.

Chapter 2, "Indians under Colonialism and Postcolonialism," traces the history of Diriomo and other Indian communities in the Granada region from the conquest to the middle of the nineteenth century. My purpose is to understand the dynamics of Indian society before the abolition of Indian communities and land privatization fundamentally altered Diriomo's landscape and society. I develop two key arguments. First, population collapse and social dislocation weakened cultural markers of Indianness in the pueblos surrounding Granada. By the nineteenth century, Indian identity was predominantly defined by common land rights and subjugation to forced labor. Second, the structure of rule in colonial and postcolonial Nicaragua perpetuated conflict between Indian leaders and ordinary *comuneros* (members of the Indian community). The chapter explores the riots that shook the region in the 1840s. Extrapolating from primary and secondary sources, I argue that opposition to land privatization fueled rebellion in the Granada region. I describe the riots' repercussions in Diriomo and official attitudes toward Indian leaders. In Diriomo, the riots represented the Indians' last stand. Never again did Indians and poor ladinos and ladinas fight against land privatization.

✗   Chapter 3, "Patriarchal Power in the Pueblos," argues that following Independence, in the virtual absence of a nation-state, local state making was to a remarkable degree gender politics. Men of Diriomo's rich peasantry, the ladino elite, accumulated political power by regulating gender. I describe how elite ladinos sought to impose a double morality on women of the pueblo, one for richer ladinas, another for indias, and how poorer men and women resisted the expanded reach of municipal rule.

Chapter 4, "The Private Property Revolution," argues that land privatization fundamentally altered the landscape and society in Diriomo but did not dispossess the peasantry. The private property revolution all but ended Indians' common land rights and gave birth to a heterogeneous landed peasantry that coexisted uneasily with large coffee plantations. I describe how rich Granadans used their power and influence to appropriate peasant property, how Indian leaders collaborated with local officials to regulate the privatization of land, and how Diriomeños and Diriomeñas gradually accepted the private property regime. The chapter ends with an examination of the pattern of land tenure in the pueblo at the cusp of the twentieth century, when common land rights had all but disappeared and private property was the norm.

Chapter 5, "Gendered Contradictions of Liberalism: Ethnicity, Property, and Households," traces the multiple and sometimes contradictory effects of liberalism, understood in a broad sense, on gender relations in Diriomo. In contrast to the prevailing view that liberalism ushered in progress for women, I argue that liberal reforms to marriage and property laws had regressive as well as progressive gendered effects. On the positive side, the elimination of male common property rights benefited Indian women as they acquired rights to own and control private property in land. On the negative side, measures that undermined women's guarantees to an equal portion of family property and wealth seem to have diminished female land-owning in the upper peasantry. At the turn of the twentieth century, 14 percent of property owners were women. Although female ownership was largely concentrated in the lower ranks of the peasantry, data from Diriomo challenge the prevailing view that females were all but excluded from peasant proprietorship in rural Latin America.

Chapter 6, "Debt Peonage in Diriomo: Forced Labor Revisited," analyzes laws requiring the rural poor to work in plantation labor and the everyday practices of debt peonage in Diriomo. It examines, in particular, labor contracting, methods of policing the labor regime, and peasant resistance. I argue that structurally debt peonage was a forced labor regime; nevertheless, in Diriomo planters deployed consensual as well as coercive practices to forge a labor force for the coffee sector. By design, peonage was a class-based system; however, there is some evidence that in Diriomo discrimination against Indians played a part in its everyday operation. In contrast to the prevailing view of Latin American peonage, I argue that in Granada debt peonage impeded more than facilitated capitalist development in the countryside. Although privatization and plantation agriculture destroyed old relations of land and labor, in the new agrarian order labor was not a commodity, it was not freely bought and sold.

Chapter 7, "Patriarchy and Peonage," examines the ways patriarchal privileges were reworked to fortify planters' control over the peasantry. It describes the ways planters' control over the peasantry and peons' acceptance of their authority were conditioned by gendered understandings of social norms. I investigate the double-sided class character of patriarchy: the patriarchal powers of planters and of male peasants. The former I call patriarchy from above, the latter, patriarchy from below. Patriarchy was double-sided in a second sense: it coupled senior male control over female and male sub-ordinates with responsibilities to protect them. The chapter traces conflicts between planters and peons over patriarchal privileges and obligations, and concludes that patriarchy was central to the longevity of debt peonage in Diriomo.

The conclusion draws out connections between the theoretical framework and the history of Diriomo. In light of my findings about social change in the pueblo, I reassess theories of capitalist development, patriarchy, and mestizaje. This discussion compares my conclusions with other studies from the region to highlight the ways Diriomo's history was typical and atypical of social change in Nicaragua.

The Sandinistas' portrayal of themselves, and of the nation's history, rested on the thesis that Nicaragua's capitalist transition occurred in the late nineteenth century. When the Sandinistas came to power in 1979, agrarian policy reflected this view. The FSLN promoted state farms and refused to distribute land to the peasantry prior to 1985, in part because they believed that peasant production was anachronistic, a legacy of premodern social relations virtually eliminated a century earlier. However, widespread demand for land distribution belied that historical view. Peasants opposed the Sandinistas' state-centered agrarian reform, leading some to support the contras. In the end, peasant opposition played a part in the Sandinistas' electoral defeat in 1990. The epilogue, and the book as a whole, aim to demonstrate that history matters. Possibly, if the Sandinistas' official history had not emphasized the capitalist character of rural society, the leadership might have listened to voices in the countryside demanding land before U.S. military intervention turned into civil war.

CHAPTER ONE

Theories of Capitalism, Class, Gender, and Ethnicity

At the turn of the twentieth century class, gender, and ethnic upheavals radically altered Diriomeños' everyday lives. In the years between 1870 and 1930 the state abolished common property to promote private property, Indian comuneros became ladino peasant proprietors, Diriomeños and Diriomeñas were drawn into debt peonage, and the rise of private landed property had contradictory gendered effects. A patriarchal duality underpinned the social order. Patriarchy from above, coffee planters' patriarchal power, regulated class and gender relations in the plantation economy. Patriarchy from below, the senior male's familial authority, governed household relations in the peasantry. In addition, privatization ended males' common land rights on the one hand, but extended property rights to Indian women on the other. The new social order that emerged in Diriomo was the product of political intention, social struggle, and forces beyond anyone's control.

My interpretation of social change in Diriomo in the era frequently described as Nicaragua's capitalist transition rests on a set of theoretical understandings about the nature of capitalism, class, gender, and ethnicity. This chapter sets out the theories that underpin the study, some drawn from explicitly theoretical literature, others from complementary historical studies. Theory is not only useful, it is necessary to explain the manifold social forces at work at a particular place and time. Historical research throws up masses of information about events, people, places, perceptions, and ideologies. Without a theoretical framework, a thesis or argument about dynamics of social change, it is impossible to make sense of the messiness of everyday life. Theory is developed by distilling patterns from the wealth of historical particulars, and the patterns facilitate analysis of historical transformation.

This process allows researchers to compare empirical findings to theoretical hypotheses and thereby assess whether research conclusions support or contradict the theoretical argument. My research for this book began with a set of theoretical hypotheses about the dynamics of capitalism, class, gender, and ethnicity. In the process of research I held up empirical findings to the light of theory and evaluated the degree to which the former fit the latter. In the conclusion I draw out connections between the theoretical frameworks and my interpretation of historical change in Diriomo.

The first section of this chapter reviews controversies about capitalist development in the colonial and neocolonial world and presents a definition of class. Drawing largely on Karl Polanyi's conceptual distinction between the role of markets in capitalist and noncapitalist societies, I argue that the question of capitalist transition turns on the nature of markets, in particular on the presence or absence of markets in labor. The next section rehearses theories of patriarchy and gender that influenced my interpretation of historical change, particularly Steve Stern's thesis that gendered understandings of patriarchal relations sustain political authority over the long term. Building on Joan Scott's classic definition of gender, I emphasize the materiality of gender relations and explain why gender analysis is fundamental to understanding society. The third section analyzes theories of ethnicity and mestizaje, understood as social (as opposed to biological) processes of Indian assimilation into a society's dominant Hispanic cultural patterns. Recent historical literature has tended to emphasize cohesive forces within Indian communities that fortify resistance to mestizaje. However, finding mounting evidence that Diriomeños and Diriomeñas largely accepted ethnic integration, I considered theories that explore divisive forces in ethnic politics and the undoing of community.

Capitalism and Class

TRANSITION DEBATES

Classic debates about imperialism and colonialism long centered on the nature and timing of capitalist development. Broadly speaking, in the first half of the twentieth century leading socialist scholars argued that the countries of Latin America, Africa, and Asia were underdeveloped because they were not capitalist. Their arguments rested on the premise that capitalism unleashes social forces and technological changes that accelerate industrialization and growth. In the second half of the century, many radical scholars turned that analysis upside down and argued that underdeveloped countries have long been capitalist. They concluded, therefore, that capitalism, not its absence, blocked development. The second paradigm dominated Latin American studies from the 1960s to the 1980s.[1] My purpose here is not to resurrect those debates, but to situate this book within the major currents in Marxist historiography.[2]

The Comintern, a world federation of communist parties founded in the 1920s by the Bolshevik Party of the USSR, held that the countries of Latin America, Africa, and Asia were predominantly feudal. Feudal, in this sense, meant societies ruled by landlord and merchant classes whose power and wealth derived from exploiting subordinate classes by coercive, nonmarket means. Leading scholars inside and outside the communist tradition argued that forced labor was the antithesis of capitalism; therefore, elimination of overt coercion was a precondition for capitalist development.[3] In line with this interpretation, the Comintern propounded a formula for two-stage revolution—first capitalist, then socialist—for the liberation of colonial and neocolonial countries. Notwithstanding its stagism and rigidity, the Comintern's official interpretation of Marxism influenced development theory well beyond the communist movement.

In the 1960s a revolution in scholarship overturned the classic Marxist view of imperialism and colonialism.[4] A new generation of socialist scholars argued that with the expansion of empire, markets, and trade, capitalism had developed throughout the world.[5] Their revision rested on a major reconceptualization of the nature of capitalism. In classic Marxism, the distinctive feature of capitalism is the particular form of class exploitation: the appropriation of surplus value from free wage laborers in production.[6] In the revised version, the distinguishing feature of capitalism is the spread of exchange relations through global trade.

The paradigm shift gave rise to two major intellectual currents: dependency theory and world systems theory. I suggest, however, that the two can best be understood as a theme with variations. The theme is that international trade and the expansion of capitalism are the self-same process. The variations are that (1) capitalism is a relationship among countries in which surplus is appropriated from one country by another, and (2) European trade spread capitalism throughout the world. In this paradigm, surplus appropriation through trade caused underdevelopment in the colonies and neocolonies and development in the imperialist countries.[7]

A third way in the capitalism controversy attracted scholars who rejected the dichotomy between precapitalist and capitalist societies. They empha-sized the articulation of modes of production. In its classic definition, a mode of production is a social system stamped by the prevailing class relations of exploitation or, paraphrasing Marx, by the way surplus labor is pumped out of the direct producers, coupled with the political and cultural institutions that facilitate exploitation.[8] However, instead of viewing the sweep of his-tory as the replacement of one social system by another, articulation theorists stressed the continuous interaction between different modes of production in one country. They argued that instead of free wage labor necessarily re-placing unfree labor and capitalism replacing noncapitalist systems, the two often coexisted over the long term.[9] In this paradigm, sometimes peasants struggled to preserve noncapitalist social systems to stave off the ravages of capitalist exploitation;[10] sometimes the precapitalist order survived because it bore most of the costs of survival of the labor force, allowing employers in the capitalist sector to pay wages well below the level of subsistence;[11] and sometimes capitalists endeavored to preserve precapitalist class relations be-cause it was more profitable to exploit peasants via sharecropping or peonage than by means of free wage labor.[12]

Drawn by the politics of anti-imperialism but weary of theories insuffi-ciently grounded in the study of history, scholars of Latin America, Africa, and Asia reinvigorated the Marxist canon by emphasizing the contradictory nature of agrarian development.[13] Borrowing elements from the three post-1960s paradigms, they criticized the notion of a contemporary feudalism and the idea that history unfolds in linear fashion from feudalism to capitalism.[14] Influenced by theories of articulation, they emphasized the contradictory and zigzag character of capitalist transitions in postcolonial countries. Evi-dence from Diriomo lends weight to the thesis that social upheavals in the modern era were not necessarily steps on the road to capitalist development. One of the principal conclusions of this study is that the revolutions in land and labor, in gender and ethnicity, in Diriomo in the era from 1870 to 1930 did not give birth to a capitalist social order. Diriomo's new society rested on the direct exercise of patriarchal coercion and consent, not the indirect compulsion of market forces.

THE SOCIAL NATURE OF MARKETS

My interpretation of late capitalist development in Diriomo turns on an understanding of the class relations of peonage and the social character of markets. My premise is that societies are distinguished by their class character, which is constituted, in the first instance, by social relations in production.[15] I define class as the shared relationship of a group of people to ownership and control of the means of production (production inputs, i.e., land, water, natural resources, machinery, tools), to their own laboring activities, and to other classes. Class is also the shared relationship of a group of people to political institutions and cultural norms. In this framework, class relations are constituted through the appropriation of surplus products or labor, which under capitalism takes the form of socially mediated labor time (surplus value), and class hierarchies are sustained by the exercise of political power. For most people, class is a relationship of exploitation: the classes that control the means of production systematically extract surplus labor or products from the producing classes, with surplus meaning labor in excess of what people perform in order to live. Whereas noncapitalist elites appropriate labor directly, often using personalized forms of coercion and consent, capitalists appropriate labor indirectly through market mechanisms.[16] In all societies, class relations develop within historical constraints, contain within them gender, race, and ethnic contradictions, and are altered by collective activities.

The premise of Marxist approaches to understanding markets is that a society's class character conditions the nature of markets; ergo, the forms and meanings of exchange are embedded in class relations.[17] Notwithstanding apparent similarities in forms of exchange in capitalist and noncapitalist societies, these mask differences in the substance and significance of market relations. A unique feature of capitalism is that most people have to sell their labor (or more precisely, their ability to labor, their labor power) to survive, and the buying and selling of labor is regulated by market forces. This aspect of market regulation is represented as freedom: workers' freedom to sell, or not to sell, their labor. However, notwithstanding people's formal freedom in the marketplace, in everyday life freedom is constrained by the need to work for wages. Under capitalism, market forces gradually transform social interactions into commercial exchanges, and in the process markets come to regulate the dynamics of the social order.

In noncapitalist societies, by contrast, because subordinate classes generally have access to land, natural resources, and tools, they are able to produce their own food and necessities. Consequently, rather than regularly bringing their own ability to labor to the marketplace, they irregularly buy and sell *things* in the market. Therefore, unlike in capitalism, where markets dominate people's way of life, in noncapitalist societies markets and exchange relations are subordinated to the workings of society. The dynamics of price formation is illustrative of this difference. Whereas in capitalist societies prices are largely regulated by market competition among companies, in noncapitalist societies prices are largely regulated not by market forces, but by custom, social hierarchy, kinship, power, and chance.[18]

This analysis of the critical difference in the role of markets between capitalist and noncapitalist societies is drawn from Karl Polanyi's classic *The Great Transformation: The Political and Economic Origins of Our Time*, first published in 1944. As Joseph E. Stiglitz writes in the foreword to the 2001 edition, "Because the transformation of European civilization [that Polanyi describes] is analogous to the transformation confronting developing countries around the world today, it often seems as if Polanyi is speaking directly to present-day issues."[19]

Polanyi's understanding of capitalism and its transformative character is rooted in an analysis of the historical and social nature of markets, which he captures in the distinction between *market societies* and *societies with markets*.[20] He argues that although markets are not unique to capitalism, the role they play in capitalism is unique. Although markets, money, and wage labor predate the development of capitalism, this trinity regulates economic and social life only in capitalist societies. In *societies with markets* (Polanyi's term for noncapitalist societies), although people may intermittently work for wages or sell products, most households have direct access to land and produce most of what they consume. Under these conditions markets play a marginal role in social reproduction and govern neither class relations nor the wider society. However, *market societies* (capitalist societies) are decisively different. Under capitalism, most households are landless or land poor and cannot subsist on their own production. Consequently, necessity drives a majority to regularly sell their capacity to work, their labor power, in order to survive.

In contrast to Polanyi's analysis of the historical and social nature of markets, and his differentiation between market societies and societies with markets, writers who equate capitalism with markets understand markets to be ahistorical, asocial institutions. In their view, markets operate in much the same way regardless of class relations between buyers and sellers and regardless of the wider social and historical context in which they are embedded.

Polanyi's insight into market dynamics rests on a Marxist interpretation of free wage labor under capitalism, understanding *free* in a contradictory sense. When landowners and the state expropriate the peasantry, people are *freed from* their land. This same process might also *free* peasants from traditional social bonds, for instance, from landlords' coercive control. Following expropriation, people find themselves *free to* sell—or not to sell—their labor. However, and here's the rub, they may well find themselves free in yet another sense: *free to starve*.[21]

As capitalism engenders landlessness and as markets permeate rural life, a corresponding process unfolds. Subsistence peasants turn into what Sidney Mintz calls *store-buyers*.[22] Households that once bought and sold foodstuffs and other necessities intermittently now find it necessary to buy and sell continually because they lack the means of producing their own livelihood. This explains a paradox of capitalism: although it appears that individuals enter into exchange relations by their own choosing, freedom is largely negated by necessity.

Consequently, a critical difference between noncapitalism and capitalism is not that the former rests on coercion and the latter on consent. Both social systems rest on a duality of coercion and consent, but of different types, and the distinction is crucial. In noncapitalist societies landlords tend to deploy direct coercion (extraeconomic coercion), as opposed to the compulsion of the marketplace, to mobilize a labor force, and they attempt to elicit peasants' manifest consent to the appropriation of their labor. In capitalist societies companies tend to rely on the compulsion of the marketplace to mobilize a labor force, and market forces partially obscure the appropriation of surplus labor. Consequently, societies with markets and market societies both rest on coercion, but of different types. In the former, coercion tends to be transparent and direct, whereas in the latter it tends to be concealed and indirect.

Polanyi's Great Transformation is the seismic shift from societies with markets to market societies. He argues that prior to capitalism markets were an adjunct to society; as capitalism developed, society became an adjunct to the market.[23] In contrast to bourgeois economic thought, Polanyi refutes the thesis that capitalist markets developed through the natural workings of supply and demand: the famous invisible hand. In *The Great Transformation* he describes how governments in Europe deprived the majority of households of their land and livelihood, thereby fostering capitalist development. Polanyi's book presents a powerful indictment of the ways politicians and property-owning classes remade the world to ensure that every transaction became commercial, every open space a market, every person a consumer, and everything had a price.

However, as Polanyi repeatedly reminds readers, not all social upheavals in modern times were steps in the development of market societies. Although in hindsight, it might be tempting to see each and every great so-cial change as a part of the historical process of capitalist transformation, other social tendencies emerged and subsequently submerged that were not compatible with the dynamics of capitalist society. In short, Polanyi warns against teleological, or linear, interpretations of development that see all so-cial transformations as precursors of capitalism.[24]

THEORIES OF LANDLORD-PEASANT RELATIONS

Three broad theoretical currents have dominated debates about transi-tions to capitalism in landlord-peasant societies. The first seeks to explain how market pressures give rise to capitalism; the second, how market pres-sures block capitalism; and the third, how peasants impede the advance of capitalism through everyday forms of resistance.

Classic Marxist controversies on the agrarian question focus on how mar-ket pressures give rise to capitalism in the countryside. Some historians have emphasized the ways capitalism developed from above, when landlords ex-propriated the peasantry and forged a rural proletariat to expand commercial production.[25] An outstanding example of this interpretation is Wheelock's *Imperialismo y dictadura*. Others have stressed capitalist development from below, describing the ways richer peasants expanded commercial production by appropriating the land and labor of poorer peasants. Florencia Mallon's *The Defense of Community in Peru's Central Highlands* is a persuasive account of the second scenario, analyzing how peasant differentiation gave rise to free wage labor. Mallon details the ways that expanding commercial oppor-tunities, combined with intervention by local politicians, gradually under-mined the subsistence economy of peasant communities. Over time, richer peasants appropriated the land and labor of poorer neighbors to produce foodstuffs for regional markets, thereby generating an agrarian bourgeoisie and rural proletariat. Rather than locating a radical rupture in social rela-tions, Mallon's interpretation emphasizes the ways market forces slowly ate away at the fabric of peasant communities. Despite their differences, both sides in the classic agrarian debate accept as a premise that agrarian producers are able to take advantage of market incentives to reorganize the social and technological conditions of production, thereby setting in motion capitalist development.[26]

In contrast to the widely held view that commercial incentives give rise to capitalism, whether from above or from below, Robert Brenner argues that market pressures in landlord-peasant societies have the opposite effect. They block the social and technological innovations that necessarily pave the way for a capitalist transition. Unlike his earlier work on Europe, which argues specifically against the notion that demographic changes drive agrarian transitions, in a later essay, "The Social Basis of Economic Development," Brenner poses different questions about barriers to agrarian capitalist development.[27] He elaborates three theses about class struggles in landlord-peasant societies to determine whether capitalism can develop within precapitalist societies where production is organized for the market. First, to safeguard survival, peasants systematically prioritize subsistence production over plantation labor and allocate family labor accordingly. Second, peasants' preference for subsistence production drives landlords to divert resources away from modernizing their enterprise to fund a politicomilitary apparatus to coercively appropriate peasants' labor. Third, as a consequence of the class struggle between landlords and peasants, commercial production does not stimulate technological change and capitalist development; instead, it results in the atrophy of both the subsistence and export sectors. On the basis of these propositions, Brenner concludes that struggles between landlords and peasants necessarily thwart the rise of agrarian capitalism. Therefore, in response to market incentives, capitalism cannot evolve out of precapitalist societies. In his words, transformations to capitalism require an "exogenous shock" and "rarely if ever" evolve out of nonmarket relations.

In contrast to writers in the Gramscian tradition who emphasize the construction of consent, Brenner maintains that landlords are driven to respond to peasant evasion with totalizing coercion. Accordingly, the role of labor discipline is starkly different in precapitalist versus capitalist societies, and, he argues, this dichotomy is key to understanding why market societies *rarely if ever* evolve out of societies with markets. Whereas under capitalism the ultimate labor discipline is to fire workers, in noncapitalist societies the objective of labor discipline is to bond workers. He argues that even though bonded labor reduces profits, landlords have no choice but to tie peasants to their enterprises. In Brenner's paradigm, this paradox represents a contradiction in noncapitalist societies that cannot be resolved. Consequently, where capitalism emerges it does so not on the basis of modernizing landlord-peasant relations in response to market incentives, but by destroying the old society and forging an entirely new one.

In contrast to Brenner's theory that landlords are driven to coercively control the peasantry, James C. Scott shifted the terms of the agrarian debate by exploring peasant resistance to the depredations of advancing capitalism.[28] Criticizing Gramscian interpretations of hegemony that stress the ways ruling classes control subaltern groups, Scott emphasizes the importance of peasants' strategies to undermine class exploitation.[29] He argues that peasants are not passive victims, but active agents who collectively negotiate the terms of their subordination. He warns against misrepresenting class conflict in the countryside by misconstruing peasants' daily compliance as acceptance of planters' power. According to Scott's thesis, peasants resist the elite's ideological domination by counterposing an alternative normative framework rooted in the morality of the precapitalist order. This, he argues, generates a counterhegemonic ideology that imposes restraints on landowners' subordination of the peasantry.

Scott's theories of peasant agency and everyday forms of resistance inspired a major revision of a canon that, through omission or commission, largely had portrayed the rural poor as passive victims of landlord domination. However, where Scott's work explored class contradictions, other writers reworked his theory of weapons of the weak and in the process ignored class. This reworking gave way to a new agrarian romanticism. Claiming to follow in Scott's footsteps, some scholars embraced a peasant populism that uncritically celebrated the agency of the oppressed, paid insufficient attention to the power of the oppressors, and ignored the everyday forms of exploitative class relations.

Patriarchy and Gender in Agrarian Transitions

It is frequently said that gender analysis does not simply add missing pieces to the historical puzzle; it fundamentally changes our understanding of the past.[30] This book argues that the revolution in property and labor in Diriomo can be understood only by analyzing the ways that gender, class, and ethnicity interacted in the making of a new social order.

A critical turn in feminist scholarship was the development of gender theory in the 1970s. Before then, feminists emphasized the ubiquity and endurance of patriarchy, understood as systematic male domination of women, and controversies centered on why and how women were oppressed by men.[31] After the turn, most scholars in the field analyzed male-female difference, or gender, and emphasized the ways that gender is constituted by sociopolitical, not biological, conditions.[32] Joan Scott's two-part definition of gender as "a constitutive element of social relationships based on perceived differences between the sexes" and "a primary way of signifying relationships of power" became the template for the field.[33] With the rise of gender theory scholars broadly repudiated the concept of patriarchy, arguing that emphasis on the systemic character of male domination and female oppression tended to camouflage the ways gender is differentially constituted in the sociopolitical realm. Repudiation of patriarchy was compounded by the linguistic turn to discourse and representation, with its neglect of class relations and material structures.

However, there is no inherent contradiction between patriarchy and gender theory. On the contrary, a unity of the two underlines the historically contingent nature of gendered structures of domination and the ways representations of gender reinforce and undermine those structures. Therefore, to bring material conditions back into research on gender, I modify and expand Scott's classic statement. First, gender is "a constitutive element of social relations based on the perceived differences between the sexes" *and on the sexual divisions of labor and behavior in society's interconnected public and private domains*. Second, gender is a primary way of *structuring and reproducing* relationships of power.

In this book, patriarchy is understood as systemic senior male control over and protection of subordinate females and males in society's public and private domains.[34] It may no longer be fashionable to combine patriarchy and gender, as the two frequently are seen to be incompatible.[35] Yet Latin American historians have gone against the grain. Rather than seeing patriarchy and gender as mutually exclusive, and rather than retreating from analysis of structures of male domination to focus solely on representations of gender, Latin Americanists have fruitfully combined the two theoretical approaches.[36] In keeping with that tradition, this book integrates analyses of patriarchy and gender.

In addition to patriarchy's once privileged position in feminist theory, the term appears in the Marxist classics. But the concept of patriarchy is invested with almost entirely different meanings in the two traditions, contributing to what Heidi Hartmann famously called "the unhappy marriage of Marxism and feminism."[37] In the traditional Marxist canon patriarchy had no gendered meaning; the term connoted neither sexual difference nor male domination. Marx and Engels described class relations between lords and serfs as patriarchal if they seemed more consensual than antagonistic.[38] In this sense, patriarchy connoted class relations that rested on landlords' paternalist practices and peasant deference.

Early on, Max Weber proposed a proto-gender analysis of precapitalist class relations.[39] He argued that patriarchy was a system of senior male power in which the authority of male heads of lineages was institutionalized through patrimonial networks. Furthermore, in premodern societies, structures and ideologies intrinsic to patrimonial relations partly explained why people in the lower social orders tended to privilege loyalty to superiors over class solidarity. Weber's analysis of patrimonialism was influential among anthropologists; however, Marxist historians largely overlooked Weber's linkage of senior male power and class domination until recently.

The work of E. P. Thompson is an outstanding case of omission. Thompson studied patrician society in eighteenth-century England and pioneered new understandings of the ways ruling classes construct consent and subordinate classes negotiate compliance—what he called the moral economy of the poor. However, he conceptualized this dynamic exclusively in terms of class structures and ideologies.[40] Examination of the ways that laws, practices, and ideologies of gender domination and difference shaped relations of power is absent from Thompson's work. My point is not to blame Thompson for writing before gender analysis revolutionized social theory, but to point out that not so long ago scholars sought to explain the dynamics of patriarchal societies without analyzing the ways that gender and class interacted. That approach is no longer valid.

Steve J. Stern's *The Secret History of Gender: Women, Men, and Power in Late Colonial Mexico* analyzes gender and takes a Thompsonian approach to moral economy, uniting hitherto separate strands of patriarchy theory.[41] Like Thompson, Stern seeks to understand the construction of consent and the negotiation of compliance; unlike Thompson, he places gender at the heart of the matter. To explain why the Mexican lower classes partially accepted the legitimacy of elite rule, Stern rejects the standard thesis that landlords elicited loyalty from peasants with empty promises of benevolence and subjugated them with violence. Instead, adapting James Scott's interpretation of moral economy, Stern argues that the legitimacy of elite rule was constituted through struggles between landlords and peasants over gendered practices and the meanings of patriarchy. Stern understands patriarchy as a cluster of competing pacts through which elites attempted to impose an absolutist vision of senior male rights and duties, and plebes countered with a contingent version that linked acceptance of elite authority to patriarchs' protection of subordinates.[42] For Stern, patriarchal pacts rested on reciprocal but unequal rights and obligations, and his premise is that the gendered dynamics embedded in patriarchal domination and contestation were central to the constitution of political power in Mexico over the long term. As he says, politics in the broad sense was gender politics.[43]

The Secret History of Gender influenced my interpretation of landlord-peasant relations in Diriomo. Stern's analysis of the ways gender politics contributed to landlords' power and peasants' acceptance of authority helped me understand the resilience of debt peonage. However, my understanding of patriarchy departs from his in several ways. First, Stern keeps the faith with the linguistic turn, defining gender culture as languages of argument. I emphasize the legal and material foundations of patriarchal domination and the concrete ways peasant men and women challenged landlords' patriarchal power. Second, Stern's central analytical distinction is between absolutist and contingent understandings of patriarchal authority, and he concludes that lower-class males had an absolutist view of patriarchal authority, while females of the same strata insisted that their obedience to patriarchs was contingent on males' fulfillment of certain responsibilities. To understand social dynamics in Diriomo, I analyze competing understandings of patriarchal authority. But I do not draw a line between absolutist and contingent views. My approach reflects research findings suggesting that Diriomeñas' perceptions of the legitimacy of patriarchal authority did not fit Stern's paradigm. Instead, I emphasize the double-sided class character of patriarchy. To this end, I analyze the gendered character of planter-peon relations and call this patriarchy from above, and of peasant household relations and call this patriarchy from below.

Ethnicity and Assimilation

"Ethnicity in operation is like all else social, a tool in the hands of men; it is not a mystic force in itself." With this quasi-poetic statement, Joan Vincent pioneered the view that ethnicity is a social, not a biological, category.[44] Ethnic identities develop and change in long-term processes of domination and subordination. In Spanish America, Indian identity was constructed at the time of conquest and changed dramatically ever since. In the colonial era, the Spanish state institutionalized a tripartite system of separate estates in which legal obligations and entitlements varied according to a person's *raza*, or racial status. The colonial authorities differentially regulated land use, taxation, labor obligations, even dress codes for Indians, mestizos, and creoles (people of European descent). One of the major dilemmas facing national elites following independence was how to govern the racial order inherited from the colonial era. Postcolonial ruling classes' responses to the racial legacy of colonialism varied depending on the creoles' political power and on the militancy of subordinate ethnic groups.[45]

Liberal tenets of universal male citizenship and equal rights before the law accentuated dilemmas of race. As governments moved cautiously in the direction of expanding citizenship and legal equality, the race question became more acute. Postcolonial states tried to juggle political modernization with continued subjugation of the lower classes, largely composed of Indians, Blacks, and mestizos. In *Trials of Nation Making*, Brooke Larson analyzes ethnic politics in the Andes in the nineteenth century and argues that in Peru and Bolivia a binary language of race developed that reinforced the Indian-Creole (or "white") divide.[46] This reflected ruling class attempts to subjugate the Indian population by imposing a type of internal colonialism, and efforts by Indian communities to defend the cultural traditions and entitlements to land inherited from the colonial era. In Mexico and Central America postcolonial elites pursued different racial politics. In Mexico after the 1910 Revolution, politicians sought to assimilate Indians and forge a mestizo national identity.[47] In Guatemala, racial politics was akin to internal colonialism.[48] In Costa Rica, elites forged a national identity based on the idea that the population was white, not mestizo.[49] In the rest of Central America, race politics tended to be a softer version of the Mexican model.[50]

Recent writings on mestizaje, understood as ethnic assimilation by political means, stress Indian resistance to assimilation and the survival of indigenous identity in Latin America.[51] Jeffrey Gould argues that Nicaraguan Indians resisted assimilation until the mid-twentieth century. In contrast to the widely held view that the indigenous population had been peacefully assimilated in the eighteenth and nineteenth centuries, Gould describes how Indians deployed ethnic politics to resist expropriation of their land and labor. In *To Die in This Way*, he argues that memories of resistance kept alive Indian identity long after Indians had supposedly disappeared.

Historical evidence from Diriomo reveals a different story. There Indians did little to resist the state's elimination of their political organization and dismemberment of the commons. Rather than collectively organizing to oppose privatization and abolition of their community, individuals endeavored to secure private titles to land. Paradoxically, in the Granada region, the voices opposing Indian assimilation came less from the comunidades indígenas than from government officials. Ladino politicians opposed abolition of the indigenous communities because their leaders had served the state. The apparent discrepancy between Diriomo and other Nicaraguan communities raises important questions about assimilation and resistance.

But before analyzing approaches to ethnicity, a word about semantics. Because *raza* was used to differentiate among Indians, Spaniards, and mestizos in the colonial era, I use *race* in writing about colonial society. For the postcolonial era, Peter Wade's usage of *ethnicity* referring to Indians, and *race* referring to people of African descent, is compelling but not useful for analyzing Diriomo.[52] Although nineteenth-century censuses listed a significant minority of Diriomeños as mulattoes, having African ancestry held no meaning for them. The ethnic distinction that mattered was between Indians and non-Indians; therefore, when describing life in the pueblo, I use *ethnic*, *racial*, and *racist*.

Richard Adams's classic definition of an ethnic group combines three fundamental conditions: (1) belief in myths of common origins, (2) collective self-identification and identification by outsiders, and (3) identifying markers.[53] Anthropologists traditionally took distinctive language, dress, and customs to be the primary identifying markers of Latin American Indians and emphasized that cultural traits displayed a stubborn resistance to change. Recently, critics of this view have stressed instead the subjective, fluid, and historically situated character of ethnic markers. Many now argue that distinguishing traits assume new forms that reflect social conditions and political struggles.[54] Gould, for example, argues that in the absence of distinctive Indian languages and dress, a collective memory of resistance to mestizaje was the key ethnic marker of Nicaraguan Indians in the twentieth century.

In the case of Diriomo, I concluded that the central ethnic marker of Indianness in the late nineteenth century was common property rights. This partially explains why, following land privatization, when Diriomeños lost the material means that held their community together, they ceased to identify as Indians. Nevertheless, Granada's oligarchs continued to refer pejoratively to Diriomeños as Indians.[55] Joan Vincent's theory that structures of ethnic domination are determined early and tend to be self-perpetuating may help account both for the persistence of ethnic discrimination and for Diriomeñas' desire to escape the Indian stigma after the state had eliminated the material benefits associated with Indian identity.[56] Paul Gilroy's thesis, consistent with Vincent's, holds that one of the contradictions of race is that identification by outsiders frequently outlives a group's self-identity. In part this is why he describes race politics and racism as a "changing same."[57] Gilroy's and Vincent's theses that racial oppression tends to be tenacious and highly resistant to change provide a framework for understanding Diriomeños' willingness to assimilate into Nicaragua's dominant mestizo culture.

Gould expands on Adams's definition of ethnic group by adding a fourth indispensable condition: the existence of a political organization that speaks in the name of the ethnic group, though not necessarily representing its interests.[58] Gould's emphasis on the role of ethnic political organizations in perpetuating identities of difference is useful, as is his analysis of the ways ethnic leaders endeavor to represent the group vis-à-vis outsiders. As Gould argues, leadership sometimes promotes community cohesion, and sometimes fragmentation. Following Gould's insistence on the importance of political organization and leadership in analyzing ethnicity, this history of Diriomo draws out these issues. However, unlike the communities Gould studied, I concluded that the politics of Diriomo's Indian leaders partially explained why the community's rank and file accepted assimilation. Furthermore, divisions between ethnic leaders and followers pose the question of whether these represented class or proto-class differences.

The relationship between ethnicity and class has a distinguished intellectual history.[59] John Comaroff has argued that ethnicity is an analogue for class; in his words, "Ethnicity is a representation in culture of the social division of labor."[60] In his formulation, ethnic groups tend not to be internally divided by class; rather, class antagonism characterizes extraethnic relations, that is, the relationship between the group, taken as a whole, and the dominant classes. Comaroff proposed that "ethnicity refuse[d] to vanish" in the face of the transformative forces of capitalism in the twentieth century because capitalists played on ethnic differences to divide the working classes and to superexploit ethnic groups.

At one time, Comaroff's formulation was broadly consistent with the orthodoxy in anthropology. However, recently most writers in the field argue that ethnicity and class represent different, though often overlapping, forms of oppression.[61] I propose that a prime characteristic of ethnicity is its very heterogeneity, in particular in relation to class. As ethnic identities and relations are variously constituted historically and socially, their relationship to class is also highly variable. Under some circumstances, Comaroff's thesis that ethnicity is an analogue for class holds, in others not.

CHAPTER TWO

Indians under Colonialism and Postcolonialism

The classic colonial dilemma for local leaders in a country run by foreigners is how to balance collaboration with the occupying authorities with representation of their people's interests. Indian leaders across the Americas grappled with this dilemma during three centuries of Spanish rule and in the postcolonial nation-states born of independence. In Mesoamerica Indian authorities negotiated this double role. They represented their communities to the state, and they were agents of the state within the Indian pueblos. Sometimes pressures from below forced Indian leaders to resist the demands of their overlords; at other times, Indian authorities accommodated more than resisted the colonial regime. It is impossible to understand the transformation of Diriomo's social order in the crucible of the great nineteenth-century coffee boom without understanding its society before.

In Nicaragua the colonial state segmented society into three main racial groups—Spanish, Indian, and mestizo—and vested each with different obligations and entitlements. Within this governing structure, Indian was a colonial category constructed by the Spanish state to facilitate the exploitation of labor and the imperial policy of indirect rule. As a consequence of the almost total collapse of indigenous society in Nicaragua after the conquest, Indians' shared cultural or ethnic markers waned, contributing to the prominence of land rights and labor exploitation in Indians' self-identity and identification by others.

In this chapter I describe life in the Indian pueblos surrounding Granada over the course of the colonial period. My analysis focuses on four themes: the collapse of indigenous society after the conquest; the land, labor, and tributary policies that defined and regulated Indians; why the Spanish system of indirect rule generated conflicts between Indian leaders and comuneros; and the racial fluidity of late colonial society. I then analyze the transition from colonial to neocolonial rule and highlight Indian resistance to encroachments on their common lands, and the continuing tensions within Indian society between leaders and comuneros.

Colonial Rule

The conquest wreaked havoc on native societies throughout the Americas; however, the speed and scale of devastation was greater in Nicaragua than in other areas. Thirty years after the Spanish occupation, the aboriginal population of the region had plummeted by more than 92 percent, from approximately 546,000 at the time of conquest to 43,700 by 1555.[1] The demographic collapse was first unleashed by epidemics unwittingly spread through contact with Europeans and then intensified by slavery, brutal labor exploitation, and endemic flight by the surviving native peoples. Spanish settlers enslaved Nicaragua's indigenous population to carry cargo across the isthmus of Panama and, according to a horrified Spanish official, to build great ships for the journey to China.[2] To avoid exploitation and almost inevitable death, many Indians escaped to regions beyond the reach of Spanish rule.

In 1550, the Crown sent an inspector to find out why population decline in Nicaragua was more extreme than in other areas.[3] Fearing that the native population would become extinct, as happened in the Caribbean, Spain's imperial council ordered Spanish settlers to import African slaves for heavy work.[4] But the native population continued to fall because, in the words of Nicaragua's governor, "even clerics and friars maltreat the Indians for personal benefit. They make Indians work with no rest for an entire year, without paying them or providing their food. The fate of these sad Indians is to live in a state of perpetual captivity and oppression."[5] Over the years, royal officials tried to stem the alarming decline of Nicaragua's Indian peoples less because of humanitarian concerns than because they knew that success in the imperial venture required the labor of Indian people.[6]

To exploit and at the same time protect the native population of the New World, the Crown implemented a strategy of indirect rule whose centerpiece was an implicit social contract between the state, Indian authorities, and the indigenous people. The Crown appropriated Indian tribute and labor, and in exchange granted common land rights to indigenous communities. Indigenous leaders were required to supply the pueblo's quotient of tribute and labor and in return were granted a degree of autonomy in the governance of their communities. A contradictory feature of the system was that Indians could escape the tribute burden if they abandoned their pueblo, but this severed their claim to common land rights and the associational character of Indian society. In sum, in the Spanish colonial system, "Indian" was a juridical and administrative category, not a cultural or ethnic one. Although the two largely overlapped in some parts of the Spanish empire, in Nicaragua the combination of population collapse and social upheaval eroded Indians' shared cultural identity. This gave prominence to the material conditions of land rights and labor exploitation in defining those who considered themselves, and were perceived by others, to be Indian.

The Province of Nicaragua was a poor outpost on a colonial frontier; nevertheless, the city of Granada acquired a certain regional prominence as a mercantile hub.[7] With circuitous access to the Atlantic Coast by way of the San Juan River and Lake Nicaragua, Granada was a licensed port in the imperial trading system. To protect the city and its commerce from piracy, the Crown established forts along the length of the river and stationed soldiers in the city and throughout its hinterland. Diriomo and the other pueblos de indios in the vicinity bore the brunt of Granada's growth, as the colonial state required local Indians to provide labor and tribute to the city and the garrisons that linked Granada to the distant Atlantic Coast. Diriomeños supplied an array of products, including corn, beans, plantains, cotton thread, cloth, henequen rope, chickens, honey, fodder, and firewood, to Granada and the far-flung forts.[8] Although the population of the pueblos was shrinking due to the effects of flight, disease, and exploitation, the Crown ratcheted up Indian tribute to supply the city and its trade route. This created a vicious cycle: as indigenous tribute became more onerous, more Indians deserted the pueblos, thereby intensifying the exploitation of those who remained.

Within the terms of the colonial contract, the tribute owed by each pueblo de indios was calibrated according to the size of its population. With the number of inhabitants shrinking, Indian authorities in the Granada region repeatedly petitioned the Crown for a recount of the tributary population. According to the census of 1682, more than half of the region's Indians had fled their pueblos: Diriomo's inhabitants numbered 167 Indians, of whom only 70 were adult tribute payers.[9] Around this time, the Spanish overlords (*encomenderos*) in the region regularly complained that they were unable to collect the tribute granted them by the Crown. In 1655, Doña Mariana de Artaza, the encomendera of Nindirí, protested, "My pueblo is virtually depopulated because most Indians have taken refuge outside its jurisdiction."[10] Doña Mariana went to extraordinary lengths to retrieve her tributaries: first, she begged the Crown to deploy soldiers to capture and return her Indians; when that failed, she hired her own armed agents to do the job; finally, she proclaimed that she would reduce the tribute of any Indian who came to live in Nindirí. Unsuccessful in all her efforts, Doña Mariana complained that "due to their evil nature the Indians are staying away." As a last resort, she petitioned judges of the high court to abrogate the link between residence in the pueblo and Indian tribute. Demonstrating their flexibility, and her considerable influence, the judges ruled that Nindirí's Indians had to pay tribute to Doña Mariana regardless of where they resided. Nevertheless, Doña Mariana remained dissatisfied with the judgment, declaring that she would never be able to collect tribute from Indians scattered throughout the province.

About the same time, the *alcalde indígena* (leader of the Indian community) of Diriomo appealed to the Crown to reduce the pueblo's tribute burden. He argued that Indians of the pueblo were not able to supply the 81 bolts of cloth, 126 boxes (*medios*) of beans, 188 *fanegas* (282 bushels) of corn, 126 chickens, and 534 pounds of sisal (*carbuya*) the Crown levied.[11] He also complained that to fulfill the labor obligation, Indian men worked one week per month on grandiose building projects underway in Granada and along the river. Finally, he objected to the requirement that Indian women weave cloth and work as cooks, laundresses, and servants for Granada's far-flung civilian and military population. He pointed out that according to the census of 1694, although the pueblo had a population of 207, the number of tribute payers had fallen to a mere thirty. The crisis in Diriomo was repeated throughout the district. Linda Newson estimates that at the end of the seventeenth century the Indian population of Nicaragua reached its nadir.[12]

The scissors effect produced by plummeting population and rising exploitation exacerbated social tensions within Indian society, as it fell to Indian authorities to squeeze tribute from the remaining inhabitants of the pueblos. As a consequence, Indians in the pueblos blamed their own authorities for the exploitation they suffered rather than the wider system of imperial rule. The Crown Court regularly received petitions from the Indian pueblos surrounding Granada denouncing local leaders. Pedro Bautista of Jinotepeque accused the alcaldes indígenas and labor recruiters (*mandones*) in his pueblo of exploiting their own people for personal gain.[13] He alleged that in violation of Spanish law and Indian custom, the mandones forced him and his wife to work half of every year in Granada. Bautista claimed that this far exceeded their obligations under the labor draft and that the Indian leaders personally profited from the arrangement. He complained that as a consequence of their long absence from the pueblo, he and his wife had been unable to harvest their own crops and his family faced dire poverty. He closed his case by petitioning the Crown Court to protect him from the vices of Indian leaders. The court responded by ordering the indigenous authorities in Jinotepeque to curtail their illegal traffic in Indian labor.

Similarly, Simón López, one of the elders (*indios principales*) of Niquinohomo, appealed to the Crown Court to protect him from abuses perpetrated by Indian leaders. López explained that although he was above the age of fifty-five and legally exempt from the labor regime, the alcalde compelled him to provide personal services to the local encomendero. After López refused, the alcalde whipped and jailed him, forced his sons to pay the costs of his imprisonment, and continued to abuse his entire family. López concluded his petition by asking the court to intervene on his behalf, "even though I am nothing more than a poor and miserable Indian." The court ruled in the plaintiff's favor and ordered the alcalde of Niquinohomo to cease demanding labor services from López.[14]

The Spanish system of domination was built on the classic colonial strategy of indirect rule. The system tends to generate conflicts within the subjugated population and to camouflage the brutality of those at the top echelons of power. Rather than being an oddity, this imperial arrangement is commonplace; it has been called "the good king syndrome." The good king is the apparently benevolent ruler whose kindness is traduced by nefarious lower-ranking officials. Within the colonial structures of power in Nicaragua, appeals by comuneros against Indian authorities were channeled through the Crown Courts, thereby institutionalizing the system of divide and rule. It is not my purpose to assess the Crown's success in promoting the idea of a benevolent head of state undermined by corrupt indigenous authorities. Rather, my point is that frequently ordinary Indians perceived they were oppressed by their own kind and turned to imperial institutions to mitigate their suffering.

In the late seventeenth century, the bishop of León denounced Indian authorities for their systematic collaboration with the state. However, unlike petitions by Indian comuneros that put some faith in Spanish officials to deliver justice, the bishop declared that the Crown's representatives regularly connived with Indian officials to exploit comuneros. The bishop described corruption involving the provincial governor, regional officials (*corregidores*), and the Indian elite in promoting the forced sale of merchandise (*repartimiento de mercancías*) in pueblos de indios. On the role of Indian authorities he declared, "The Indians regard their homelands [*patrias*] as despicable and flee from them because they are neither able to pay for the goods they are forced to buy, nor can they endure the mistreatment and punishments they suffer at the hands of the alcaldes indígenas."[15]

The colonial state regularly rewarded Indian leaders' collaboration. For example, after loyally serving the Crown, Pedro Hernández, the alcalde in Nindirí, became Indian governor of the region. In recognition of his service to the Crown, Hernández was given three *caballerías* of land.[16] However, the comuneros of Nindirí protested that the land grant violated the customary principle that Indian land was common property. Furthermore, they objected to rewarding Hernández for his abuse of power and corruption. To appease opposition from below rather than purvey the property as a gift for services rendered, the Crown sold the land to Hernández at a concessionary price.[17]

Steve J. Stern argues persuasively that in early colonial Peru the Spanish Crown constructed hegemony by drawing Indians into extended litigation over the terms and conditions of rule.[18] Instead of being excluded from the state, Indians participated in the everyday workings of the Crown bureaucracy through involvement in the justice system. As a result, Andean peoples often sought reform within the colonial structures of domination rather than seeking to overthrow the imperial overlords. Put simply, Stern concludes that the Spanish system of justice tended to co-opt Indians into accepting the legitimacy of colonial rule. Stern's theory helps explain why, rather than challenging the colonial system, Indian comuneros in Nicaragua turned to the Crown Courts to seek reform within the structures of power. Because outside institutions arbitrated conflicts between indigenous leaders and ordinary Indians, the Spanish system of justice aggravated, more than arrested, conflicts within the pueblos de indios.

A court case involving local authorities in Jalteva, the Indian barrio of Granada, lays bare the inner workings of the system of indirect rule in the late colonial period. The case is carefully documented by the historian Germán Romero Vargas.[19] In 1769 the provincial governor instructed the Indian *cabildo* (governing council) in Jalteva to reelect Gregorio Centeno to the post of alcalde indígena. The cabildo refused to comply, arguing that Centeno was a tool of the city's ruling elite, not a representative of Indian interests. Explaining their opposition, the cabildo documented Centeno's abuses of power: he embezzled community funds, forced Indians to work far in excess of the labor draft, and used common property for personal gain. Notwithstanding continuing opposition, the governor reappointed Centeno, and the cabildo reluctantly agreed under threat of reprisals. Centeno celebrated his victory by jailing his opponents. Almost immediately riots erupted throughout the barrio and unrest continued to simmer as Indian comuneros declared their support for the opposition. Confident that colonial authorities would help him stamp out the unrest, Centeno formally charged his opponents on the cabildo with insubordination. Giving its full backing to the Crown's representative in the Indian barrio, the high court ruled in favor of Centeno and sentenced the leaders of the opposition to a public flogging in the plaza of Jalteva.

The case provides a window on governance toward the end of Spanish rule. As alcalde indígena, Centeno purportedly represented Indian interests to the state; in fact, he was a blunt tool of the state in the Indian community. Centeno's flagrant abuse of Indian comuneros was not merely tolerated, it was fully supported by Crown officials. In this case, Centeno resolved the classic colonial dilemma by categorically collaborating with the occupying forces and trampling the interests of his community. Centeno's activities might well have been extreme; nonetheless, the case demonstrates the extent to which Indian authorities were prepared to challenge opposition from below. Furthermore, the court ruling suggests that Crown policy in the province had shifted from appeasement of grassroots protests to repression. As a result, judicial channels previously used by comuneros to redress abuses of power by Indian elites were closed. It is not difficult to imagine that Centeno's triumph, and the public humiliation of his opponents, sent a powerful signal to comuneros throughout the region that the colonial government was prepared to unconditionally support Indian leaders in the face of opposition.

Late colonial society became more racially fluid as a consequence of population growth and the erosion of everyday divisions between creoles (Spaniards born in the colonies), Indians, and castas. The Bula de la Santa Cruzada, an ecclesiastical census of 1776, records Diriomo's population as 1,117, of whom the vast majority (92 percent) were Indian.[20] Although census officials noted that the population was probably higher than their count indicated, even their figures demonstrate a sixfold increase over the preceding hundred years. Before the late eighteenth century, Diriomo's inhabitants were Indian by virtue of their residence in a pueblo de indios. However, according to the 1776 census, 8 percent of the population was composed of

Spaniards (or "whites"), mestizos, mulattos, and castas, with the last two categories accounting for most of the non-Indians. Reflecting the colonial strategy of divide and rule, most of the soldiers in the region were mulattos, and according to contemporary observers, Diriomo's mixed-race population was a consequence of former soldiers settling in the pueblo.

Various factors contributed to increasing racial fluidity in the region. Seeking refuge from the bands of pirates that regularly sacked Granada, mestizo families fled the city and moved to Diriomo and other nearby pueblos. Although census officials labeled them Spanish, frequently they were described as mestizo.[21] In addition, racial exclusion was breaking down in the colonial bureaucracy. Legally, posts in the Crown and the church remained restricted to creoles. Nevertheless, to overcome barriers to employment, Indians and castas regularly petitioned the royal court to amend their racial status in exchange for a fee. Men seeking appointment to the priesthood and to the upper reaches of the royal bureaucracy, at one end of the spectrum, and to posts such as scribe, pharmacist, and letter carrier, at the other, frequently petitioned the Crown to change their racial status.[22] For example, Diego López, town crier in Granada, was assigned at birth to the contradictory category indio-ladino. But because employment by the city government was forbidden to Indians, López petitioned to alter his ethnic status to "pure ladino."[23] Francisco Fernandez of Masaya paid 40 pesos to "rid [himself] of the condition of being mulatto [quitarme de la calidad de mulato]" to become a pharmacist.[24] Even some members of society's upper echelons believed that racial exclusions were anachronistic. The bishop of Granada inquired whether he might permit mulattos into the priesthood and lesser posts within the church if he was "confident they were free of the bad blood [limpios de la mala raza]."[25] Many requests for racial conversion were granted, demonstrating that if a person had sufficient funds and was prepared to pay the Crown, he or she could change his or her race status. Extraofficial acts of ethnic conversion were also common. Andrés de Marzilla, a mulatto-indio of Managua, asked the alcalde indígena to stop forcing his nieces into the labor draft because they were more mulatto than Indian. The alcalde readily agreed in exchange for a fee.[26]

It is plain that some inhabitants of Nicaragua were able to move without too much difficulty from one race category to another. Of equal significance, people's descriptions of their racial status demonstrate an ideology of race in the process of change. Indio-ladino and mulatto-indio suggest race mixtures that did not conform to the official categories designed to divide people in colonial society. Furthermore, the bishop implied that some mulattos, if not all, were "free of bad blood," suggesting some erosion of the colonial ideology of good and bad races.

Examples of increasing racial fluidity are numerous. In Diriomo, *cofradías* (Indian associations to administer common property) founded under the auspices of the church had once been exclusively Indian fraternities, but in the late eighteenth century a visiting bishop noted that Indians and ladinos worked side by side in the cofradías.[27] Masaya and Managua, also pueblos de indios, experienced similar changes. Although Masaya's alcalde indígena, Manuel Bermudez, ordered Indians to live in separate barrios in strict accordance with the colonial apartheid laws, the inhabitants of the pueblo defied his authority and resided in racially integrated neighborhoods.[28]

Although late colonial society in Diriomo was more racially diverse than before, the change was not reflected in differences in wealth. The same bishop who reported that Indians and ladinos participated jointly in the cofradías noted that Spanish and ladino families in Diriomo "planted only small plots for their own subsistence and appeared almost as poor and miserable as the pueblo's Indians." The largest property in the pueblo was a small sugar plantation owned by the parish priest. Evidently the padre was imbued with the entrepreneurial as well as the holy spirit, as he deployed the forced labor services of his parishioners to produce cane liquor (*guaro*), which he sold for a tidy profit.[29]

Despite population growth and increasing racial diversity, Diriomo remained "a poor and miserable place in a lamentable state."[30] Although stratification by wealth was insignificant, differential land and labor systems continued to divide Indians from non-Indians. Indians retained access to their common lands. However, because the community had more land than Indians needed for their own use, it rented parcels to the non-Indians of the pueblo for a nominal annual fee. In another mark of continuity, Indians remained subject to oppressive tribute and labor obligations. As Bishop Morel wrote in 1751, "The Indians of Granada are overburdened by labor drafts and tribute demands."[31]

After centuries of population crisis and social dislocation, cultural markers of Indianness were weak in the pueblos surrounding Granada. On top of this, the imperial system of separate racial estates was crumbling. Nevertheless, on the eve of independence, differential land rights and labor exploitation continued to divide Indians from non-Indians. Within Indian communities, the structures of colonial domination fostered conflicts between leaders and comuneros because the indigenous authorities remained accountable to the state for the extraction of tribute and labor.

Indian Resistance to Expropriation of the Commons

It is frequently said that Latin American societies have always been characterized by struggles over land. However, as a consequence of the demographic collapse, before the nineteenth century labor, not land, was regularly in scarce supply. In rural Granada, the first recorded struggles over land took place in the last decades of Spanish rule, when Granada's oligarchs wanted to produce cacao for regional markets. Pressures on Indian land took various forms. Sometimes entrepreneurs simply encroached on the commons, and sometimes they attempted to acquire Indian land legally. Community responses also varied significantly: at one extreme, Diriomo's alcalde indígena surreptitiously sold land on the Mombacho Volcano without consulting the community;[32] at the other, Masaya's alcalde indígena militantly resisted encroachment on the commons. The Indians of Masaya collectively petitioned the Crown Court to stop the appropriation of their land. The case, with arguments for and against expropriation, provides a vivid account of early attempts to privatize property and of Indian resistance.[33]

Don Francisco Alvarado, a merchant and landowner from Granada, planted cacao on land that bordered the *tierras comunales* in Tisma that belonged to Masaya's pueblo de indios. To expand his cacao plantation, Alvarado proposed to the Indians that in exchange for relinquishing their land in Tisma, he would give them four caballerias of land in another area. Exasperated by the Indians' repeated refusal, in 1807 Alvarado filed suit in the Crown Court arguing that because the Indians did not cultivate their land in Tisma, the Crown should expropriate it. After royal judges ordered Masaya's governor to intervene on Alvarado's behalf, the Indians sent this declaration to the court:

> We, Masaya's Indian elders [indios principales], met to consider [Alvarado's] offer. We decided not to accept the proposal because of the damage it would inflict on the interests of the Indian community [*común del pueblo*]. Don Francisco wants us to believe that he would not benefit by the exchange of our common lands for the land he offers us. [But] this gentleman has no reason to benefit us; he is motivated entirely by self-interest . . . Although he says that our lands are uncultivated, they are of

great use to us and are necessary for this community [*este común*] because our principal commercial activity is making straw hats and mats . . . We gather the materials for this activity on our common lands in Tisma, and in addition people cut wood from this part of the commons [*los ejidos del común*] to construct houses . . . The land Don Francisco offers us in exchange might well be useful for individual cultivation, but it is entirely useless for our collective purpose. We request that this gentleman leave us in peace with what we have. We are completely satisfied with our common land.

But Alvarado did not leave the Indians in peace. He continued to press his case through the Crown Courts, arguing that if he owned the land it would "contribute to the wealth of the entire community." Furthermore, he argued, "the land in question forms only a small part of the seventy-four caballerías belonging to the Indians of Masaya that remain uncultivated, and I am offering to pay double the normal value of the land." To strengthen his case, Alvarado cited a recent study by Granada's Junta de Sociedad Económica (Economics Society), which warned, "The greatest obstacle to progress in the region is scarcity of land for the production of cacao. Granada will prosper only if the ejidos and the common lands of the Indians are divided up into proportional landholdings." Alvarado's petition was endorsed by prestigious members of the cabildo de Granada.[34]

Despite pressure from the oligarchy, the Crown judges decided that it was not a propitious moment to expropriate Indian land. Facing popular uprisings against Spanish rule in Masaya, the judges recommended the case be deferred.[35] However, the dispute foreshadowed changes that would alter the fabric of Indian communities. At the end of the nineteenth century, common lands throughout the region were divided up into just the sort of "proportional landholdings" that Granada's ruling elite advocated. In a sense, the struggle between Alvarado and Masaya's Indians was a dress rehearsal for state-sponsored land privatization, the elite's agrarian reform.

Rather than waging an anticolonial struggle against Spain, Central America gained independence by default.[36] The region was of so little importance to Spain that when Mexico secured independence in 1821, the Spanish government ceded Central America as well. For the next four decades Nicaragua was wracked by political instability: first it was annexed to Mexico, then it was a state within the Central American Federation. In 1838 Nicaragua became an independent republic. Until the 1860s, the elites of Granada and León were locked more or less continually in internecine warfare, and Nicaragua had no central institutionalized authority deserving of the name nation-state. E. Bradford Burns calls this period Nicaragua's "rustic enlightenment" because intraelite battles so preoccupied the rich that they were unable to systematically appropriate the labor of the poor.[37]

Independence set in motion a process that unevenly altered the racial order. Although racial descriptors fell into disuse in official documentation, paradoxically ethnic distinctions took on a new importance in everyday life in the pueblos. Following Independence, perhaps the most significant change in Nicaragua was the nature of governance. With the disappearance of the highly centralized colonial state, political power devolved to the regions and locales. In implicit recognition of their inability to rule, national politicians invested local governments with wide-ranging authority. They ensured that municipalities were governed by a town council (junta municipal) that was headed by a municipal mayor (*alcalde constitucional*, or alcalde municipal).

In contrast to Spain's colonial policy of indirect rule, whereby the Crown governed the pueblos through Indian authorities, following Independence ladinos assumed control of local government in many pueblos de indios. In Diriomo, with the birth of the junta municipal, diverse racial identities that coexisted prior to independence tended to harden into a binary divide between Indians and non-Indians. Previously mestizos, mulattos, and castas variously constituted the non-Indian population of the pueblo. However, with the formation of the junta municipal those groups tended to gel into ladinos, a generic category implying non-Indian. Although Indian men were not explicitly excluded from the new municipal institutions, they did not participate in the life of Diriomo's junta municipal. The alcalde constitucional and the men who served on Diriomo's junta municipal were chosen by ladinos of the township, who perceived themselves as not-Indian. Indian and ladino subsistence producers were divided not by political fiat, but by everyday practices into the rulers and the ruled within the pueblo.

Although political institutions changed after Independence, the Indian labor draft continued much as before. Diriomo's new junta municipal ordered the alcaldes indígenas to mobilize the Indians to build roads, clean wells, and repair the church.[38] Frequently, ladino politicians admonished Indian leaders if the tasks were not done well.[39] Although Indian authorities largely accepted the neocolonial arrangement, on occasion they objected to particular aspects of the labor draft. Minutes of meetings of the junta municipal in 1845 demonstrate rising tensions between ladino and Indian authorities. Complaining that the pueblo was "dirty, miserable and a disgrace to the people of Diriomo," the ladino mayor reminded his Indian counterpart that it was the "customary responsibility" of the indígenas to clean the plaza and the town center. After Diriomo's mayor ordered the alcalde indígena to organize a labor draft, the latter objected, albeit timidly. He argued that because most Indians lived in the rural hamlets (caserios and *comarcas*), and ladinos near the plaza, the junta should pay the Indians for their labor. Diriomo's mayor brushed aside the objection, saying the project was for the common good of "el pueblo." With these words, he asserted a unity of purpose increasingly at odds with the ethnic differentiation of power within the pueblo.[40]

Soon afterward, Diriomo's Indian leadership requested a joint meeting of the ladino and Indian cabildos. The Indian authorities protested that their community was unable to bear the brunt of organizing the annual celebrations for Diriomo's patron saint, the Virgen de Candelaría. The alcalde indígena, who was also the patron (*mayordomo*) of the Fiesta de Candelaría, complained that he and his people were too poor to pay the church fees plus provide food, liquor, firewood, cloth, decorations, and music for the celebration.[41] After haggling unsuccessfully with the junta municipal the alcalde indígena resigned, saying, "I am poor and my responsibilities are the ruin of me and my family." The junta immediately appointed his successor, but as a concession promised to provide some supplies for the fiesta.

The dispute is important for two reasons: first, it provides evidence of rising conflicts between ladino and Indian officials; second, instead of adhering to custom and allowing Indians to name their own authorities, the town council appointed the alcalde indígena. Over the next years, Indian and ladino political spheres became increasingly separate, the former subordinated to the latter. The junta municipal developed into an instrument of ladino rule that fortified the political and economic power of the pueblo's emergent elite.

A land dispute that attracted considerable attention in the pueblo in 1846 throws light on early moves to privatize land. Although constitutions of 1826 and 1832 ratified both common and private property, the dispute shows that in the pueblos common land rights were threatened. Two Diriomeños claimed land rights to the same woodland (*monte*) within the boundaries of the común del pueblo.[42] On one side, the Indian comunero José Cano testified that his ancestors long enjoyed use rights (usufruct) to the woodland;

on the other, Don Pablo Espinosa, a ladino and the town's former mayor, claimed the land was his private property. Espinosa, who wanted to sell the land to Don Francisco Cuadra of Granada, said his father had purchased the woodland sometime before the turn of the century from the alcalde indígena, Francisco Pérez. Both sides in the dispute called witnesses to support their claims. Cano's neighbors testified that if Pérez had in fact sold the land, he had done so surreptitiously and illegally, as the woodland was part of the Indian commons. Because Espinosa had no document recording the sale, Diriomo's mayor, also the judge of first instance, dismissed the case. Although the land in question remained within the común del pueblo, the dispute foreshadowed wider struggles to erupt across Nicaragua. The next year, Indians and poor ladinos violently protested creeping moves to privatize land, impose new taxes, and create state monopolies and the expanding powers of local politicians.

Prior to the 1860s, the Nicaraguan state ruled in name only, as intraelite warfare prevented consolidation of central political institutions deserving of the name nation-state. After Independence, intense partisan rivalry, family feuds, and personal reprisals perpetuated political instability and internecine warfare.[43] Taking advantage of the anarchy that permeated the country, elites encroached on Indian common land and the ejidos belonging to the municipalities. Between 1845 and 1849, a string of local uprisings took on the character of a national rebellion. Nicaragua's infamously partisan nineteenth-century historians, led by José Dolores Gámez and Tomás Ayón, viewed the riots singularly through the lens of the profound divisions within the elite.[44] In their accounts, common people were mere pawns in the endemic struggles between Liberals and Conservatives, as politicians incited peasants and plebes to riot in favor of, or against, one or another faction. In their interpretation, the uprisings demonstrated the ease with which elites were able to manipulate the poor.

More recently, social historians have argued that the rebellions were manifestations of popular politics. E. Bradford Burns and, to a lesser degree, Rafael Casanova described the riots as an agrarian revolt against official and extraofficial moves to privatize the commons.[45] In their view, the uprisings were authentic popular protests by peasants and plebes against taxes, state monopolies, and an assortment of policies designed to undermine customary entitlements inherited from the colonial order. In *Nicaragua: Identidad y cultura política (1821–1858)*, Frances Kinloch Tijerino argues against the revisionist approach. Drawing on the writings of Gámez, among others, as well as on court records from the trials of rebel leaders, her interpretation of events largely confirms the traditional view. In her account, politicians enlisted common people into their camp and incited them to murder and ransack and destroy the property of their partisan rivals. Furthermore, elite politicians cynically sought alliances with the self-styled caudillos of the poor to cajole Indians and peasants to take up arms in support of different factions within the governing classes.

In fact, because of a scarcity of primary evidence about the events and people involved in the uprising, all interpretations of these crucial years remain tentative. My account, pieced together from documents in Diriomo's municipal archives and secondary sources, lends support for the revisionist view. There is ample evidence that peasants and plebes in different parts of Nicaragua took advantage of the breakdown in political authority to avenge long-standing grievances and to protest new ones. The rebels, as well as their demands, reflected the diversity of the lower stratum of society. Indian and peasant leaders denounced labor drafts, land enclosures, state monopolies of alcohol and tobacco, taxes, and the expanded reach of local government in the regulation of everyday life. By all accounts, rioting was localized, often spontaneous, and usually directed against the abuses of particular landlords and political officials. Two ladinos with popular followings, Bernabé Somoza and José María Valle, gave the uprisings some minimal leadership, political ideology, and practical continuity. Calling themselves liberators and generals of the poor (*los caudillos de los pobres*), they condemned abuses by the rich, oppression of the poor, and the plight of "los tristes indios infelices [the sad, unhappy Indians]."[46] Although contemporary accounts claimed that many landlords and officials were murdered, Casanova believes the figures are grossly exaggerated. He estimates that fewer than twenty men from the upper echelons of society were killed over the four years, far fewer than the number killed in the oligarchic civil wars. Nevertheless, the uprisings engendered fear in the ruling classes.

The pueblos surrounding Granada were at the epicenter of the rebellion and provided support to Bernabé Somoza, a local caudillo. Peasants rioted in Diriomo, Diriá, Masatepe, and Nandasmo; in Nandaime the population attacked soldiers garrisoned in the pueblo. The inhabitants of Jalteva rebelled after a *hacendado* (large land owner) fenced in part of the Indian common lands. Although the Jalteva riot was quelled, sporadic violence continued in the barrio.[47]

Terrorized by the specter of peasants in arms, the oligarchs of León and

Granada briefly interrupted their intraelite warfare and forged a common military force to defeat the rebellion. The national government struggled to station soldiers throughout the country to bring the rebellion to an end, and individual landowners hired private guards to defend their property. Notwithstanding a sometime alliance between elite politicians and Bernabé Somoza, after their falling-out a warrant was issued for Somoza's arrest. For several years Somoza managed to avoid capture, alternately fleeing the country and hiding out among supporters on the Meseta de los Pueblos just outside Granada. Some historians take this as a sign not only of indigenous support for Somoza, but of the Indian character of the rebellion. However, others believe that evidence in support of this interpretation is thin, coming mainly from contemporaries who claimed that several of Somoza's lieutenants were Indians who enjoyed wide support in Jalteva.[48]

I propose that part of the dilemma as to whether some of Somoza's lieutenants and supporters were Indian arises from the fact that distinctive Indian language and dress, ethnic markers that denoted Indianness in other parts of Mesoamerica (Guatemala and Mexico, for instance), had long been absent from the pueblos of Granada.[49] There the defining conditions of Indianness were common property rights, labor exactions, and the existence of Indian authorities in the comunidades indígenas. Consequently, insofar as the rebellions were motivated in part by resistance to land privatization, it would be surprising if they did not have, to some degree, an indigenous character. Similarly, it would have been surprising had Somoza and his lieutenants not appropriated the language of Indian rights to a movement that claimed to defend the customary entitlements of the lower social orders in postcolonial society.

The uprisings flared on and off for four years, indicative of the weakness of the state and the endurance of popular opposition to elite policies. Toward the end of the cycle of rebellion a riot erupted in Diriomo. The governor (prefect) of Granada requisitioned horses and cattle for what he called "the regional war" and levied a forced loan from citizens of the pueblo deemed able to pay. A number of ladinos refused to pay the war tax, and they were joined by four comuneros indígenas who contested their inclusion in the list of Diriomeños who owned more than 100 pesos' worth of property.[50] In 1849, in response to rioting in the pueblo, Diriomo's junta municipal asked regional officials to send in soldiers to restore order.[51] The local uprising set off a flurry of correspondence between Diriomo's mayor and the prefect of Granada about how to calm the situation. The mayor wrote that although he did not know what had sparked the violence, the prefect's demands on the pueblo "had intensified the misery of the population." Correspondence between the mayor and the prefect suggests that although few of the township's richer peasants made common cause with the rioters, they were not willing to shoulder the costs of repression.

Against the backdrop of regional uprisings, letters between Diriomo and Granada stopped abruptly. When correspondence resumed, the prefect told Diriomo's mayor to write nothing of importance and to send nothing of value in the post because the rebels regularly attacked the mail.[52] Just weeks before Somoza was apprehended, the government finally stationed soldiers in Diriomo. This was a mixed blessing for the junta municipal and a curse for the alcalde indígena: the junta had to pay the soldiers and provide auxiliaries to help them keep the peace; the alcalde indígena had to collect food and fodder from Indians of the pueblo to provision the troops.[53]

In 1849, Bernabé Somoza and some fifty insurgent leaders were captured, convicted of fomenting insurrection, and sentenced to death by firing squad in Granada's central plaza. Although government officials called for militarization of the countryside, the central government proved incapable of institutionalizing its authority in rural areas because it lacked funds, a national army, and an effective nation-state. To fill the void, ladino elites moved to reassert their control in the pueblos by expanding the reach of municipal government, thereby consolidating ladino domination and Indian subordination in the countryside.

Although official decrees and charters drafted prior to the uprisings recognized the legality of common property, in the climate of endemic anarchy constitutions and legality mattered less than the politics of power. In the Granada region landlords and elite politicians turned a blind eye to officialdom and moved to appropriate the commons, and Indians resisted the expropriation of their property. Although rioting in the pueblos surrounding Granada did not congeal into an organized agrarian revolt, I propose that a motif tying events together was anger at the continuing encroachment on the commons. The uprisings in Diriomo and surrounding pueblos de indios might be interpreted as the Indians' last stand, for never again did poor people in the pueblos, Indians as well as ladinos, organize militarily to defend common property rights and their customary entitlements.

State responses to the uprisings were contradictory. Divisions within the elite played out in part in ideological differences over the politics of common property and Indian entitlements. Nevertheless, at the highest and the most fragile echelon of power the state moved hesitantly to erode common land rights and the authority of Indian elites. In contrast to the constitutions of 1826 and 1832, draft charters of 1848 and 1854 did not explicitly guarantee common property. In 1862, the direction of change in state policy was clear: the government decreed that all land be surveyed to facilitate buying and selling and the state oversee the redistribution of common lands.[54] The decree sent an unambiguous signal of political intent, but the nation-state was in no condition to implement the ambitious program it outlined for another twenty years. However, at the lower echelons of power, the provincial and municipal levels, politicians engaged in a contradictory process of wresting power from Indian leaders on the one hand, while shoring up their standing in the comunidades on the other.

After the rebellion politics returned to business as usual in Diriomo. The municipal mayor ordered the alcalde indígena to organize labor contingents to rebuild wells and repair roads.[55] Several years later, when fighting between Liberals and Conservatives raged in the city of Granada, the department's governor (*jefe político*) repeatedly ordered Diriomo's mayor to send him more draft laborers. In the midst of the war in 1856, he wrote, "I need 45 laborers who are good workers. They will earn 4 reales per day. I expect you to comply without fail to my orders and deliver the workers on Monday next. This order takes precedence over all others, because as you know this work is of maximum importance."[56] Following custom, Diriomo's mayor ordered the alcalde indígena to fulfill the requisition.[57]

The juxtaposition between pressures on the common lands and business as usual exacerbated social tensions in the pueblos. In the colonial era the link between common land and forced labor was the centerpiece of the social contract between Indians and the state. But Nicaragua's postcolonial regime was moving to sever the historical connection between land rights and forced labor. Finding themselves squeezed between demands for labor and threatened land loss, a number of Indian alcaldes resigned.

Traditionally, Indian alcaldes were part agents of the state in their communities and part representatives of their communities vis-à-vis the state, and their role was mirrored in the formalities of selection. In the mid-nineteenth century, Indian alcaldes supposedly were chosen by senior males of their community before being sworn in to office by the junta municipal. However, in Diriomo, municipal officials increasingly intervened in the selection process.[58] After midcentury, the number of Indian men prepared to serve as alcalde of their community dwindled, apparently in response to heightened tensions between Indians and the ladino leadership.⁵⁹ Explaining that Indian comuneros had threatened him with machetes when he ordered them to participate in a labor draft, Mercedes López resigned as *mandón* of Diriomo's Indian community.⁶⁰ Teodoro Pérez resigned as *alcalde natural*, saying he was "so poor that he had no clothes for himself or his wife and children." His wife offered a different explanation for his resignation: "He fled and is in hiding because the mayor of Diriomo is persecuting him and forcing him to take possession of the post."⁶¹

Throughout the Granada region, local officials doggedly struggled to prevent the wholesale resignation of Indian leaders. Francisco López had been a compliant leader of Diriomo's Indian community for a number of years; therefore, the prefect of Granada was alarmed by the rumor that López had resigned. To find out what was afoot in Diriomo, the prefect sent this letter to the alcalde municipal:

> According to current laws and customs, we are mandated to protect the customs of the Indians, and because one of those customs is that there are alcaldes naturales indígenas, the *prefectura* requests the following information:
>
> 1. Was Sr. Francisco López reselected as alcalde natural of the pueblo?
>
> 2. Is he or is he not currently in possession of the post and carrying out its duties?
>
> 3. If the response to the above is negative, who removed him and why? Please supply details as to the causes.
>
> 4. Is there a functioning alcalde indígena in the pueblo, and if not explain the reasons why not?

The letter concludes, "López is a friend of the authorities and efforts should be made to ensure that he remains the alcalde natural."⁶²

In the mid-nineteenth century, successive prefects in Granada acted as protectors of the Indian alcaldes. They intervened in the internal affairs of Indian communities to support leaders who were facing criticism from below.⁶³ They also instructed ladino officials to honor the special privileges granted to Indian leaders.⁶⁴ The prefects were motivated by two factors: first, they aimed to guarantee that Indian leaders would continue to provide labor contingents; second, they wanted to ensure that loyal representatives of the state remained in Indian communities to serve as a conduit of information and authority, a transmission belt, between the government and the Indians.

What it meant to be Indian changed substantially over the course of the colonial and early postcolonial periods in the Granada region. Nevertheless, structures of domination displayed a remarkable continuity. The defining features of Indianness in the colonial era were common land rights, common subjection to labor and tribute exactions, and common representation by political institutions. These features largely survived independence. With the long-standing weakness of cultural markers of Indianness, what it meant to be Indian continued to be principally defined by land rights, labor exploitation, and communal representation. In the postcolonial period, common land rights served as the glue that held Indian communities together. However, as encroachments on the commons became more pronounced, conflicts between indigenous leaders and comuneros threatened to tear the communities apart.

CHAPTER THREE

Patriarchal Power in the Pueblos

To a remarkable degree, local politics in Diriomo in the mid-nineteenth century was gender politics. After Independence, ladino peasant men took control of the municipal government and accumulated authority largely by regulating domestic life. Before coffee production put pressure on land and labor, Diriomo's politicians directed their attention to governing the gendered norms and behavior of people in the township. This chapter analyzes the rise of patriarchal politics in the pueblo and argues that regulation of gender was central to the constitution of state power at the local level.

The state is the array of official institutions involved in governance. Although states represent themselves as presiding over the general interest, frequently class, gender, ethnic, and racial divisions belie that claim. Except under extraordinary circumstances, states promote the common good of particular sectors of the dominant classes. How states accomplish class rule depends on the balance of power in society, which is conditioned by historical and conjunctural factors. Subordinate groups endeavor to minimize their disadvantages, and ruling classes ordinarily construct consent by acceding to some demands from below. However, except in rare moments of upheaval, states operate within a "field of power" in which the sway of the upper classes far outweighs that wielded by the lower classes.[1]

This chapter analyzes the ways rich ladino peasants accumulated political power in Diriomo. Municipal governments in Nicaragua in the middle of the nineteenth century were not outposts of a national state; given the virtual absence of a nation-state, they were a substitute. Diriomo's municipal institutions fostered the authority of men from the upper strata of the peasantry who endeavored to govern the pueblo in their own interests. Although Diriomo's peasant elite claimed they ruled in the common interest of el pueblo, it was rarely so. The needs and desires of Indians and poor ladinos regularly clashed with the class, ethnic, and gender interests of Diriomo's emerging patriarchal elite.

Philip Corrigan and Derek Sayer have argued that state formation is a process of cultural revolution.[2] Drawing on their approach, this chapter examines the ways local government contributed to the construction of new—and the destruction of old—social relations and ideologies. By regulating the mundane activities of everyday life, Diriomo's municipal council forged a specific form of class, gender, and ethnic domination in the pueblo. Throughout Central America, between Independence and the coffee boom, municipal governments took the lead in regulating the social order. As the vanguard of emergent nation-states, they were central to the consolidation of authority in the public sphere. There are, of course, major conceptual and historical differences between the rise of the English bourgeois state that Corrigan and Sayer describe and local state making in nineteenth-century Nicaragua. Nevertheless, adapting their framework of state formation as cultural revolution provides insights about how, following the collapse of the Spanish colonial regime in Central America, a ladino, male peasant elite consolidated its domination in rural townships throughout Nicaragua. Local regulation of everyday life is part of the history of state formation in Latin America.[3]

Reforming Patriarchy

Corporate patriarchy stratified along lines of class, race, and gender underpinned late colonial society in Spanish America.[4] The patriarchal character of colonial society derived from Spanish laws dating from the thirteenth century.[5] These doctrines invested fathers and husbands with authority over and obligations toward women and younger males in their household. Patriarchal privilege inscribed in the principles of patria potestad granted senior men wide-ranging powers to control the labor, bodies, and property of their dependents and required patriarchs to protect their subordinates. Although patriarchal practices changed substantially over the course of the colonial period, the dialectic between authority and protection remained a central element of the patriarchal order. The ideology of governance in the colonial and postcolonial periods rested on the idea that a well-ordered society was composed of well-ruled families in which the senior male represented the state within the household and acted for family members vis-à-vis the state. In a sense, the relation between senior males and their dependents mirrored that between the Crown and its subjects: the patriarch exercised power, controlled labor, and demanded obedience; in return, he was expected to protect the men and women in his domain.[6]

Within the confines of the patriarchal regime, females in colonial Spanish America enjoyed greater privileges than women in other parts of the world. Partible inheritance laws guaranteed daughters and sons an equal share of their parents' wealth, including land, and the common marital property regime guaranteed wives an equal share of property acquired in marriage. In addition, females enjoyed a legal existence (*personería jurídica*) independent of their husband or father, which meant they were allowed, in principle, to sign contracts and speak in court. But few women were permitted to exercise these privileges, as married women and unmarried daughters remained subordinated to their father's or husband's patriarchal authority. In practice, widows composed the only group that decidedly benefited from the gendered privileges inscribed in the Hispanic legal tradition, as their husband's death legally freed them from direct patriarchal control.

In the nineteenth century liberal politicians across Latin America aspired to modernize their societies, and to that end they promoted two great reforms: land privatization and the secularization of marriage.[7] Both affected gender relations in significant ways. However, contrary to the prevailing view that liberalism unequivocally benefited women, I argue that property and marriage reforms had regressive as well as progressive effects on the gender order, with the outcome differentiated according to a woman's class and ethnicity. On the progressive side, the assault on corporate property allowed indigenous women to acquire private property in land. In Diriomo, as in other Indian communities across Mesoamerica, common property was a male right. Under customary law, usufruct or the right to use the commons was invested in male heads of household. As a consequence, Indian women's access to land was mediated through their male kin. However, after land privatization and abolition of the common property regime, national law replaced customary law and Indian women in Diriomo acquired the right to directly own and control land, albeit within the confines of the patriarchal order.

Liberal reforms also had regressive effects on women. In the late nineteenth century, some Latin American governments undermined legal provisions inherited from the colonial period that had guaranteed women an equal portion of inherited wealth and property, both parental and marital. The reforms, or more aptly, the counterreforms, aimed to lay the foundations for modern society by liberating property from archaic constraints. In particular, politicians hoped to diminish the fragmentation of land and wealth implied by the colonial inheritance system, because, to their way of thinking, the concentration of wealth and property was a precondition for development. While politicians heralded the positive effects of inheritance reforms, although these same reforms diminished the property protections women had enjoyed "since time immemorial," there was no public debate about their possible negative impact on women.

Concurrent with changes to property law, the Civil Code of 1871, enacted by a Conservative government, spelled out the terms whereby a husband controlled his wife's body and sexuality. To facilitate the inheritance of property, the law sought to simplify identification of biological parents. To that end it granted a husband legal control over his wife's womb, and thus by extension over her sexual practices.[8] A wife's legal rights, such as they were, pertained only if she was "decent," understood as monogamous and obedient to her husband. In cases of marital separation, a husband could confine his wife to live under the supervision of an "honorable" family for ten months. Although the code does not elaborate here, it seems fair to assume that the objective was to ensure that if she gave birth, the child would be the husband's heir. State regulation of gender norms went further: Nicaragua's civil codes granted impunity for uxoricide, or wife killing, if a husband could demonstrate that his wife was an adulteress. However, if he committed adultery, so long as his infidelities were not flagrant, his wife had no legal recourse. Impunity for uxoricide finally was struck from Nicaragua's new Civil Code in 1904. However, male adultery was legally sanctioned for another fifty years, which may partly explain why extralegal polygamy long remained widely practiced and tolerated.[9] It was not accidental that property reform coincided with intensification of patriarchal control over women's bodies and sexuality. The latter was meant to ensure the legitimacy of heirs for the transmission of private property.

Secularization of society, the second great transformation effected by many emergent liberal regimes, also had regressive repercussions for women. Across Latin America, incipient nation-states in the nineteenth century sought to legitimate their authority by wresting power from the church. In important ways, this battle was played out in the realm of gender. Successive governments throughout the region appropriated for themselves powers previously wielded by the Catholic Church, such as the regulation of marriage, annulment, sexuality, and legitimacy of birth. Insofar as the state claimed for itself the authority to regulate such central and tradition-ally sacred areas of life, it was a bold move. In Nicaragua, the Civil Code of 1871 initiated the transition from ecclesiastical to state control over mar-riage, a process that culminated in 1904, when only civil marriage was legally recognized.

Lewis Namier warned against imagining the past in terms of our own experience.[10] This caveat is particularly relevant for studying the histori-cal construction of gender. It is often argued that the Catholic Church has always undermined gender equality. The conclusion scholars draw from this interpretation is that moves toward secularization always represent steps in the modernization of gender relations.[11] But neither the former nor the latter proposition is necessarily true. In nineteenth-century Latin America, secularization had contradictory gendered effects.[12] To the extent that Catholicism naturalized the notion that motherhood was the sole pur-pose of women's lives, the church played a reactionary role. However, Catho-lic doctrine held that the marriage sacrament was a union of equals, and to the extent that the church upheld this article of faith, secularization tended to expand legal inequalities between men and women, particularly over the terms of marriage, separation, and sexuality. Consequently, in important ways the expanding reach of state regulation of gender reinforced patriarchal authority.[13]

Gender Politics and Local State Making

The one square league of common land granted by the Crown to Diriomo's pueblo de indios in the colonial period remained under the jurisdiction of the comunidad indígena until the late nineteenth century. Held in the name of the community and administered by its leaders, *el común* included fer-tile valleys, arable uplands, fields and pastures, forests on the slopes of the Mombacho Volcano, and a lake, La Laguna del Apoyo. Ladinos in Diriomo tried to purchase property from la comunidad, but until the late nineteenth century non-Indians had to make do by renting land at modest prices and under long-term arrangements from the comunidad. Although landed prop-erty was not privately owned, differential wealth in the form of *mejoras*, or improvements to the land such as hedgerows, fruit trees, crops, and cattle, internally stratified both Indian and ladino society.

Prior to land privatization, stratification by wealth was modest in Di-riomo. However, property differentiation by gender was stark both within and between the Indian and ladino groups. In the ladino community, women's property rights were regulated by national laws; in Indian society, property rights were regulated by customary laws that allocated common land rights to male heads of household. Similarly, membership in the comunidad indígena was restricted to adult males and mejoras were owned by men.

Evidence about the gendered character of the indigenous land tenure system comes from a number of sources. In a land claim from the 1860s, the claimant described the old system of rights to el común, saying that land rights were distributed among the men inscribed in the Indian community.[14] In the 1840s, when the municipal mayor itemized property in mejoras owned by individuals in the Indian community, no women (*indias*) appeared on the list.[15] The absence of females is significant as it demonstrates that partible inheritance laws did not apply among the indigenous population. Finally, petitioning for land titles in the course of the late nineteenth-century agrarian reform, Indian men and women invoked their father's traditional usufruct rights to the commons.[16] These sources indicate that Indian women's formal access to the commons derived from male kin. This contrasts with the principles underlying men's membership in the comunidad indígena, which regulated inheritance through matrilineal descent. In other words, rights to common resources passed through women, yet passed them by.[17] Cofradías, which owned and administered an important part of the collective wealth of the community, in particular cattle herds, also concentrated property in domains from which women were excluded. Thus, Indian women's formal access to the material resources of the community was indirect and mediated through senior males.

Political power in the comunidad was another masculine domain from which women were excluded. Governance of the community was entrusted to male authorities under the leadership of the alcalde indígena, who allocated usufruct rights, adjudicated disputes, administered the treasury (*caja de comunidad*), and organized religious fiestas.[18] Furthermore, as a number of sources indicate, only adult males participated in communal deliberations and the wider political life of the community.[19]

After Independence, with a vacuum of power at the level of the nation-state, political authority in Nicaragua devolved to the regions and locales. Municipalities, with their governing body, the junta municipal, were superimposed on comunidades indígenas, a prior ethnopolitical jurisdiction. Tensions inherent in the coexistence of the Indian and municipal jurisdictions intensified in Diriomo when it became apparent that municipal politics was becoming de facto a ladino sphere. Nicaragua's early constitutions conferred citizenship and the vote on men with property or a profession.[20] Although those charters did not explicitly exclude Indians from citizenship, no man of the *casta indígena* participated in Diriomo's *corporación municipal*. Indian and ladino political spheres were separate and increasingly unequal, the former subordinated to the latter.

Diriomo's ladino citizens, fifty or so men of the rich peasantry, elected the junta municipal. At its head sat the alcalde municipal, who was simultaneously the town's mayor, civil and criminal judge, bailiff, notary, and sometimes scribe. At midcentury, no man on the junta municipal claimed private ownership of land, yet paradoxically all fulfilled the property requirement for citizenship. Like the Indian leaders, they owned mejoras, or the products of labor; however, unlike Indians, their property included more substantial items such as mills, carts, and a small distillery.[21] Property in the products of labor, modest though it was, formed the economic basis of class stratification within the Indian and ladino sectors in the pueblo. Most people, whether Indian or ladino, had little private property besides their clothes, rustic houses, small domestic animals, and machetes.

Although the vast majority of Diriomeños were Indian, migration and disintegration of the colonial caste system ate away at the ethnic divide in the pueblo. Whether families were Indian or ladino increasingly depended on a mix of wealth, the social relations of landed property, and politics. The first provided the possibility for social mobility, which could effect ethnic conversion. The second was manifested concretely in land rights and served as the primary basis for identifying Indians and non-Indians. The third reflected the role and relative power of the comunidad indígena, the Indians' political organization, and its relationship to the junta municipal. Diriomo's junta municipal became the motor of peasant differentiation and ethnic assimilation, although in the mid-nineteenth century these processes were still at an early stage.

Gender relations, both within and between the Indian and ladino communities, rested on a mixture of material, ideological, and biological elements. In terms of the first two, control over property was central to gender differentiation, although it was ruled by different customs and laws in the two ethnic communities. In the case of indias, exclusion from direct access to property was customary and pertained to all females of the comunidad regardless of marital status. In the case of women in the ladino community (*ladinas*), access to or exclusion from property was regulated by national laws, which differentiated women by marital status. All ladinas were entitled to own property, but only widows were permitted to control it.[22] In sum, the nature of patriarchy, understood as senior male authority over and protection of females and males, was substantively different in Diriomo's two ethnic communities.

As the municipal junta consolidated its power in the pueblo, it eroded preexisting ethnic differences in the two gender regimes that coexisted in Diriomo. However, the erosion of gender differences developed unevenly, reflecting both the process of mestizaje and resistance by poor Diriomeñas to the morality imposed by the emergent ladino elite. Tribunals, composed of the alcalde and two men from the upper reaches of the town's ladino peasantry (*hombres de bien*), adjudicated disputes in the pueblo. Most cases decided by the local court involved domestic conflicts pertaining to women's honor, marital violence, rape, and child support. Before coffee, thus before conflicts over land and labor engrossed the attention of the junta municipal, a small clique of ladino men increasingly imposed their moral ethos on the community at large. In the first decades of ladino rule, the tribunals tended to regulate two codes of conduct for women of the pueblo: one for elite ladinas, another for poor women, mostly indias. The junta enforced an honor code for the former, which included sexual purity before marriage and monogamy afterward. For the latter, Diriomo's ladino fraternity tolerated a more flexible model of sexuality.

Both gender regimes precipitated an assortment of struggles in the juridical sphere. A case involving two ladina matrons provides a window on the meanings and practices of female honor among the rich peasantry. In a trial that polarized the elite of the pueblo, Juana Carballo accused Olaya Vásquez of "bringing about the loss of my publicly recognized honor as a good wife and mother."[23] The heart of the dispute was whether Carballo had had sexual relations with Vásquez's husband many years earlier. At the trial Carballo declared, through the intermediation of her husband, that "as the public judges people's honor, I cannot allow the evil that directly spoiled my person and reputation to pass in silence." Seventeen witnesses, all male, provided testimony about the conduct and reputation of both women, as well as about their husbands and families. In the end, the tribunal ruled that Vásquez had defamed Carballo with malicious intent, and the judge imposed a prison sentence for slander.

The case is interesting for a number of reasons. It demonstrates the power of the pueblo's male elite to regulate gender norms, an authority gradually appropriated by the junta municipal from the church. Furthermore, it underlines the public nature of a woman's honor and its importance to the extended family. Litigants, witnesses, and judges all described honor as a public virtue. This stood in stark contrast to the fact that the two litigants, because they were married women, had no legal persona in the public sphere. In the eyes of the law they were virtually their husband's chattel. Finally, married women's legal invisibility was evident in the courthouse rituals. Both women stood silently while their spouse spoke for them.

Diriomo's modest courtroom was the scene of Kafkaesque dramas in which married women had no voice and where their existence was acknowledged only through the words of their husband. In addition, as the courtroom was one of the few public spaces in Diriomo aside from the church, testimony played a significant role in constituting what Diriomeños came to perceive as normal and abnormal gendered behavior. Finally, the town's patriarchs sat in judgment on morality. By regulating the intimate aspects of Diriomeñas' everyday lives, they extended their power in the pueblo.

In a different vein, in his role as local magistrate, the alcalde municipal regulated the lives of poor women. Humble women frequently accused ladinos of the town's upper crust of sexual assault. Between 1851 and 1873, 102 accusations of rape, sexual assault, and battery were lodged by women in the township. However, more than 80 percent of the charges were dismissed by the tribunal for insufficient evidence, suggesting that elite ladinos of the township imposed a double-sided morality: one for females of their social strata, another for poorer women.[24] Nevertheless, the large number of accusations stand as evidence that women and men of the popular sectors did not condone the elites' customary abuse. Few plaintiffs were as successful as Gertrudis Banegas, who accused a member of the junta municipal of raping and kidnapping her daughter. In keeping with local custom, her denunciation was first dismissed by Diriomo's tribunal, but after pressure was brought to bear by Banegas's patrón, the case was transferred to Granada for a second opinion.[25]

When the junta municipal was consolidating its power in the community, there were many accusations that elite ladinos sexually abused poor women, who, because of the demographics of Diriomo, we can assume were mainly Indian. These charges can be interpreted in two ways: first, the patriarchs routinely, possibly systematically, violated indias, and second, sexual violence was a means, directly or indirectly, of fortifying ladino authority in the pueblo. Although the latter hypothesis might seem extreme, it is well known that the systematic rape of women has been a part of strategies to consolidate political and military domination throughout history. In addition, as historians have routinely demonstrated, the sexual abuse of Indian women was endemic to the exercise of class and ethnic domination in Latin America since the conquest. With this in mind, possibly what increased was not the incidence, but the reporting of sexual violations committed by the town's ladino elite.[26] On a practical level, the establishment of municipal tribunals in pueblos formerly ruled by Indian authorities presented women and men of the lower orders with new opportunities to pursue justice.[27] In Diriomo, public denunciations of sexual abuse demonstrate that ordinary people used the court system to contest the morality of the town fathers. Taken together, these cases suggest that Indians and the poorer strata of the ladino peasantry endeavored to assert a gender regime that differed markedly from the norms the elites attempted to impose. With the political transformation of the pueblo, it seems that men and women of Diriomo's lower orders resisted accumulation of power by the rich peasantry by contesting the sexual morality they attempted to impose.

In a case that occupied Granada's civil and religious leaders, the regulation of gender norms and the exercise of political power are intimately connected. In 1869 Marcelino Cano accused Diriomo's parish priest of abusing his wife.[28] Cano alleged that the priest forcibly detained his wife to avail himself of her labor and sexual services. Although the curate struck Cano for attempting to rescue his wife, initially the peasant tried to resolve the situation privately. He did not want to publicly accuse the clergyman of abuse because, in his words, "the priest is a person of dignity." However, after the priest beat him a second time, leaving him blind in one eye, Cano appealed to the bishop of Granada to intervene. Cano filed a formal complaint in the ecclesiastical court accusing the curate of raping his wife. According to Cano and his neighbors, the priest regularly mistreated townspeople, especially Diriomeñas, but his abusive behavior had been long tolerated. After appeals to the church fell on deaf ears, Cano sought justice from the town's secular tribunal. However, the elite ladinos who presided over the municipal court refused to adjudicate the case, but not because it fell within the ecclesiastical jurisdiction. Permitting the case to proceed, said the alcalde, "would encourage men of Cano's social standing to show disrespect for people in authority." The case demonstrates that men of the lower orders opposed the morality of the elite, but their protests frequently were ignored. Cano's case is particularly noteworthy as it reveals complicity between the church and local governing institutions to sustain the class and gender hierarchies that underpinned rule by the town's rich ladino peasantry. In matters of state making, by regulating sexuality and morality the alcalde municipal fortified the power of the township's patriarchs.

Between Independence and the coffee boom power was exercised mostly at the local level in Central America. This was an era when local elites consolidated their authority and extended the reach of municipal government by policing gender norms. With the emergence of the nation-state, weak though it was in Nicaragua, the mid-nineteenth century saw early moves toward the secularization of society. Where before the church had monopolized the regulation of marital relations and sexual behavior, incipient municipal governments took on this role as their own. Insofar as this allowed elite ladinos to regulate marriage and sexuality, it marked a major change. In Diriomo the junta municipal combined the customary powers of the church, the colonial state, and the family patriarch to govern the everyday lives of people in the community.

We know little in the case of the ladino minority, even less in the case of the Indian majority, about gender relations in households. I am not suggesting, therefore, that social control over women and regulation of gender norms occurred mostly in the public sphere. My argument is that patriarchal households were not the only, nor even the primary site of regulation and contestation of gender relations. The constitution of gender roles and relations is a social, not a private process. In rural Granada efforts by the elite to regulate gender, and struggles by the lower classes against the norms they imposed, were an important part of everyday politics in the nineteenth century. Municipal juntas took on the role of adjudicating gender norms and sexuality, and in exercising that authority they fortified their political domination. In Diriomo the politics of governance was gender politics.

Efforts by Diriomo's rich ladinos to legitimate patriarchal authority in the township chimed with the dominant ideology of the nation's political elite. According to Nicaragua's constitutions, men with property or a profession became citizens at a younger age if they were married.[29] In a similar vein, citizenship could be suspended if a son showed ingratitude toward his father.[30] Such conditionality underlined the importance Nicaragua's founding fathers accorded patriarchal authority inside and outside the home. In addition to institutionalizing family patriarchy, the country's founding charters codified the public authority of elite patriarchs cum fathers. The Republic of Nicaragua was in a true sense a polity of propertied males who governed their subordinates, male and female, in and beyond the confines of their family.

In the mid-nineteenth century, church and state in Nicaragua unleashed a campaign to shore up patriarchal authority. In the 1840s, when society's lower orders were rebelling against land enclosures, taxes, and local governments' expanded reach, Padre Agustín Vijil, curate of Granada, declared that society was in upheaval because people no longer respected patriarchal authority. Vijil stated that social unrest was caused by a decline in sexual morality and that "only marriage can preserve society."[31] He argued that patriarchs were the bulwark against disorder, and he concluded that consolidation of patriarchal authority in the family and the larger society would bring the chaos to an end.

Padre Vijil's condemnation of people's disregard for patriarchal authority was echoed in many quarters. In 1851 a pamphlet reminded young men that "a father's will is law in domestic society" and warned that "public order rests on the respect due the father and on the subsequent tranquility of the family."[32] In his inauguration as supreme director (i.e., president) of Nicaragua in 1853, Fruto Chamorro underscored these themes: "I consider myself as a loving but rigid father of the family [who] always seeks the welfare of his children . . . I will maintain peace, but like a good father I will punish the wayward son who disturbs it."[33] Chamorro's vision of the Nicaraguan nation as a family and his portrayal of presidential responsibilities as those of an authoritarian yet benevolent father mirrored the patriarchal politics of the times.[34]

Family Patterns

Upheavals in rural society, combined with reform of property and family law, affected marriage patterns and household composition in Diriomo. Nonmarrying behavior was a feature of local society at least since the late colonial era. According to the Bula de la Santa Crusada of 1776, the census administered for religious purposes throughout Central America, about 30 percent of adult Indians in Diriomo were unmarried.[35] The figure is largely consistent with patterns of nonmarrying behavior found throughout Latin America at that time, especially among the popular classes.[36] By the end of the nineteenth century, in Diriomo the unmarried adult population had increased to 50 percent.[37] Faced with an ever larger number of single mothers in the pueblo, governance of gender norms took on a different character as ladino elites turned their attention to regulating paternity and maternity. By adjudicating conflicts over child support and inheritance, Diriomo's elite men became arbiters of sexual norms and family morality. The tribunal's ideological role was particularly conspicuous in the many cases involving single women who claimed child support from wealthy ladinos of the pueblo. These cases demonstrate the extent to which so-called private life was publicly regulated. Taken together, child support cases from Diriomo lend support to the argument that the line between private and public spheres is highly permeable, if one exists at all.[38]

Some two hundred child support claims were filed with Diriomo's civil tribunal between 1850 and 1875. In one, Señora Josefana Bermúdez asked the alcalde to compel Sr. Eufreciano Alfaro to support his infant son, the offspring of their extramarital union. Nicaragua's civil code required fathers who accepted paternity to support children over the age of three, the customary age of weaning. Although the infant was under the statutory age, Señora Bermúdez petitioned the judges to compel the father to fulfill his paternal obligation immediately because she was too poor to support her children.[39] The señora explained that as a single mother living in conditions of extreme poverty she was unable to provide food for her four children. Although Señora Bermúdez testified that she had never married, she is described as *la señora* in the court records. Diriomo's scribes regularly listed women with children as señora, regardless of their marital status. It would seem the practice was intentional; it was certainly significant as it reinforced the ladino elite's ideal of matrimony in a pueblo where marriage was far from universal.

In the course of the trial the defendant, Sr. Alfaro, struck a deal with the alcalde. He offered to pay child support in return for future custody of his son. Such bargains were commonplace in Diriomo, where men regularly bartered recognition of paternity for custody. For some, willingness to assume responsibility for out-of-wedlock children might have stemmed more from material than from sentimental reasons. Diriomo's richer peasants frequently complained that they found extrafamilial labor hard to come by. With prospects for commercial production expanding, they faced a shortage of labor because Diriomeños mostly worked within their household economy. In a milieu where children might have been seen to be a productive asset, it is possible that aspiring peasant entrepreneurs regarded paternity, at least in part, as a social relationship of production.

In the Alfaro-Bermúdez dispute, the town's patriarchs presented the señora with a Faustian bargain. Either the father would pay child support and in return receive custody of his son when he reached his tenth birthday— the age poor children in Diriomo frequently were sent to work outside the family—or she could keep her son but receive nothing from the child's father. This was a dilemma shared by many poor peasants in Diriomo, who resorted to giving away or selling their children. For example, Santiago López asked the alcalde to order the return of his two sons. In López's words, "Last year my poverty forced me to give away [regalar] two of my sons, but the boys are too young to work incessantly from morning to night, as they have been forced to do, at tasks too onerous for their ages."[40]

State regulation of parental obligations was not always pro-patriarchal. Luiza Vallecío, a ladina artisan of some standing and a single mother, de-manded that Andrés Marcía, Diriomo's former mayor, recognize paternity of his two illegitimate sons (hijos naturales) and pay child support (pasarle ali-mentos, meaning literally "provide them with food").[41] Marcía agreed, stipu-lating the usual patriarchal bargain: he would supply food now in exchange for custody later. Throughout the trial Vallecío flouted the gender norms promulgated by the town fathers. She repudiated the patriarchal bargain, declaring that under no circumstances would she surrender custody of the children. In addition, she refused to pretend that her behavior conformed to the patriarchal ideal of womanhood. On the contrary, Vallecío scandalized the judges by describing her various sexual and household arrangements. After two years of litigation the tribunal ruled in favor of Vallecío: it ordered Marcía to pay child support and awarded Vallecío permanent custody of her children. Yet justice remained beyond her reach. Although the tribunal issued various writs demanding that Marcía comply with the ruling, he per-sisted in ignoring the court's orders. Vallecío finally demanded he be served with a prison sentence, but the tribunal turned a blind eye, perhaps because Marcía was part of the ladino fraternity that governed the township. Sev-eral years later Marcía was reelected by his peers to serve as Diriomo's mayor for a second time. In a measure of elite ladinos' gendered morality, Marcía's well-publicized sexual exploits inflicted no long-term damage to his political career.

In Diriomo, municipal government regulation of motherhood was con-tradictory. In the main, judicial decisions fortified an ideal of the patriar-chal family, a model that did not fit the life experiences of the many single mothers in the pueblo.[42] However, despite the tribunal's bias in favor of the patriarchal model, single women—and not exclusively those of the middle and upper strata—continued to turn to the legal system to resolve conflicts in their domestic arrangements. Women who brought cases before the local tribunal held out hope that the patriarchs would administer justice. Their expectations were grounded partly in tensions in family law between provisions that fortified patriarchal authority and those designed to protect women and children from poverty and abuse. A few women, Luiza Vallecío among them, even hoped to persuade the town fathers to recognize a gender arrangement that differed markedly from the patriarchal vision of morality. These tensions, both legal and social, made the tribunal an arena of struggle over the ideology and everyday practices of sexuality and family life. In Diriomo municipal intervention did not always have negative consequences for the individual woman embroiled in the judiciary. Yet class, race, and gender biases so infused the law, and Diriomo's social order, that the overall effect of municipal regulation was to fortify the gender, class, and ethnic domination of the male ladino elite.

Local court cases demonstrate some of the ways Diriomo's ladino patriarchs established family values. Interpretation of the civil codes, with all of their intricacies and contradictions, gave the junta wide berth to legitimate particular class, gender, and ethnic norms pertaining to the family, motherhood, and fatherhood. In Nicaragua, marital, family, and property law was explicitly differentiated by gender; in practice it was also differentiated by class and ethnicity. As a result, the tribunal's regulation of paternity and maternity generally reinforced the patriarchal ideals of the rich ladino peasantry in the township. Furthermore, by virtue of their political and juridical power, patriarchs were able to put pressure on poorer peasants, both ladino and Indian, to adhere to the gender norms constituted by the male elite.

Gender Politics in Transition

Politics in the rural pueblos of Nicaragua was not high in the sense of a rarefied sphere that touched only the lives of the elite. Municipal institutions dominated by rich ladino peasants regulated people's everyday practices of birth, child rearing, work, leisure, marriage, sex, and death. This gave the local elite wide-ranging authority in the community, which in turn fortified their expanding political power. The governance of gendered norms was an important aspect of everyday state formation in Nicaragua in the mid-nineteenth century.[43] The emerging local state, with its ample powers of regulation and surveillance, reshaped the mundane activities of people's lives. The authority of the tribunal to call in endless witnesses to testify about the sexual behavior and family mores of their neighbors was a daily reminder of the sway of local politicians. People knew that the powers of the alcalde, the junta municipal, the hombres de bien, and local courts extended into the domain of domestic life. Some behaviors they encouraged, others were tolerated, and quite a number were branded as deviant.

The interval between the collapse of colonial rule and the rise of the coffee economy was a period of political change in the pueblos, including changes in the politics of gender. The fabric of community, family, and household in the Indian pueblos unraveled and was rewoven under the direction of the municipal government. The process of negotiation and consolidation of power at the local level was as much about reconfiguring the gender order as it was about reconstructing class and ethnic relations. The emergent society in rural Granada in the mid-nineteenth century was marked by new forms of patriarchy. In Diriomo, just before the coffee economy transformed land and labor, the upper strata of the ladino peasantry fortified the junta munici-pal and made it into an instrument of class, ethnic, and gender rule. Pub-lic contestation over gender norms took place predominantly in the judicial sphere, which enhanced and legitimated the regulatory powers of the local state apparatus. Possibly of greatest significance, the local tribunal endeav-ored to fortify—ideologically and materially—the patriarchal ideals of the upper reaches of the ladino peasantry.

This history of gender contributes to new ways of thinking about local state formation. Gradually, in what once were Indian pueblos, a ladino peas-ant elite established its authority. With a hold on municipal government, they reshaped social relations and regulated people's everyday lives. Through the array of regulatory powers at their disposal, over the course of the nine-teenth century the municipal elite played a role in suppressing communal relations and Indian identity and in consolidating patriarchal norms that be-came the foundation of labor relations on coffee plantations.

CHAPTER FOUR

The Private Property Revolution

In the late nineteenth century land privatization transformed landscape and society in Latin America more than any other event since the conquest.[1] In Nicaragua before 1870 most land was common property; by 1920 most land was privately owned.[2] The momentous shift from common to private property developed unevenly across the country, sometimes constrained by conflicts within the dominant classes, sometimes by Indian resistance.[3] Around Granada, land privatization gave rise to large coffee estates and cattle ranches owned by members of the oligarchy and to socially differentiated peasant holdings. Unlike in other regions of the country, following the uprisings of the 1840s there was little organized Indian resistance to the privatization of property. In Diriomo, after initial protests against enclosure of the commons, Indians put their efforts into acquiring title to land. In the early years of the twentieth century the comunidad indígena ceased to play a political role in the pueblo, and Diriomeños gradually stopped thinking of themselves as Indian.

The history of privatization in Diriomo is not a romantic story of collective resistance to the appropriation of common property. Rather, it is a story of planters wielding power to amass large coffee estates, of collaboration between local officials and the leadership of Diriomo's indigenous community, and of the ways ordinary Diriomeños struggled to acquire title to small plots of land. After the demise of common property and the indigenous community, little by little ethnic distinctions within the pueblo were forgotten and Diriomeños considered themselves simply Nicaraguan peasants.

Liberalism and the Politics of Land

In nineteenth-century Latin America liberals generally sought to dismantle the corporate structures inherited from the colonial era.[4] Under Spanish colonialism, the state established differential land rights for corporate groups defined largely by race. In colonial Nicaragua, the vast majority of land was held by Indian communities, the church, and the Crown, which awarded land grants to individuals in return for services rendered.[5] Private landed property in the modern sense of individual dominion in perpetuity with rights to buy and sell land did not exist.[6]

Roughly cotemporaneous with the decline of Spanish colonialism in the New World, European political theorists advocated the idea that to establish the foundation for economic progress modern governments needed to strip away customary constraints on buying and selling, thus allowing market forces to regulate economic and social interactions.[7] Applying principles of economic freedom to political institutions, they envisaged the development of new modes of citizenship in which individuals' political rights would be a product not of their birth, but of differential property ownership and participation in the marketplace. Accordingly, European liberal theorists believed that altering the workings of the economy would transform the nature of state-society relations.[8] Ideas born of the European Age of Enlightenment crossed the Atlantic. Inspired by European writings about the advantages of market freedoms, many Latin American liberal theorists called for the abolition of corporate landholding to liberate property and the wider society from constraints inherited from the colonial era.

In Nicaragua, politicians on both sides of the partisan divide debated the merits and demerits of corporate versus private property in land and whether principles of citizenship in the new republic should tend in the direction of political inclusion or exclusion.[9] Both camps recognized, however, that government policies needed to reflect the realities of their country, not imported ideals. Consequently, although Conservatives and Liberals continued to argue over the ideology of corporate versus private landholdings, in practice frequently they advocated similar policies. Significantly, a majority of Nicaragua's most ardent Liberals recognized that labor freedom, one of the principles born out of the Enlightenment, was compatible neither with social conditions nor with their own economic interests. For that reason, leading Liberal politicians often went to great lengths to justify the gap between the tenets of liberalism and their policy prescriptions.[10]

After Independence Nicaraguan governments moved steadily, if un-evenly, to eliminate corporate control over land and to establish the rule of private property. Between 1830 and 1910 successive administrations en-acted some sixty land laws. The sheer quantity of legislation was a measure of disagreements between Liberals and Conservatives over the limits of pri-vate versus common property, of the state's inability to implement the laws of the land, and of the importance all accorded to the property issue. Not-withstanding continued tactical differences, the nation's elites soon came to embrace a common purpose: to privatize land in order to promote export agriculture. Thereafter, the labyrinthine ins and outs of land legislation dem-onstrate the intent—and the impossibility—of governmental regulation of the minute workings of the new private property regime.[11]

Following thirty years of land laws drafted by governments severely debilitated by intraelite warfare, Nicaragua's first peacetime constitution marked a watershed in the transformation from common to private land rights. Ratified in 1858, the constitution emphasized the inviolability of pri-vate property.[12] Over the next fifty years, land laws progressively eliminated corporate land rights and established private property as the principal form of land tenure. Successive laws regulated the sale and commercial use of landed property formerly under the domain of the state and the church and dissolved comunidades indígenas. To eliminate Indians' control over large tracts of land, repeated decrees demanded that half of Indians' common lands be sold at public auction and the remainder converted into private property and distributed to members of the comunidades. Furthermore, to ensure enclosure of the commons, the government stipulated that if the new owners did not fence their property and register their titles, they would for-feit the land.

Hand in hand with legislation to privatize land, the government pro-moted coffee production. After a series of halfway measures meant to en-courage coffee cultivation, in 1862 the government made a bold move and decreed that land suitable for coffee might be expropriated "in the national interest."[13] Over the next decades, the state promoted larger-scale produc-tion by subsidizing plantations with more than ten thousand trees, by estab-lishing a tariff regime that encouraged importation of processing machinery and exportation of coffee, and by implementing a tax system that favored large plantations.[14]

Crowning fifty years of legislation designed to curtail corporate landhold-ing and debilitate Indian communities, in 1906 the Liberal government of

President José Santos Zelaya decreed, "All common lands and Indian communities [are] extinguished forever more."[15] To that end, the Decree on Indigenous Communities and Ejidal Lands ordered municipalities to carry out a census of persons and a survey of lands that remained under the domain of Indian communities. It instructed local officials to divide up and distribute half of the Indians' common lands to individuals of *la casta indígena* and to sell the other half to buyers "preferably not of the indigenous caste." The law spelled out how various kinds of land should be surveyed, divided, and sold: it established a schedule of differential land prices based on soil quality, environmental conditions, and the social character of buyers and sellers, and it conditioned how proceeds from the sales could be spent. The decree concluded, "Once the division of communal land has been completed, the [Indian] communities will be extinguished and their members will be integrated into the population of the cities, towns and pueblos as individuals with the same rights and obligations as the other inhabitants of the region . . . and the authority of Indian mayors [alcaldes indígenas] will be null and void."

The 1906 decree was the death knell for Diriomo's Indian community. Although privatization of common lands started in the 1870s, the decree was keenly felt in the township. It hastened transfer of the remaining communal lands, terminated the authority of the alcalde indígena, and all but ended the political life of the Indian community. Following Zelaya's overthrow at the hands of partisan rivals in league with Washington, a Conservative government annulled abolition of the comunidades indígenas in 1914. It was but a temporary reprieve and had little impact on Diriomo. Never again did Indian organizations play a political role in the pueblo; never again did Diriomeños organize to defend their rights as Indians.

Although Nicaraguan land laws were a morass of contradictions, the direction of government policy had long been clear. Following Independence, the dominant classes moved to eliminate Indians' common land rights and to establish the rule of private property. But popular riots, internecine warfare, and foreign intervention had conspired against them. However, by the turn of the twentieth century, the government accomplished its goal: most of the country's best coffee lands were in the hands of large landowners, with the remainder owned by peasant proprietors.[16] The triumph of private property in Nicaragua was achieved not through the workings of the market's invisible hand, but through relentless state intervention to divest Indians of the common property rights they had enjoyed since the conquest.

Pioneers on the Frontier of Private Property

The property revolution began slowly in Diriomo, sowing discord and confusion. In the first place, the concept of private property in land was alien to Diriomeños, both Indian and ladino. On a more practical level, no one in the pueblo quite knew the boundaries or the legal status of the common land. Because corporate landholding had prevailed in the community since the proverbial time immemorial, and because there had been no scarcity of land, Diriomeños had paid little attention to the formalities of land tenure. Although national elites had been trying to eliminate corporate landholding since Independence, they had been largely unsuccessful in the vicinity.

In 1855, in one of the junta municipal's first discussions about the implications of the new property laws, the township's richer ladino peasants expressed skepticism about the touted advantages of private landholding.[17] At the same time, they found themselves in a dispute with the Indian authorities in the pueblo, but not about privatization per se. The dispute turned on the dual nature of corporate landholding in the pueblo. After Independence, municipal governments had been superimposed on the older ethnopolitical jurisdictions of the comunidades indígenas and allocated *ejidos*, or municipal lands.[18] Apparently, ladinos in Diriomo had done little to assert their authority over ejidal land. It seems that with the uprisings of the 1840s and no scarcity of land in the pueblo, the municipal junta decided to refrain from stirring up conflicts over land rights. Consequently, confusion as to the jurisdiction and the sociopolitical significance of dual systems of corporate landholding simmered for decades.

In the 1850s Diriomo's municipal junta decided it was time to sort out how ejidal lands assigned to the municipality corresponded to the Indians' common lands: whether the two jurisdictions overlapped or whether separate authorities ruled separate areas of land. A national decree ordering municipal authorities to survey Indian lands brought the matter to a head in 1854, when Diriomo's junta municipal resolved to comply with the law. However, their decision sparked a disagreement with Indian leaders as to where the Indians' common land lay in relation to the ejidal land.[19] Sidestepping that conflictive issue, the junta created a committee to oversee the surveyors and appointed as one of its members the alcalde indígena. It is likely that by including the alcalde the junta bowed to Indians' objections to the enclosure movement underway. But the nomination had a different outcome; it served to co-opt the Indian elite and exacerbated tensions between the leaders and comuneros of the comunidad indígena. From that time forward Diriomo's alcaldes indígenas generally acted as junior partners of the town's elite in managing the privatization of land.[20]

At that same meeting, the junta first mooted possibilities for coffee cultivation in the pueblo. The juxtaposition of coffee production and the need to survey the commons surely was not coincidental. It foreshadowed things to come. However, for the time being, nothing was done on either front because partisan warfare once again engulfed the region.[21] The National War culminated in 1856 in the siege of Granada, described by Bradford Burns as "a seventeen-day orgy of destruction."[22]

Over the next decade Diriomo's ladino elite redrew the political landscape of the pueblo and consolidated its control over the commons. In the 1860s, the junta municipal received the occasional land claim (*denuncia*) that set in motion the process of privatization. As there were few local precedents to guide the procedure, the junta approached each case in an ad hoc fashion. The practice as well as the concept of private property in land was still foreign to inhabitants of the pueblo. Even members of the municipal junta, men who soon acquired private property in land, initially believed that private landholding was contrary to the natural order.[23]

The meaning of private land evolved slowly in the municipality, in concert with the bureaucratic process. From early on, Granada's leading citizens registered claims to substantial tracts on Mombacho.[24] However, Diriomo's ladino elite filed most of the original petitions in the pueblo, and at first they worded their requests for land grants in the only frame of reference they knew: the buying and selling of mejoras, or improvements to the land. Petitions trickled in to privatize a *huerta* (a vegetable plot), a pasture, a *rastrojo* (field cleared for cultivation), a *parcela* (small plot of land), and a "*milpa* [subsistence plot of corn and beans] that yielded five *medios y cuartio* [five and a quarter boxes] of maize." Diriomeños still thought of land in terms of what it produced, not its size.[25] Claimants sometimes deployed the new vocabulary of private property, calling themselves owners (*dueños*), but their testimony reveals that they had usufruct rights to the commons, as they and their ancestors had exercised common property rights in the pueblo. Pioneers on the frontier of private property, Diriomeños did not grasp its revolutionary character. They petitioned for something new, private land, but framed it in the older tradition of usufruct and mejoras. Claimants' petitions and decisions by Diriomo's junta municipal referred randomly and interchangeably to los ejidos (the municipality's corporate land) and el común (the Indian common land), suggesting that people continued to confuse the two. Perhaps the junta encouraged ongoing confusion, as it served to erode the Indians' claim and to enhance their own authority.

Tensions between the old ways and the new generated conflicts in the pueblo. One of the first issues to confront municipal authorities was whether public rights of way took precedence over private land. In 1861, Francisco Básques brought suit against Procopio López, a former alcalde indígena, for fencing a plot in the ejidos del pueblo. Básques accused López of "appropriating el común to the prejudice of many [Diriomeños] by enclosing the right of way used from time immemorial to reach the common pasture land."[26] Unable to imagine an agrarian culture dominated by private landholding, Básques ended his testimony by predicting that "enclosing the commons will destroy the very basis of agriculture."

López responded to the accusations with a jumble of contradictory arguments. First, he claimed there was no right of way. Then he conceded that "in remote times there may have been a pathway but it had fallen into disuse." Finally, after the judge said he would see for himself if the path existed, López warned him that it was unnecessary, "because Básques's accusation is evil and intended only to promote discord in the pueblo." In the end, after refusing to cooperate with the tribunal, López requested that the case be transferred to Masaya, presumably because he thought the judge there more sympathetic. However, experts from Masaya examined the site and found "a very old pathway obviously heavily used which cut across the fenced milpa." Guided by the principle that common land use took precedence over private property, the judge ruled in Básques's favor.[27]

The judgment would seem to represent a victory for common property rights. However, emblematic of the revolution underway, the two men settled their dispute: Básques agreed to drop charges if López paid him eighteen *pesos sencillos*. The last line in the court transcript reads: "The land is considered to have been sold and the right of way remains closed."[28] So, rather than a defense of the common property tradition, the case symbolized its approaching defeat. In the end, private property rights took precedence over public access.

Land privatization was more advanced in the township than anyone in Diriomo realized. Behind the backs of the municipal council, in 1855 Granada's prefect awarded two large land grants on Mombacho to Don Juan Cuadra and Don Dionesio Chamorro to establish coffee plantations (fincas).[29] But the National War interrupted the oligarchs' plans to develop coffee estates and the land remained idle. In the interim, Diriomo's junta granted the same land to local claimants. The confusion of claims and counterclaims came to a head in suits lodged thirty years later by the oligarchs' descendents, who called on national politicians to ratify the original land grants. Diriomo's ladino elite also mobilized support, but of a different sort. The junta municipal called on Diriomeños to rally in front of the town hall "with the important purpose of declaring that the lands in question are part of the ejidos of Diriomo." To counter threats from outside, as opposed to those from within, the junta set aside its differences with the Indian authorities and appealed for a show of unity between the pueblo's Indians and ladinos. Although ladinos exercised local political power, they felt they still needed the support of the pueblo's Indian majority.[30]

The court appointed a surveyor to investigate the various claims. After interviewing inhabitants of "a hamlet of Indians" (*un caserío de indios*) on Mombacho, the judge decided that the original land grants to Chamorro and Cuadra were valid, even though part of the land fell within Diriomo's ejidos. Significantly, the dispute was part of a proxy war between Granada's oligarchy and Diriomo's elite over the rich coffee lands on Mombacho. In 1882 the national government ratified the boundary line dividing the two municipalities. Despite pressure from Granada, government surveyors ruled that about half the land on the volcano fell within the municipality of Diriomo and half within Granada.[31]

This case, and others like it, has contemporary as well as historical resonance. After the Sandinistas lost state power in 1990, owners whose land had been confiscated under the Sandinista Agrarian Reform moved to reclaim their land. Some hired private soldiers to expel beneficiaries of the agrarian reform; others pursued their claims through the courts; most did both. Invariably, their demand for restitution rested on the argument that their ancestors had purchased the land and the Sandinistas had desecrated private property rights. However, as land records from Diriomo and Granada reveal, Nicaragua's first coffee barons did not purchase their land; they marshaled political influence to expropriate land from the peasantry. The oligarchy created their landed domains by violating the common property rights of Indians and poor ladino peasants.

In the late nineteenth century, tensions within the property revolution gave rise to an array of conflicts: between old and new forms of land tenure, between claimants from Granada asking for larger tracts and people from Diriomo requesting smaller ones, and between Diriomeños who successfully petitioned for private property and their neighbors who lost age-old land rights. Notwithstanding the confusion that reigned with regard to land tenure, throughout the 1860s Diriomo's municipal junta generally upheld two principles. First, land was not a commodity to be sold; land would be distributed at the discretion of local politicians. Second, only petitioners who previously cultivated plots within the boundaries of the township were eligible for land grants. As events unfolded, the former principle was upheld, but the latter was ignored. Increasingly, the success of larger claims rested on the deployment of power, wealth, and patronage.

In the 1870s the trickle of petitions for private property in Diriomo became a torrent. Following verbal claims and a bewildering assortment of affidavits, testimonies, surveys, and fees, the junta often awarded claimants *derecho de posesión*, or right of possession.[32] At first this itself was a vague claim that, by emphasizing possession, not ownership, failed to clearly distinguish it from the earlier usufruct tradition. In hindsight, however, derecho de posesión marked a significant step in a process that ended, though often not until many years later, in legal title to private property in land. Some Diriomeños never reached the end of that labyrinthine process. Some bartered or sold their claims. Others never had that opportunity because larger planters simply appropriated their land. Still other Diriomeñas were forced to abandon claims halfway through the process either because they were unable to muster sufficient money to pay the assorted fees or because the teacher or scribe who had helped them navigate the bureaucracy turned their attention to other things. Nevertheless, contrary to the great emphasis in the Latin American historiography on expropriation of the peasantry, the vast majority of Diriomeños managed in the end to acquire private property in land.

The Tide Turns

With the tide definitively turning toward private property, richer peasants in the pueblo accommodated themselves to the new regime. Although Diriomeños with fewer resources and political connections continued to press for protection of common land rights, with the Indian elite collaborating in the privatization process, attempts to stave off the property revolution were individual and largely futile. Some Diriomeños looked to the justice system to block encroachments by larger landowners; others fended for themselves by uprooting coffee trees. In one notorious case, a peasant threatened with expropriation murdered a coffee planter.[33] Although individual acts of resistance plagued coffee planters, they did little to hold back the tide of change. Perversely, at the same time that the junta municipal was dismantling Indians' common land rights, it invoked the ethos of Diriomo's comunidad indígena to legitimate its authority outside the pueblo, particularly vis-à-vis Granadans who sought to usurp land and power from Diriomo's rising ladino elite.

The 1870s marked a watershed in the property revolution in Diriomo. The municipal junta's annual plan of 1873, the Plan de Arbitrios, demonstrates that Diriomo's political elite was coming to terms with the enormity of the shift from common land to private property. The Plan reproduced verbatim assorted national laws pertaining to land privatization, incongruous statements about landholding, and lists of taxes that did not apply to enterprises in the pueblo. It laid down provisions for auctioning public lands (*tierras baldías*) but stated that none existed within Diriomo's boundaries.[34] Yet despite the Plan's many inconsistencies, it demonstrates that Diriomo's elite was struggling to master the complicated regulations governing the property revolution.

The press of land claims—and of self-interest—soon pushed the municipal junta to draft an annual plan that corresponded more closely to realities at hand. The second master plan institutionalized the process of privatizing land by establishing procedures for registering claims.[35] Significantly, the Plan states that only the junta municipal had authority to distribute the resources of the pueblo, thus resolving any ambiguity that might have persisted with the Indian elite. Article 15 stipulates that a grant could not exceed ten *manzanas* (or 17 acres), although in fact the junta had already ratified larger grants and would continue to do so.[36] Members of the junta awarded themselves grants that, though not as generous as those secured by Granada's oligarchs, considerably exceeded the modest ceiling.[37] The everyday politics of land is reflected in the 1905 census of Diriomo's medium and larger landholders. Virtually all of the larger landowners in the district had served on the junta municipal in the preceding decades.[38] Reflecting the uneasy passage from a morality of common to private property, the Plan established equitable principles rarely upheld in practice. For example, Article 58 required successful land claimants to reimburse former occupants for fences and other improvements. However, the junta municipal did not back peasants who sought compensation.

The budget attached to the second Plan demonstrates indirectly that political power governed distribution of land. The budget includes a schedule of fees that correspond to the various steps involved in privatizing land. The fees were modest and changed little in subsequent decades, suggesting a certain democracy at work in the property revolution. However, Diriomeños who owned sizable fincas in the township in 1905 acquired them because they wielded power in the pueblo, not because of their ability to pay the fees.[39] The 1874 municipal budget also levied taxes on land and coffee trees and stipulated that the proceeds would be used to build a new municipal hall. Evidently the junta wanted to lay the foundations literally as well as figuratively for its authority. Finally, although the junta directed its attention primarily to managing the transition to private property, the Plan recognized the continued legality of common property rights and included a schedule of fees for planting a milpa, grazing cattle, hunting animals, and gathering firewood in the town's ejidos.

In keeping with past practice, the junta appointed Francisco Pérez, the alcalde indígena, "as representative of la clase indígena" to two commissions: one to survey the tierras edijales, the other to calculate the value of property for tax purposes.[40] His appointment provides further evidence that the Indian and ladino elites worked hand in hand to transform land tenure in the pueblo. Overall, the junta's second municipal plan played an important role in consolidating the political power of the ladino junta, and in codifying the rule of private property in land. Perhaps most important for the future of land privatization in the pueblo, it sustained cooperation between the ladino and Indian elites by granting a measure of authority, but no independence, to the alcalde indígena.

Although ladinos on the junta municipal embraced private property in land, a proposal to privatize the town's water supplies took them by surprise and caused considerable consternation. The low water table on the Meseta de los Pueblos was traditionally a problem; ironically, before the property revolution water had been a far scarcer resource than land. Recognizing the possibility of profiting from the water scarcity, an enterprising Granada merchant, Don Nilo Ortega, petitioned the junta to privatize water in the municipality. He offered to buy the town's wells on condition that the junta close the rights of way that provided public access to the streams and lakes within the boundaries of the pueblo. But the junta decided that a private monopoly on water was a step too far, and it met with leaders of the comunidad indígena to formulate a joint response to Ortega.[41] Together they created a commission to defend the "rights of the pueblo" (*los derechos del pueblo*). The commission issued a statement condemning the takeover bid, declaring that

Ortega's plan to privatize water would "deprive the pueblo of the freedom to take with complete liberty the principal element without which life itself would be reduced to a most lamentable state."[42] It is noteworthy that to resist the outside threat the junta again appealed to the ethos of community, asking Diriomeños to set aside their differences in the interests of the common good. The immediate struggle was successful: public rights of way and access to the town's wells were saved, but only temporarily.

In 1884, Don Yndalecio Morales, a former mayor of Diriomo and a member of the very junta that had rejected the earlier proposal to privatize water, asked the municipal junta to approve a similar, but grander, plan.[43] Morales pledged to direct the new enterprise himself and promised to sell clean water at cheap rates from carts that would cruise the town center from sunrise until sundown. This time the junta approved the project. Two factors might explain its change of heart: first, privatization had gone so far so fast that what once seemed unthinkable a decade later appeared reasonable; second, whereas the initial proposal represented an outside threat, Morales was one of the town fathers.

Another challenge from outside also prompted Diriomo's ladino elite to seek the support of Indians in the pueblo. In 1875, Diriomo's municipal junta was engaged in a dispute with its counterpart in Granada concerning control over the Mombacho Volcano. After the slopes of Mombacho were found to be ideal for coffee cultivation, Granada's junta municipal claimed that the volcano fell within its municipal jurisdiction. As in the past, Diriomo's junta sought allies in the comunidad indígena to resist the power of the oligarchs. At a meeting to discuss the controversy, the junta asked the Indian alcalde, Francisco Pérez, and others of la clase indígena to argue its case before Granada's junta municipal. The document they prepared argued that the area in question had been part of el común that had belonged to Diriomo's comunidad indígena since time immemorial.[44] Again Diriomo's ladino elite appropriated the discourse of community, but their appeal to the common interests of Diriomeños, and to the pueblo's indigenous heritage, stood in stark contrast to the very process at hand, itself a negation of the rights of the Indian community.

The junta's struggles with Granada's oligarchs reveal the contradictions of ethnic and class relations both within the pueblo and outside it. The junta justified its claim to Mombacho on the grounds that the land belonged to the comunidad indígena. However, the junta wanted to convert those lands to private property and commandeered indigenous leaders to serve as the public face of its endeavor. This confrontation coincided with a turning point in ethnic and class relations. Whereas within the sphere of local politics Diriomo's ladinos were progressively defining themselves in opposition to the comunidad indígena, to outsiders they continued to uphold the traditional rights of community when it served their interests. In confrontations with the Granada elite, Diriomo's ladino leaders adopted the discourse of Indian rights to protect resources they considered rightfully theirs against encroachments from the oligarchy.

In the initial stages of the dissolution of the commons, most poorer Diriomeños and Diriomeñas, Indian and ladino, were largely unaware of the transformation in the world around them. Between 1865 and 1875 the local tribunal was overwhelmed with complaints from individuals who had bartered their rights to the commons for paltry sums: five bags of salt, one bag of rice, two pesos. As one woman claimed, "Simplicity had made her blind to the fact that land could have value," and she asked the alcalde municipal to undo her mistake.[45] In the flood of land grants, the fields that Indian families had cultivated for generations and thought of as the foundation of their community were privatized, often without their knowledge. Frequently, only after hedgerows or coffee trees were planted did they discover that the municipal junta had awarded their fields to someone else: a rich ladino from the township, a grandee from Granada, or simply another Indian peasant from the pueblo. Initially, many poorer Diriomeños tried to stop the process. In the 1870s and 1880s people threatened with land loss appealed to the municipal junta. In a series of individual petitions, Diriomeños testified to their historical rights to the common lands. Some won their cases, but most people with a milpa or a *platanal* (stand of banana trees) in an area on the volcano ideal for coffee, or in the valley bottom, failed in their attempt to preserve their land rights.[46] Diriomeños with neither political clout nor a patrón who could influence the town council found it difficult to negotiate the bureaucratic maze involved in registering and contesting claims. Also, townspeople without sufficient connections or cash to enlist a teacher, scribe, or literate neighbor to argue their case before the agrarian tribunal tended to lose out in the race to acquire private property in land.

Most subsistence agriculturalists (*parceleros*), Indian and ladino, who had the misfortune to cultivate land on the volcano had their land expropriated silently. Most left few traces; paradoxically, often their losses were recorded only by the tell-tale words in a claimant's affidavit that although once the land had been cultivated, it had long been abandoned. Not all parceleros who lost land accepted their fate in silence. Litigation by those who fought against privatization shows that their land had not been abandoned; on the contrary, it was cultivated according to the prevailing custom of slash and burn agriculture that included a long fallow period.

Marcos Aguirre was in the front ranks of the resistance to expropriation by powerful interests. Aguirre claimed usufruct rights to five manzanas on Mombacho within the town's ejidos. In 1875 Celendino Borge of Granada, the regional military commander (*comandante*), petitioned the junta to grant him sixteen manzanas on the volcano to expand his coffee finca. After the junta approved Borge's claim, which encompassed Aguirre's parcela, the latter óbjected, saying the land rightfully belonged to him because his father and grandfather had cultivated the area and paid tribute for generations.[47] Furthermore, Aguirre explained that despite Borge's contention, his parcela had not been abandoned. Four years earlier he had hired peons to clear and plant a milpa, and following three years of cultivation the field was purposefully left fallow. Finally, Aguirre declared that if the town councilors granted Borge's request, they would demonstrate just how corrupt they were, because Borge had been employed by the junta to survey the ejidos and supervise the process of privatization.

When Comandante Borge took the stand he reminded the alcalde municipal that the junta had promised to award land to anyone who planted large stands of coffee. He had already planted two hundred trees and had four thousand seedlings waiting to go in, he said, as soon as the litigation was resolved. Throughout his testimony Borge emphasized three reasons he deserved the land grant. First, he extolled the modernizing virtues of coffee cultivation and boasted of being the first in the township to use barbed wire, instead of hedgerows, to fence his land. Second, turning Aguirre's accusation on its head, he argued that he should be given the land in recognition of his years of service to the junta. Third, he described his close connections to the country's leading politicians. This last seems part promise, that he could wield influence to benefit the junta municipal, and part threat, that the same influence could be brought to bear against Diriomo's inconsequential politicians. In contrast to the modest witnesses who spoke for Aguirre, two former alcaldes municipales testified on Borge's behalf. Before announcing his verdict in favor of Comandante Borge, the judge stated that although Aguirre had a legitimate claim to the land, the junta had the right to expropriate land for the purpose of planting coffee.

Aguirre appealed the decision to a higher court in Granada, where, unsurprisingly, Borge's influence was even more closely felt. The final judgment confirmed the earlier verdict, with the proviso that Aguirre pay Borge's damages and legal costs. Evidently, the authorities wanted to deter peasants from contesting the expansion of coffee estates. Defeated but still defiant, Aguirre said he had expected that the courts would "protect his legitimate possession of land from powerful men who tried to appropriate it." He, too, deserved preferential treatment, he said, as he and his father had supported the party in power by voluntarily contributing to the Conservative war effort. When the alcalde refused to reopen the case, an embittered Aguirre declared, "Not even a campesino can swallow such bitter pills without pliers [Ni un hombre del campo puede tragarse píldoras tan deformes sin las tenazas]."[48] Although Aguirre lost the battle over land, he persisted in resisting the power of large planters. Some twenty years later, Aguirre again sought justice through the courts, demanding that coffee planters respect the rights of indebted peons.[49]

It would be tempting to romanticize Aguirre, to portray him as a humble campesino who believed that property was theft. In fact, Aguirre was a middle peasant, apparently more intent on acquiring private land than on preserving common property rights. In the ensuing fifteen years he registered six land claims, and on two occasions poorer neighbors accused him of usurping their land.[50] In Diriomo the rise of coffee accelerated the social differentiation of the peasantry. Aguirre was one of the many who tried but failed to become a rich peasant. His repeated misfortunes seem to have been less the result of poverty than of not having a political patron to support his pursuit of upward mobility. Aguirre's case also raises important questions about ethnicity. Because Aguirre's ancestors paid tribute, it would seem fair to conclude that they, and probably he as well, were Indian. Although the issue of ethnicity is absent from the court record, it is possible that his Indianness contributed to his lack of success.

Aguirre was not the only peasant in Diriomo to resist privatization of land. He was, however, one of the most persistent in defending his rights through legal channels. Aguirre's insistence that he satisfied all of the requirements for a land grant provides a window on the political process underway. For poorer residents of Diriomo, prior usufruct rights and continuous cultivation were necessary but not sufficient conditions for successful claims. For more powerful claimants neither the former nor the latter was required, as the ruling classes had redefined productive land use to mean coffee cultivation, which, as one of Diriomo's mayors proclaimed, "would bring about national progress."[51]

In Diriomo resistance to the privatization of land was neither collective nor organized. I found no evidence that leaders of the comunidad indígena opposed privatization. The hierarchy of Diriomo's Indian community long had collaborated with the municipal junta, and it seems that in the process of privatization both sides saw the advantages of maintaining the tradition. Francisco Pérez remained alcalde indígena throughout this key period, and so far as I know, he consistently served the interests of the ladino elite.[52] In 1889 the municipal junta again named him to a commission charged with surveying land on the slopes of the volcano, which was a precursor to conceding large land grants to Don Gregorio Cuadra and others of the Granada oligarchy.[53] In this role, Pérez was an accomplice in expropriating land from Diriomo's poorer peasantry. Rewarded for services rendered to the local elite, he received a modest land grant on Mombacho, squeezed in between coffee fincas owned by Granada's oligarchs and men of Diriomo's elite.[54] Collusion between Diriomo's ladino and Indian leaders postponed rising class and ethnic tensions in the township but did not eliminate them. Ordinary Indians and ladinos resisted the junta's drive to turn common property of the masses into private property of the few.

Without leadership from Indian authorities, resistance to the property revolution was largely left to individuals. Some, like Aguirre, fought through the courts, a domain dominated by the ladino elite. Recourse to the judiciary undermined the possibility of collective resistance, as those who sought justice via the legal system hoped to escape the fate of their neighbors. But the majority of peasants who turned to the court to resist expropriation were disappointed, and even the occasional success in the judiciary did little to stem the tide of privatization. Working within the system pressured litigants to seek elite patrons, instead of alliances with Diriomeños of their caste and class. Furthermore, the judiciary often ensnared litigants in costly and drawn-out proceedings. Those whose cases were argued in court tended to be a favored group within the peasantry. Most people in the pueblo were too poor and too intimidated by the power of the alcalde to take their struggles into the legal domain. In addition, perhaps they believed that ultimately the judiciary favored those the system was designed to serve.

Most poor Diriomeños recognized that resistance in the legal sphere was fruitless without the support of a ladino on the town council or, better yet, one of Granada's grandees. Consequently, most people who struggled against the new property system simply tore down hedgerows and uprooted coffee trees. The authorities meted out harsh punishments to the few they managed to apprehend.[55] But the municipal junta frequently complained that petty crimes against property had become common and local officials were all but powerless to stop them. After a coffee planter was murdered on Mombacho in 1889, Diriomo's agrarian magistrate (*juez de agricultura*) created a civil patrol to police the volcano.[56] Diriomeños never organized collectively to resist privatization, and everyday forms of resistance—destroying property, legal appeals, petty insubordination, even the occasional murder—were insufficient to obstruct the forces of change. Accepting the inevitability of private landholding, Diriomeños and Diriomeñas joined the property revolution en masse. They worked the system as best they could to secure titles to small plots scattered over the hillsides and plateaus surrounding the town center.

Consolidation of Private Property

By the early twentieth century private property prevailed in rural Granada. Sensing that the tide had definitively turned, Diriomo's Indians and poor ladinos and ladinas endeavored to transform their corporate land rights into private holdings. At the same time, larger planters expanded their estates.[57] Political influence was key to the acquisition of land at both ends of the spectrum. In Diriomo, the process of land privatization was neither linear nor rapid. It was fraught with conflicts not only between large planters and poor peasants; it also generated struggles within the elite and within the peasantry. In other words, conflicts unleashed with the coffee revolution were not exclusively class- and caste-based. The majority of court cases involved disputes between elites over competing land claims and between peasants over boundaries.

Once private property was the norm, those at the top of the social pyramid grew bolder. Coffee planters petitioned for larger land grants and did little to hide the fact that the politics of property was driven by influence and power. Between 1889 and 1896 General Agustín Avilés, a Conservative war hero from Granada, pieced together two large coffee plantations on Diriomo's side of the volcano. He successfully petitioned the junta municipal for land grants totaling 150 manzanas and thereafter simply encroached on the surrounding properties.[58] Avilés had his land surveyed and fenced, and in 1900 he harvested about 200,000 coffee trees. Diriomo's junta wanted to curb the general's appetite for land and appointed a commission to investigate the legality of his later acquisitions. However, the investigation was aborted after General Juan Bodán, jefe político of Granada, informed the junta that he had approved Avilés's land grants, though unfortunately both he and the general had mislaid the papers. In recognition of the reach of Avilés's power and influence, Diriomo's junta accepted that Avilés was legal owner of the plantations.[59] After 1894, all land claims involving more than fifty manzanas in the Department of Granada needed approval of the regional governor, the jefe político.[60] In keeping with tradition, when Don Dionesio Chamorro requested a land grant on the volcano some twenty-five years later, he wrote to the minister of state asking him to approve the claim.[61] In the Granada district, politics and patronage regulated landholding well into the twentieth century.

Political influence was not new to the process of land privatization. Somewhat earlier General Bodán had given twenty manzanas on Mombacho to his comrade in arms from the National War, Santiago Rodríguez of Honduras, "in honor of their illustrious friendship." Although Diriomo's junta approved the grant, peasants expropriated by Bodán's generosity were not so accommodating. They took matters into their own hands and murdered Rodríguez.[62]

As coffee planters were assembling large properties, peasants were working their way through the bureaucracy to acquire titles to their small holdings. For the poor as well as the rich, political influence rather than the market's invisible hand regulated the process of privatization.[63] While the rich called on important government officials to substantiate their claims, Diriomo's peasants frequently turned to town councilors to help them secure titles to private property.[64] It was customary for poorer peasants to make use of patron-client networks in the township to avail themselves of the scribes, notaries, and surveyors needed to prepare the thick documentation that prefigured a final title deed. At the turn of the twentieth century, Diriomo's municipal mayor and scribe both helped peasants regularize their titles in exchange for a small fee.

Historians have often found that securing land titles was a necessary step prior to the development of large coffee estates. Taken as guarantee of an owner's domain, titles were regarded as a fundamental prerequisite for financing. Consequently, aspiring planters refrained from investing heavily in saplings until they secured title to the land. In Granada it seems that the system worked the other way around: having an ongoing coffee concern facilitated title acquisition. At the turn of the twentieth century, some planters in the Diriomo-Granada district had yet to secure title to their land, but this did not prevent them from establishing large plantations. In Diriomo, often an entrepreneur's first step was to plant coffee trees. Then he (in one case, she) would petition for the right of possession based on the argument that, unlike the subsistence peasantry, he was putting the land to productive use. In 1889 two of Diriomo's midsize coffee planters, Luis Felipe Tífer and Jacinto Fernández, petitioned the junta for land grants on Mombacho to regularize their domain. Some years earlier they had planted coffee groves in the ejidos del pueblo and on that basis they claimed possession. Unlike Marcos Aguirre and other peasants whose lands on the volcano had been expropriated, Tífer and Fernández were awarded the grants. Their success can be simply explained: both men boasted successful coffee plantations and both were members of the town's political elite.[65] Another contributory factor that explains the willingness of entrepreneurs to develop coffee fincas before they held land title is that Nicaragua lacked formal financial institutions before 1910. In their absence, investment funds for the coffee sector were supplied by state subsidies, supplemented by money raised through kinship and partisan networks.[66]

Documentation in Diriomo's municipal archive sheds considerable light on financing for small and medium commercial ventures in the township, but little information on the financial resources available to large coffee growers. Customarily, small commercial operators borrowed money from larger planters, or local lenders, with the promise to repay the loan after the harvest. An insidious practice prevailed in small-scale borrowing in the township: lenders ordinarily stipulated that should the borrower default, he or she would be required to repay the loan with labor on the lender's plantation. This practice regularly dragged enterprising peasants into debt peonage and contributed to the rise of social inequality in the township. In addition, disagreements between borrowers and lenders gave rise to numerous court contests between rich and poor peasants in Diriomo, which I treat at length in chapter 6, where I analyze the plantation labor system and debt peonage.

After the Upheaval

In the fifty years between 1860 and 1910, common property rights were all but swept away and private property in land became the norm in the Department of Granada. Although new patterns of landholding dominated the countryside, the process was not over. As late as 1932 elite Granadans still were pressing government officials to cede them lands remaining in the pub-

Table 1. Distribution of Land in Diriomo (for holdings < 100 manzanas, ca. 1900)

Category	HOUSEHOLDS		
	Number	Percentage	Average size
Landless* (< 4 mz.)	28	4	3
Poor peasantry (4–6 mz.)	260	37	5
Middle peasantry (7–15 mz.)	275	39	9
Rich peasantry (16–49 mz.)	134	19	27
Commercial planters (50–99 mz.)	7	1	61
Total	704	100	na

Note: Manzana, the traditional measure of land in Central America, is still used in Nicaragua. 1 manzana = 1.72 acres, or 0.7 hectares.

* Contemporaries considered holdings below 4 manzanas too small for household subsistence. Therefore, for simplicity's sake, I call this category landless.

Sources: Calculated by author from Libro de Matrícula de Fincas, Año 1905, Diriomo; Libro en que figuran las personas obligadas a pagar el canon de ley, Diriomo, 1902; and Resúmen del Censo Provisional de 1906, Departamento de Granada, Población Diriomo, Ramo Agricultura, AMD.

lic domain. Additionally, some of Diriomo's poor and middle peasants still were wending their way through the bureaucratic maze to secure titles to modest claims.[67] Nevertheless, by 1910 a new society had emerged out of the upheaval.

Turn-of-the-century property registers, compiled by Diriomo's municipal mayors (alcaldes municipales), provide a picture of landholding in the pueblo after privatization (Table 1).[68] With 704 households and a population of 4,188, acutely land-poor families (those owning less than four manzanas) accounted for 4 percent of households. This stratum of landless peasants was composed largely of Indians who had lost common land rights and who had not managed to acquire private plots, for whatever reasons. The vast majority of households (76 percent) farmed between four and fifteen manzanas. With four manzanas considered the minimum necessary for household subsistence, these families constituted the poor and middle peasantry. Families in this stratum included Indians who had previously enjoyed common property rights and ladinos. The next stratum, Diriomo's rich peasantry, farmed between sixteen and forty-nine manzanas, accounting for 19 percent of households. This group included farmers who combined cash crop farming, small-scale trade, and subsistence production. Families in this stratum were in the main ladino, though some were Indian who had previously enjoyed common property rights.[69] At the pinnacle of local society stood Diriomo's commercial planters: they farmed between fifty and ninety-nine manzanas and accounted for fewer than 2 percent of households in the municipality. These ladino planters ruled the municipality, rotating among themselves the top posts in local government.

A salient aspect of the social differentiation of Diriomo's peasantry was that families in the poorest strata became poorer and their survival more precarious. After privatization, Indians lost access to common land for cultivation and pasture, and large coffee fincas stood on the slopes of the volcano where before Diriomeños had hunted and gathered firewood. Of equal significance, private property fixed landholding in a spatial sense. Before the rise of coffee and private land, shifting slash and burn techniques predominated in Diriomo. Common land rights suited that cultivation system, for households moved their milpas every few years, allowing fields to lie fallow and regrowth to restore the soil's fertility. However, privatization spatially fixed peasant agriculture, and poorer peasants began to regard fallow periods as a luxury rather than a necessity. This accelerated soil erosion and contributed to declining agricultural productivity and ecological degradation in the district.[70]

Diriomo's variegated pattern of landholding was overlaid, almost literally, by the coffee estates on Mombacho, owned in the main by Granada's leading families. By the early twentieth century the Mombacho Volcano dominated the economic and political landscape of the region. With fifty plantations on the volcano, coffee production in the region was highly concentrated: twenty fincas with more than one hundred manzanas planted with coffee groves, most owned by Granadans, dominated the sector (Table 2). These fincas produced 94 percent of the coffee and covered 87 percent of the land planted in coffee in the department.[71] A distinctive feature of Granada's large coffee estates was their high productivity. Although Nicaragua was infamous for having the lowest coffee yields in Central America, the Mombacho mini-region was atypical. Large producers on the volcano produced on average 17 ounces of processed coffee beans per tree, whereas their competitors in Carazo and Managua produced 14 and 11 ounces, respectively. This put Granada's coffee industry almost on a par with large producers in Guatemala and Costa Rica.[72]

1. Francisco Salazar, owner of coffee fincas El Amparo and La Margarita, ca. 1900. Oil painting.

2. Margarita Castillo, wife of Francisco Salazar, ca. 1900. Oil painting.

A list of Granada's large coffee producers reads like a *Who's Who* of Nicaraguan society at the turn of the twentieth century. However, there was one anomaly: Alejandro Mejía, regularly described as "el indio Mejía" in the oral histories I recorded with older Diriomeños. Mejía was one of the first Diriomeños to claim land on the volcano and to compete with the Granada elite in the coffee industry. Before most people in the township realized that land had value, Mejía staked claims in the tierras comunales on Mombacho and subsequently consolidated his holdings by buying and bartering surrounding parcels of land. In the 1880s he controlled land sufficient to develop two large coffee fincas located alongside the estates of the nation's oligarchs. By 1910, Mejía was one of the largest planters in the region, with more than 270 manzanas planted in coffee on the volcano.[73]

Although Mejía was Diriomo's wealthiest resident and largest landowner, he never participated with the town's propertied elite on the junta municipal and he never held political office. In all likelihood, Mejía was excluded because he was Indian. Mejía's extraordinary career gave rise to countless folk

3. Coffee bushes under shade tree, finca on Mombacho Volcano, 1991.

Table 2. Coffee Estates in the Department of Granada, 1909–1910

Size of estate (in manzanas)	Number of estates	Total area (in manzanas)	Number of trees	Produc- tion*	Estates	Total area	Trees	Produc- tion
	ABSOLUTE				PERCENTAGE			
0–6	4	17	9,000	48	8.2	0.3	0.5	0.4
7–15	11	121	31,200	104	22.4	2.1	1.8	0.9
16–49	8	200	48,200	114	16.3	3.5	2.8	1.0
50–99	6	370	79,000	373	12.2	6.5	4.7	3.3
100–199	9	1,306	472,300	3,074	18.4	23.0	27.8	27.1
200+	11	3,657	1,057,000	7,635	22.4	64.5	62.3	67.3
Total	49	5,671	1,696,700	11,348	100.0	100.0	100.0	

*In quintales; 1 quintal = 100 pounds of green coffee beans = approximately 46 kilograms.

Source: Calculated from "El Censo Cafetalero de 1909/10."

stories in which he is described as "el indio Rico," shortened to "el Wico." In Diriomo's oral tradition, Mejía is portrayed as the cunning rustic who proved he was cleverer than the illustrious men of Granada's elite. At the same time, he is remembered, rightly or wrongly, as a cruel and sadistic patrón who exploited and abused his peons more ruthlessly than other planters.[74]

Despite their father's exclusion, Mejía's children enjoyed advantages conferred by wealth, property, and schooling; they became professionals of the highest standing and joined the town's social and political elite. Although shades of racism continued to permeate stories about the many grisly ways that Mejía personally punished his peons, that his sons and daughters became members in good standing of the local elite points both to the fluidity of ethnic differences in the pueblo and to their declining importance in the early decades of the twentieth century.

In the second half of the nineteenth century, Diriomo's junta tried and failed to retain exclusive control over Mombacho for the local elite. Nevertheless, down through the years Diriomo's town fathers made their peace with Granada's coffee barons. After 1910, land transactions in the district tended to reinforce the pattern of landholding that had taken shape in the preceding fifty years. That pattern remained more or less intact until the Sandinista Agrarian Reform in the 1980s.

Ambiguities of Transition

At the cusp of the twentieth century the older common property system was dying out, but it was not yet extinct. In 1902, Diriomo's alcalde municipal compiled a register of properties in the pueblo that reveals ambiguities of a land system in the throes of transition. The very name of the register belies one of its principal purposes: "Libro en que figuran las personas obligadas a pagar el canon de ley" implies that the list was composed to collect the traditional canon de ley, the fee the comunidad indígena, and later the municipality, charged for use of the community's corporate landholding.[75] However, even though the alcalde collected fees from some Diriomeños, it seems that the primary purpose of the exercise was to determine how far privatization had advanced in the pueblo. Although larger holdings listed in the register are described as private property, smaller ones tended to be in an in between state: not yet private with title deed, but no longer corporate. The document provides insights into a society in the aftermath of upheaval, where neither the status nor the meanings of private property had hardened and where many people remained unsure about the status of their landholdings.

In compiling the register, the alcalde inquired first about the legal standing of people's land. He asked a series of questions: "Are you the owner in possession of a title? . . . Do you have rights to possession [derecho de posesión]? . . . Have you filed a land claim [denuncia]? . . . Do you exercise usufruct rights in the town's corporate lands [tierras ejidales]?" In addition, he asked people to describe the size, use, and location of their holdings. A minority of Diriomeños and Diriomeñas stated unequivocally that their land was their "exclusive private property [mi exclusiva propiedad privada]," but many were less sure about the present status of their holding. Also, whereas most Diriomeños clearly described their land use, many poorer peasants tended to be vague as to the size of their plots. For example, Juana Centeno, a poor peasant woman, reported, "I grow plantain trees and animal fodder [chaguite] on a hillside [monte], and I have fields of stubble [rastrojo] located in a narrow valley some distance from the pueblo where my family will plant a milpa after the rains come. I have some land surrounding my dwelling [choza] where we raise chickens and sometimes a pig. I harvest several fruit trees, also one cacao and one rubber tree; I grow bamboo [caña de construcción] for repairing the cottage, and I cultivate small amounts of sugar cane and cotton."

However, in answer to the alcalde's question about the size of her holdings, she replied first that she did not know, then that the milpa was "more or less one-half manzana" and the land surrounding the choza was "probably about two manzanas." As to tenure, her ancestors had enjoyed usufruct (*el uso de la tierra*), and she recently filed a claim for derecho de posesión with the help of Doña Echeverry, wife of the coffee planter for whom her family worked as debt peons.

The objective of the next exercise to track property in the township was more straightforward. The 1905 register, *el Libro de Matricula de Fincas*, was compiled in order to levy a municipal tax on all enterprises in the township.[76] Consequently, in addition to land, the list includes tools, machinery, farm animals, standing crops, buildings, and the workshops owned by the town's artisans. Interestingly, a list of employees was included with assets of the enterprise. This suggests that workers were considered chattel, or property, at least for tax purposes. Certainly debt peons, or more precisely the debts of peons, legally constituted part of the property of coffee estates and were listed as such for tax and inheritance purposes. Keeping this in mind, it seems safe to assume that artisans' employees, at least if they were indebted to their master, fell into the same legal and social category.

Conclusion: Barriers to Capitalism

Land privatization revolutionized class, ethnic, and gender relations in Diriomo. Private property did not, however, usher in a capitalist market in land. Polanyi distinguishes between two types of land markets. In one, land transactions and their trappings, particularly price and supply, are directly regulated by the state. In the other, the state creates the institutional setting for buying and selling but does not directly regulate prices and designate the supply of land. In his theoretical framework, the first corresponds to noncapitalist land markets, the second to capitalism.[77] Polanyi offers a further insight that I drew on to understand social change in Diriomo. He argues that social relations of property can be understood only in the context of the wider class system in which they are embedded. Accordingly, land markets characteristically conform to whatever principles of exchange predominate in the particular society and reinforce the ascendant dynamics of that social milieu. Evidence from Diriomo supports Polanyi's definition of a noncapitalist land market. Land privatization was directly regulated by the state, acquisition of large holdings all but required intervention by authorities in the upper echelons of political power, and peasants secured titles to small land-holding by assiduously complying with regulations enforced by local politicians. In Diriomo, private property brought into being new social relations that were not regulated by capitalist markets.

In Diriomo, land privatization fundamentally transformed property relations among the peasantry, as well as in the plantation sector. Before the rise of private property most Diriomeños were comuneros who enjoyed use rights to the common lands of the community. After the property revolution, peasants owned private plots that they could buy and sell or forfeit to debt collectors. Although privatization impoverished some Diriomeños, social differentiation in the pueblo was not sufficiently advanced to forge a free wage labor force for the plantations. Critically, with landless and acutely land-poor households constituting only 4 percent of the community, few men or women relied principally on waged labor for survival.

In principle, Diriomo's poor and middle subsistence peasantry might not have posed an insurmountable obstacle to the rise of capitalism in Granada's coffee sector. Coffee cultivation is highly seasonal: planters require a large labor force only for the duration of a two- to three-month harvest; the rest of the year planters need a relatively small number of workers. Therefore, the availability of peasants who sustain themselves through subsistence agriculture might have allowed planters to hire workers at wages well below the level necessary to maintain a rural family, thereby increasing profits in the sector.[78] However, in Granada, the coffee harvest clashes with the peasants' harvest of corn and beans, their means of subsistence.[79] Although power relations between planters and peasants were key to defining the labor system on coffee estates, this "natural" factor also contributed to the making of a plantation labor system that rested on coercion, but whose effects were mitigated by patriarchy. In Diriomo, the combination of coercion and patriarchy impeded the emergence of capitalist relations of production until the 1960s.

On the question of ethnic relations, the rise of private property set in motion the demise of Diriomo's Indian community. In late-nineteenth-century Diriomo, Indian identity rested predominantly on entitlement to the common lands, and before that also on forced labor obligations. Destruction of corporate property rights undermined the Indian community and accentuated preexisting tensions between Diriomo's Indian leadership and membership. As this chapter demonstrated, the town's Indian elite collaborated in the process of land privatization, thereby thwarting possibilities for collective resistance. When Diriomo's Indians recognized that they could not preserve common property rights, they struggled in a different way: to secure private property to the lands they had cultivated in the ejidos. Although Diriomeños with parcelas on the volcano were dispossessed by coffee planters, they composed a minority of the pueblo's population. In the municipality at large, the privatization process resulted in peasantization more than in expropriation.

This chapter examined the destruction of common property and the rise of private property associated with the spread of coffee in Diriomo. It concluded that changes in the rural social order were more incongruent than congruent with the development of capitalism. It is not that this wave of land privatizations had nothing to do with the eventual capitalist transition in Nicaragua. Insofar as old ways of combining land, labor, and power came to an end, it did. But struggles over what would replace the old ways produced social relations and patterns of landholding that impeded the emergence of a bourgeois order.

CHAPTER FIVE

Gendered Contradictions of Liberalism: Ethnicity, Property, and Households

The combination of reforms to inheritance rights and land privatization radically altered gender relations of property in Nicaragua at the turn of the twentieth century. Two features of what I call the gendered contradictions of liberalism can be seen in microcosm in Diriomo. First, Indian women overcame customary barriers to land rights and many acquired title to property. After the demise of Diriomo's Indian community, 14 percent of landholdings were owned by women, mostly of the poorer peasantry. Second, females were conspicuously underrepresented among the pueblo's larger landed proprietors. Various factors combined to marginalize women from the upper reaches of land ownership, but the liberal reforms that undermined women's guarantees to parental and marital property were possibly the most important. Some authors stress the power of patriarchal culture in reproducing gendered inequalities; this study emphasizes the material and legal aspects of patriarchy that subordinated women and men to senior male domination.

Before describing how liberal reforms to property and patriarchal authority differentially affected women and men in Diriomo, I review the patriarchal character of colonial jurisprudence: the regime that liberals whittled away in their desire to establish the foundations for economic progress. Expanding on the presentation in chapter 3, I begin with an examination of the regulations that had protected women's rights to property. First, however, I clarify the sense in which I use the terms liberal and liberalism. Liberalism in Latin America, both its ideologies and practices, was famously ambiguous and multivariant, as politicians selectively adapted different strands of European liberal thought to suit their needs. In addition, in different countries members of both Conservative and Liberal parties were influenced by elements of European liberal thought and implemented what might broadly be considered liberal programs in the late nineteenth and early twentieth centuries.[1] Consequently, in this book the terms liberal and liberalism denote a political approach broadly in line with liberal doctrines current in Latin America. Foremost among these were land privatization, the uneven extension of male citizenship and political rights, the rollback of inheritance guarantees, and the dismantling of colonial regulations on trade.

As a number of authors have argued, despite bitter partisan wars that destabilized Nicaragua over the long term, Liberals and Conservatives frequently endorsed similar policies.[2] Although Conservatives ruled from 1858 to 1893, sometimes referred to as the Thirty-Year Peace, they enacted measures endorsed by liberals across the continent. In other words, Conservative governments enacted legislation I describe as liberal, and politicians advancing liberal measures might have been members of the Conservative Party. Unsurprisingly, both the underlying causes of Nicaragua's endemic partisan warfare and the extent of political osmosis between Liberals and Conservatives have generated considerable debate among historians.[3] My contribution to this controversy is modest and draws mainly on local history. Largely, but not exclusively, members of Granada's elite were Conservatives and renowned for providing the leadership of the party. Because most of Diriomo's political elite supported the Liberal Party, their conflicts with Granada politicians sometimes played out along partisan lines. In this study, I endeavor to unpack similarities and differences between the two parties by analyzing everyday rivalries over property, labor, and local politics that fueled antagonisms between Granada's ruling elite and Diriomo's politicians.

Colonial Patriarchy

Latin American elites inherited a patriarchal regime from the colonial era that subordinated women and sons to senior males who were vested with authority to control and obligations to protect their dependents. Fathers and husbands exercised extensive patriarchal powers as they represented members of their household to the state, and were the state's representative within the family. Decrees spelled out the scope of senior male authority over the property, behavior, and bodies of the women and men in their domain. This included the power to sign contracts, allocate labor, and manage land, and also the obligation to maintain order in the patriarchal sphere by punishing dependents when necessary. However, patriarchal authority over females and males differed in a crucial respect: guided by the principle that females were incapable of governing property, their children, or even themselves, the rules of patria potestad, meaning fathers' rights over their children, and potestad marital, husbands' rights over the person and property of their wife, subordinated most women to men throughout their lifetime.[4] On reaching adulthood, sons were freed from a father's control and inherited the authority to govern women and younger men, but the only women permitted to manage their own affairs and govern themselves were widows and adult unmarried daughters who had been formally emancipated by their father. The idea that women were incapable of governing others was so tenacious in Nicaragua that mothers were not granted parental authority over their own children until the 1940s, when patria potestad was radically reworked.[5]

Notwithstanding the extensive power of senior males, in Latin American countries women's legal subordination was markedly less severe than in other parts of the world, particularly with respect to property. The Hispanic legal tradition permitted women to own property and protected women's share of inherited family and marital wealth. Under mandatory partible inheritance laws, the testamentary regime included provisions guaranteeing daughters a dowry and an equal portion of their parents' property.[6] Similarly, the marital property regime was favorable to women; laws privileged a common property system whereby husbands and wives jointly owned all property acquired during the marriage. In sum, the legal system that prevailed in Nicaragua until the latter nineteenth century protected women's ownership of property while handing its governance to the family patriarch.

Liberalism and Female Landholding in Diriomo

Liberalism altered the gendered property regime in Nicaragua in contradictory ways. On one hand, it abolished the common property system that excluded Indian women from land rights, allowing them to own property; on the other, liberal legislation whittled away at women's guarantees to parental and marital property.[7] Although the effects of these two measures were contradictory, they reflected a common purpose. Liberals sought to liberate property from what they regarded as archaic constraints so that individuals would be free to buy and sell, bequeath, and manage their assets however they saw fit. In keeping with liberal tenets permeating Latin America, Nicaraguan politicians hoped that by eliminating barriers to the freedom of property they would lay the foundations for a modern economy.[8] However, reflecting the ambiguities of liberalism, the state simultaneously passed legislation to free property from constraints inherited from the colonial era and endeavored to put in place a dense regulatory framework to govern the new private property regime.

Notwithstanding disjuncture between laws and everyday practices, elimination of common land rights significantly altered the gendered property regime in Diriomo. Abolition of the male-dominated Indian common property system had an emancipatory impact on Indian women, who made up 74 percent of the pueblo's female population in 1883.[9] Two property registers compiled by Diriomo's alcalde municipal in the first decade of the twentieth century demonstrate that 14 percent of private landholdings, including properties still in the process of privatization, were owned exclusively by women.[10] I emphasize exclusively, because another 19 percent of landholdings were registered as joint marital property. Of the 704 properties registered in the pueblo, 98 were owned by women and a further 133 jointly owned (Table 3). In a community where a male-dominated common property regime had prevailed for centuries, female land ownership represented a major break with the past. Furthermore, as the incidence of marriage remained low in Diriomo and the number of female-headed households was high, evidently land ownership, however small in scale, allowed many women to maintain their household.[11]

The incidence of women's landownership is all the more remarkable because all women needed permission from their husband or father to acquire a title to land, except for widows and emancipated unmarried adult daughters. At every step in the bureaucratic process of land titling, women needed affidavits provided by the family patriarch that allowed them to sign contracts. To acquire private property in land women had to, in Deniz Kandiyoti's words, negotiate with patriarchy.[12] The fact that ninety-eight females in Diriomo claimed land as individual proprietors demonstrates that women wanted to own land in their own right, and to accomplish their goal they overcame formidable obstacles inherent in Nicaragua's patriarchal system.

Female landowning was concentrated in the two poorest groups in the pueblo: the landless and the poor peasantry. And circumstantial evidence suggests that the women who swelled the ranks of the poorer peasantry had their roots in the comunidad indígena. The fact that women proprietors were overrepresented (relative to men) among the poorest peasantry (those

Table 3. Distribution of Female Landholding in Diriomo, ca. 1900

Category	Number of owners	Percentage	Average size	Female, of total
Landless* (< 4 mz.)	15	15	2	54
Poor peasantry (4–6 mz.)	51	52	4	20
Middle peasantry (7–15 mz.)	27	28	8	10
Rich peasantry (16–49 mz.)	5	5	20	4
Commercial planters (50–99 mz.)	0	0	na	0
Coffee planters (100 + mz.)	1	1	131	5
Total	98	100	na	14

Notes: 1 manzana = 1.72 acres, or 0.7 hectares.

* Contemporaries considered holdings below 4 manzanas too small for household subsistence. Therefore, for simplicity's sake, I call this category landless.

Sources: Calculated by author from Libro de Matrícula de Fincas, Año 1905, Diriomo; Libro en que figuran las personas obligadas a pagar el canon de ley, Diriomo, 1902, Ramo Agricultura, AMD; and "El Censo Cafetalero de 1909/10."

with sub-subsistence holdings) demonstrates that for a minority of Diriomeñas ownership did little to stave off poverty. Yet the striking characteristic of the land tenure pattern is that the bulk of female proprietors (seventy-eight) owned properties of between four and fifteen manzanas. These holdings were sufficient to support household subsistence and may well have been an important part of the material base of female-headed households in the pueblo.

The weight of female landowning after the shift from corporate to individual property is a strong indicator that land privatization altered gender relations. In Diriomo's corporate property regime, women's access to land devolved from membership in a male-headed household. Common land rights deferred many advantages on women, as well as on men, but from a feminist perspective the system also reproduced gendered disadvantages, as women were dependent on men for access to the most vital resource of the community. One of the gendered contradictions of liberalism is that land privatization destroyed the very basis of the community's collective existence and created preconditions for the commodification of land. However, that same process partially freed women from dependence on men's command over property, and by extension from patriarchal control. Where women's land rights had rested on being a constituent part of a family unit, after the revolution in land, women were able to claim private property in their own name. Consequently, the liberal impulse and the politics of land privatization conferred on the women of Diriomo's comunidad indígena certain, albeit limited, individual rights. The process of decoupling women from the family, thereby expanding the possibilities for females to become self-determining individuals, has been called *individuation*.[13] In Diriomo, land privatization set in motion early and tentative but nonetheless significant steps toward individuation. In sum, the property revolution contributed to a change in gender politics in the pueblo and, in certain senses, marked an advance for women.

Another facet of liberal reform, the erosion of women's rights to family property, had regressive implications and may have contributed to female exclusion from the upper echelons of landed proprietors. According to liberal theory, the colonial system guaranteeing equal inheritance to all heirs contributed to property fragmentation and economic backwardness. While that may or may not have been the case, the mandatory equal division of property under colonial law benefited women by protecting their entitlement to inherited wealth.

In the latter nineteenth century, Nicaraguan jurists began to undermine the protective measures inherited from the colonial system guaranteeing women an equal portion of parental and marital property. The first change came with the Civil Code of 1867, enacted under Conservative rule, which slightly expanded testamentary freedom and reduced the protected status of the female dowry.[14] But the great break came with the Liberal Code of 1904, enacted under the government of President Zelaya. It established testamentary freedom, thereby allowing people to bequeath property and wealth as they saw fit, and ended the enforced joint marital property system. The 1904 code established the separation of marital property as the default regime (what governs if not otherwise specified).[15] That measure lifted colonial restrictions, and gave couples considerable leeway in defining the terms and conditions of property ownership within marriage and upon the death of a spouse. Ergo, the state encouraged something on the order of a prenuptial agreement, whereby husband and wife could choose from a range of marital property regimes. On the assumption that men tended to acquire more property and wealth over the course of a lifetime than did women, the shift from joint to separate marital property would have decidedly negative consequences for females.[16] In the main, liberal reforms facilitated the concentration of property and wealth and undermined women's guarantees.[17]

As Anne Phillips argues in *Which Equalities Matter?* the principle of individuals' equality before the law, the bedrock of classical liberal political theory, when rigidly applied might have more oppressive than progressive implications.[18] Analyzing developments in liberal theory, Phillips suggests that when the principle of equal rights before the law replaces the principle that vulnerable social groups need protection under the law, the shift might have negative practical consequences for groups that historically have suffered from discrimination and exclusion. Furthermore, she proposes that official declarations that all citizens enjoy equal rights may obscure the persistence of structural inequalities and systematic discrimination in people's everyday lives. Politicians may well justify the absence of measures that could mitigate social inequalities by pointing to the existence of formal equalities. Phillips's proposition that principles of legal equality sometimes mask and frequently perpetuate structural inequalities provides a useful framework for disentangling the gendered contradictions of liberal reforms, particularly their impact on the upper reaches of Diriomo's landed proprietors.

Liberal legislation ending guarantees of equal inheritance may have contributed to the dearth of women in the upper strata of Diriomo's landholders. Of 134 properties belonging to rich peasants, five were owned by women. Women were entirely absent from the ranks of the town's commercial planters, and only one Diriomeña owned a coffee plantation on Mombacho. While female exclusion from the upper reaches of landownership partly reflected historical discrimination, reforms undermining women's guarantees to parental and marital property intensified women's structural disadvantages. To develop commercial ventures, it would appear that Diriomo's larger planters abandoned the long-standing obligation to bequeath property in equal measure to their wife and children. Instead, they sought to concentrate landed property in the hands of a male heir. Consequently, liberal reforms restricted the possibilities for women from the upper reaches of the pueblo's social hierarchy to own and inherit land.

Not surprisingly, gendered property relations at the top of the nation's social pyramid differed from patterns of landholding in the pueblo. In 1910, none of the largest coffee estates on the Mombacho Volcano were owned by women; however, three widows had inherited substantial coffee fincas.[19]

Female property ownership in the oligarchy demonstrates yet another facet of gendered liberalism. The new wave of testamentary freedom allowed landowners to avoid the disadvantages of property fragmentation implied by the traditional inheritance regime, and apparently several planters in the Granada district bequeathed their landed property in its entirety to their widow. These few examples suggest that the freedom of property instituted through liberal reforms sometimes served to empower elite women.

Thus, in the Granada coffee district the gendered effects of liberalism and land privatization differed in the upper and lower strata of society. At the bottom of the social pyramid, the male monopoly on land that had characterized the common property regime gave way to an agrarian system in which women and men became peasant proprietors. At the other end of the social spectrum, large coffee planters took advantage of testamentary freedom to consolidate expanding commercial ventures that passed to their widow. Like the oligarchs, Diriomo's commercial planters and rich peasants seemed inclined to consolidate their landholdings; however, unlike the oligarchy, they excluded females from landed property. Three broad trends emerge: (1) for the majority at the base of society land privatization broke the male monopoly on land rights and ushered in female landholding; (2) among Diriomo's local elite, the liberal revolution seems to have restricted women's control over property; however, (3) among the large planters of the district there was a tendency to concentrate landholdings, and a few widows became coffee planters of some significance.

Female Household Heads, Artisans, and Traders

At the time poorer women in Diriomo were acquiring titles to private landholding, the incidence of female household headship in the pueblo was remarkably high. According to two censuses conducted in the pueblo in 1882 and 1883, 40 percent of Diriomo's households were headed by women, and 51 percent of the adult population was unmarried.[20] Historians of the family have demonstrated that nonmarrying behavior and its corollary, female household headship, were common features of Latin American societies in the nineteenth century. Nonetheless, the very high incidence of both in Diriomo merits attention. Even though the majority of adults listed in the census as single probably lived in extralegal or common law unions, the triad of female landownership, household headship, and nonmarrying behavior gives us a very different picture of peasant society from the one we have been routinely offered. The traditional view of the Latin American peasantry, emphasizing male proprietors and male-headed households, does not fit Diriomo or, for that matter, many other rural regions in Latin America at the turn of the twentieth century.[21]

I propose that the combination of female land ownership and participation in the expanding commercial economy provided new material possibilities for female household headship.[22] It is also possible that inclination toward nonmarrying behavior on the part of peasant women was enhanced by patriarchal law. An unmarried woman might retain control over her land and assets, whereas a married woman necessarily forfeited control. In late-nineteenth-century Diriomo, widows headed 35 percent of female-headed households, with the remainder (65 percent) headed by single women, mostly mothers. In another epoch both groups, but particularly single mothers, might have been subsumed into a male-headed household. It is possible, however, that expanding opportunities for female landholding and participation in the cash economy gave those women the wherewithal to maintain a separate household. Nevertheless, for most women in peasant society, the advantages of patriarchal independence might well have been offset by the economic, social, and cultural disadvantages associated with female household headship.

The men of Diriomo's rich peasantry and commercial planters demonstrated a higher marriage rate than any other group in the township. While a functional explanation of elite men's propensity to marry may oversimplify the complexities of rural society, their marriage behavior seems to corroborate Engels's famous theory of the family. In *Origin of the Family, Private Property, and the State*, he argued that the bourgeois family rested on a material foundation in which the wife produced legitimate heirs for the transmission of property. Although Diriomo's local elite were not embedded in a capitalist social order, the revolution in land and liberal reform laws meant that the transmission of property acquired a newfound importance in rural society.

The evidence of female household headship combined with a tendency toward nonmarrying behavior underlines connections between women's economic dependence and male control over female property, labor, and sexuality. When women enjoyed some degree of economic independence, modest though it might have been among the peasants of Diriomo, we find a society in which neither marriage nor male household headship was the rule. The fact that almost 40 percent of households in Diriomo were female-headed in the late nineteenth century is of major significance for understanding the unfolding process of peasant differentiation. Female household headship may partly explain the relatively high percentage of peasant land titles held by women and their active participation in the cash economy. However, the causal relationship might be the other way around: female landowning and participation in trade may well have laid the material basis for female household headship. While more research is needed to understand the ways gender affected social differentiation and vice versa, evidence from Diriomo indicates there was a strong link between male monopoly over productive resources and the male-headed household in the period prior to land privatization. When women became small peasant landholders and participated in the cash economy, there was a very high incidence of female-headed households in the pueblo. This history sustains the idea that property relations condition family patterns and sexual norms. Although Engels's formulation of the connection between property and the family was flawed by romanticism about gender equality in "primitive" societies, his theory is an important formulation of the links between property, the family, and male control over female sexuality.

With the development of coffee production, small-scale trade and artisanal activities expanded in Granada's rural townships. Diriomo's junta municipal sought to regulate the rise of commerce by fixing prices, licensing traders, and stipulating the location and hours of business operations.[23] Town records demonstrate that women participated on a par with men in small-scale commerce and the burgeoning artisanal trades.[24] The gendered differentiation of artisans and traders was particularly striking in one respect: females were predominantly unmarried, whereas their male counterparts demonstrated a propensity to marry in excess of local norms. About 65 percent of female artisans and traders in the township were either single or widowed, in contrast to 31 percent of their male counterparts.[25] There are two possible explanations for the low marriage rate among economically active women. The first draws on theories of the feminization of poverty that emphasize the disadvantage of female-headed households. Interpreting the data in line with these arguments suggests that Diriomo's unmarried peasant women turned to artisanal activities to supplement a fragile household economy. However, the data might be read differently. Patriarchal laws required married women to secure their husband's consent to engage in trade, while widows and unmarried females faced fewer impediments to commerce. In a real sense, single women who aspired to enter the commercial economy were in a privileged position, better placed than married counterparts to maintain a household on their own earnings. In contrast to the feminization of poverty, we might call this the feminization of privilege.

Evidence from Diriomo indicates that the incidence of female participation in trade, together with the propensity to not marry, is best explained by the feminization of privilege. Most females active in trade were in the middle and upper echelons of local society by virtue of their family and ethnic background. More important, with their own enterprises, these women had the economic wherewithal to postpone marriage, sometimes indefinitely. The feminization of privilege position is strengthened by statistics showing that marriage was more prevalent among the poor peasantry than among the middle sectors in the township, and the group most likely to marry was also the most disadvantaged: poor Indian women.

In Diriomo, women engaged in artisanal activities that reflected the gendered division of labor in the pueblo. In order of frequency, women were seamstresses, tobacconists, jewelers, and small traders. Poorer Diriomeñas served as cooks and laundresses for richer families in the pueblo, tasks universally regarded as women's work. Men's artisanal work included, again in order of frequency, carpentry, woodworking, quarrying, and smithing. Artisanal work tended to be segregated by ethnicity as well as by gender. With very few exceptions, Diriomo's artisans and tradespeople were ladino. Evidently for reasons of custom and/or the economics of poor peasant production, Indians were marginalized from artisanship and trade.[26] The gendering of work was less pronounced in commerce than in artisanal activities. Of the town's twenty-five licensed merchants, ten were women. As many authors have pointed out, commerce on a grand scale in Latin America was the province of men, petty trade of women. This pattern was reproduced in Diriomo; men were wholesale and long-distance merchants, women were shopkeepers and local market traders.[27]

Censuses frequently fail to capture, or intentionally misrepresent, people's race, ethnicity, and marital status. However, flawed categories generally derive from elite political discourses and as such provide insights about dominant ideologies and contemporary social mores in the state bureaucracy. In some ways, officials who compiled Diriomo's 1883 census conveyed more about the socialization of ladino officialdom than about society in the pueblo. The occupation of virtually every Indian woman was given as *molendera* (grinder of corn) and of Indian men as *jornalero* (day laborer). Both occupational categories reproduced gendered and racist stereotypes held by local officials and thereby obscured social realities in the pueblo. Although all Indian women worked in agrarian production and some claimed private land, in the eyes of officials Indian women represented the iconic grinders of corn. Similarly, Indian men mainly worked in subsistence household production, not as occasional day laborers, as the term jornalero suggests. Furthermore, as I demonstrate in the next chapter, when peasant men labored on coffee estates as debt peons, they generally worked side by side with their wife and children. Yet no woman in the pueblo was listed in the census as jornalera, nor *agricultora* (in Diriomo *agricultor* meant proprietor of a middle to large landholding). Paradoxically, the census takers unintentionally highlighted peasant women's double day; in addition to their agrarian activities, they devoted many hours every day to grinding corn and preparing tortillas.

Interestingly, women of the town's upper echelons dominated an activity central to the incipient commercial economy: money lending. Women of the town's elite, excluded de facto from property ownership, turned to the activity traditionally undertaken by pariahs. Middle peasants and commercial planters in the pueblo frequently borrowed from Mombacho's coffee planters, but more modest lending was the province almost exclusively of the pueblo's female elite. Several Diriomeñas became protagonists in the emerging cash economy by regularly lending small sums.[28] One of the town's leading lenders was La Niña Fernández, titled La Niña (young girl) in official documents because she never married, even though she was about fifty years old. Whereas peasants sought to guarantee loans with land, Fernández required borrowers to secure loans with labor. Consequently, peasants unable to repay La Niña became her debt peons.[29] In a region where planters regularly complained that shortage of labor was the principal obstacle to progress, Fernández's control over forced labor gave her substantial clout in the township.

Conclusion

The gendered effects of liberalism and land privatization in Diriomo were highly contradictory, and their impact on women and men in the pueblo differed substantially according to class and ethnicity. At the turn of the twentieth century, four features of the gender regime in Diriomo stand out: (1) female landholding was significant and concentrated in the poorer strata of the peasantry, (2) the incidence of female household headship and of nonmarrying behavior was very high, (3) females actively participated in artisanal activities and small-scale trade, and (4) women were largely excluded from larger landownership in the township. While a number of factors combined to create this distinctive gender order, liberalism and land privatization played a leading role in gender transformations in the pueblo.

CHAPTER SIX

Debt Peonage in Diriomo: Forced Labor Revisited

Liberals in nineteenth-century Latin America proclaimed that they stood for individual rights and personal freedom. In reality, they safeguarded the rights of large property owners and trampled the freedoms of ordinary people. The rise of liberalism and export agriculture went hand in hand across the continent and in many countries ushered in a golden age of forced labor rather than its demise. I propose, controversially, that under the aegis of liberal regimes many if not most rural Latin Americans found themselves trapped in debt peonage, slavery, and indentured servitude.

My interpretation of debt peonage goes against the grain of the revisionist literature. Revisionists stress the modernizing impact of debt labor and see it as an embryonic form of capitalist free wage labor.[1] I propose that the coercive side of peonage frequently predominated, and debt labor systems often impeded more than facilitated capitalist development. If my contention is correct, Nicaragua was quintessentially Latin American in this regard, as the production of coffee—the country's leading export—rested largely on the coerced labor of debt peons. Rather than an archaic remnant from earlier times, in Nicaragua full-blown peonage was a product of the property revolution. Debt labor had existed prior to the coffee boom, but it had been small-scale, occasional, and unregulated. To forge a large labor force for the coffee sector, Nicaraguan planters in tandem with state officials created a legally binding and highly regulated system of debt peonage.[2]

In contrast to the ideology born of the European Enlightenment that private property and free wage labor intrinsically go together, Nicaraguan liberals frequently argued that forced labor was a necessary, if unfortunate, adjunct to the property revolution. Putting their ideas into practice, the rise of private property ushered in forced labor.[3] In rural Granada privatization radically altered the class, gender, and ethnic character of property relations, but it did not dispossess the rural poor. Although many were impoverished by the loss of communal land, Diriomo's peasant economy continued to rest on household production for consumption. Consequently, privatization gave rise to tensions between Diriomo's peasants and Mombacho's coffee planters.

In coffee cultivation, as in virtually all agricultural endeavors, timing is everything. As soon as the coffee cherry (the fruit surrounding the seed or the coffee bean) ripens, it must be picked; if it is not, the coffee will rot. Harvesting coffee is a laborious process that requires a large workforce to pick the cherries off the branches, and on Mombacho the harvest was made more difficult by the volcano's steep terrain. Diriomo's subsistence peasants were not unwilling to work for wages on the fincas, but they wanted to labor on their own terms. Because cultivation of their milpa took precedence over paid labor, with the rise of coffee cultivation the fundamental contradiction of agrarian society was the clash between the subsistence production of the peasantry and the demands of plantation labor.

For almost a century, the state's highest priority was promotion of the coffee sector, and it sought to overcome this contradiction by forcing peasants to work on the fincas. Conflating the interests of large planters with the national interest, successive governments from 1860 to 1920 legalized state labor drafts and debt peonage. When poor people found ways to evade forced labor, politicians resorted to draconian measures to compel peasants to work in the plantation sector. And they denounced the backward peasantry. According to highly placed government officials, peasants were naturally idle, feckless, and lazy. If left to their own devices, they would shirk labor, turn to vagrancy, and devote their time and energies to criminal activities.[4] For the good of the nation, it was the responsibility of the government to force peasants to work in plantation agriculture, they argued.

Leading Latin American historians hold that in general, nineteenth-century peonage was a form of free wage labor and that it set in motion the great transformation to capitalism throughout the region, most notably in Chile, Mexico, and Peru. I have concluded that in Diriomo peonage was forced labor.[5] In Granada's agrarian economy, peonage was part of a social order regulated by force and overlaid with patriarchy. In other words, debt peonage on the coffee estates was neither part of, nor midwife to, a capitalist system. This chapter examines legislation that compelled the vast majority of men and women to work on coffee fincas, the repressive machinery designed to enforce labor laws, and the everyday practices of debt peonage in

Diriomo. It describes the workings of a system that rested on laws that were implemented by the state's punitive machinery, including special agrarian tribunals and a highly local and irregular rural police. The chapter also analyzes the nature of authority, work, and labor discipline on coffee estates. It focuses on planters' personalized forms of control and punishment, officially described as the rightful customs and traditions (*usos y costumbres*) of the estate, and it explores the degree to which planters' personal powers were endorsed by the state and its local officials. Finally, the chapter investigates the extent to which planters' personal authority took precedence over the public exercise of the rule of law. This history of the everyday workings of peonage in Diriomo illustrates how planters and peasants, in very different ways, sought to rework the labor regime to suit their needs. The following chapter, continuing the argument developed here, focuses on the patriarchal character of the planter-peon relationship. It argues that patriarchy was intrinsic to the social relations of peonage during its golden age and sustained the peonage system well beyond its time.

Diriomo's peasantry combined resistance and accommodation to minimize the oppression of forced labor. Resistance took various forms, but in the main peons defied planters' control by running away from the fincas. Most peons escaped simply to harvest their own corn and beans, the mainstay of household subsistence. However, when peasants found themselves in chains and having to answer charges of breaking the labor laws, most endeavored to justify their escape. Speaking before Diriomo's agrarian tribunal, composed of the local elite, the hombres de bien, poor peasants generally argued that they took justice into their own hands after their boss defied the law, and flight was the only way out of the unlawful circumstances in which they found themselves. In combination with resistance, peasants attempted to diminish the oppression of forced labor by seeking some measure of accommodation with planters. Peons frequently went to lengths to sustain a relationship with a "good patrón" who, at a minimum, abided by labor laws.

For their part, planters endeavored to veil and sometimes diminish the exercise of coercion with patriarchal ideologies and practices. Many promised to assist loyal peons who found themselves in dire circumstances. Over time, customs and traditions associated with patriarchy played a part in relations between planters and peons. There is insufficient evidence to confirm the extent to which patriarchy permeated and regulated labor relations. However, courtroom testimonies by planters and peons demonstrate that appeals to clientelism were commonly deployed on both sides. It appears that planters hoped that promises and manifestations of patronal benevolence would encourage loyalty and hard work and discourage peons from running away during the coffee harvest, when their labor was most needed. For their part, in subsequent oral histories as well as in contemporary court testimonies, peasants regularly described the value of a lasting bond with a patrón who could be counted on to assist them in times of need.

Debt peonage in Diriomo was not, by and large, the stuff of the black legend. Yet, some of the laws and practices I describe in this chapter would not be out of place in Jorge Icaza's socialist-realist novel, *Huasipungo*, B. Traven's *March to the Montería*, or the rest of his *Jungle Novels*: examples include the passbooks Diriomeños carried, which proved they complied with the labor laws, the grisly punishments meted out by coffee planters, and various nefarious activities of local officials.[6] In the main, however, the class struggle between Diriomo's planters and peons generated a labor system whose everyday operation entailed not only coercive but also consensual arrangements. Yet planter-peon relations were embedded in a social structure that rested on the exercise of force. Although debt peonage in Granada was certainly not a form of slavery, there are some telling comparisons. Slaves sometimes consented or reconciled themselves to human bondage, but no one would contend that slavery was a free labor system. Similarly with debt peonage in rural Granada. To mitigate their oppression peons tried to develop consensual relationships with planters. Nonetheless, the production system that governed the plantation sector rested on a foundation of force. Compulsory labor was inscribed in law, regulated by the state, and sustained by planters' class power. Peasants' occasional success in minimizing the disadvantages of forced labor did not fundamentally alter the character of the labor regime. Finally, in Diriomo's peonage system, neither coercion nor consent was regulated by competitive market forces. As I demonstrate in this chapter, both were embedded in nonmarket, or extraeconomic, relations between planters and peons. Consequently, the social order born out of the coffee boom was, in microcosm, what Polanyi called a society with markets: a noncapitalist society.

This chapter analyzes forced labor laws and the ways they were implemented and violated in Diriomo. I highlight how peasant differentiation was reflected in the workings of the labor regime and how middle peasants accommodated and resisted forced labor differently than did the poor peasantry. To the extent evidence allows, I explore the shrouded practices of ethnic discrimination in Nicaragua's purportedly class-based labor system.

In the conclusion, I revisit the Latin American debt peonage debates and explain why Diriomo's history does not fit the standard view that peonage ushered in a capitalist transition.

This story of debt peonage is told largely in the words of the men and women whose lives were shaped by the system. The voices of peasants, planters, officials, estate managers, and jurists long since dead have been preserved in abundance: in labor laws and contracts, in court transcripts from trials involving planters and peons, in telegraph messages, and in a mountain of official and unofficial reports and letters. The voices of modern Diriomeños come from fifty oral history interviews I recorded in the 1990s. In combination, these sources help us understand, first, the inner workings of the peonage system, or the structures that existed independently of people's consciousness and will; second, people's activities, or how different groups endeavored to work the system to suit their interests; and third, the ways planters, peasants, and local officials perceived, talked about, and remembered the labor regime that dominated everyday life in the pueblo.

The Labor Regime from Above

The 1862 Ley de Agricultura was the first in a long line of legislation designed to compel peasants to work in plantation agriculture.[7] Enacted during the infancy of large-scale coffee production, the law required peasants without employment or a means of subsistence to work for commercial planters.[8] Although earlier labor legislation had signaled the same intent, the 1862 law was the first to address the problem of enforcement. In tacit recognition of the frailty of Nicaragua's nation-state, the law ordered municipal officials to enforce the labor regime. To this end, it instructed large property owners to elect a rural magistrate (juez de agricultura) who was in charge of putting the poor to work:

> The magistrate will patrol [the municipality], in particular on mornings following festivals and at all other times as he deems appropriate. He will arrest all drunken *operarios* [contract laborers], and when they have recovered he will force them to fulfill their contracts. If they have no contract, he will put them to work. The magistrate will do the same with jornaleros, even if they are not drunk. Any person rounded up several times in sweeps of the municipality will be handed over to the alcalde municipal, who will investigate how they support themselves. If they are without

work or the means of subsistence, the magistrate will assign them work and ensure they obey.[9]

In an attempt to guarantee that planters had enough laborers during the harvest season, the law criminalized peasants who left fincas before the harvest ended or otherwise evaded plantation labor:[10]

A peon contracted . . . for any enterprise that requires uninterrupted labor cannot leave the hacienda until the harvest is completed, whether or not he received a cash advance [*adelanto*], unless he, his wife, children, or parents are gravely ill, or unless he finds a substitute to replace him. In cases where the above conditions are not met, the peon must pay the legally established fine. He must also pay the planter in money or labor, whichever he chooses, for damages he caused by not working . . . If an operario defaults on a contract, whether or not he received an advance, he will be fined and sentenced by the rural magistrate. The fine is not to exceed ten pesos, or an equal number of days in prison and/or laboring on public works. Expenses incurred in the pursuit, capture, imprisonment, punishment, and return of delinquent workers will be added to the peon's debt.[11]

Jurists who designed the labor laws were under no illusion that recruitment of plantation labor could be left to the market's invisible hand. They spelled out exactly how local officials should round up peasants and put them to work in export agriculture.

The 1862 law both outlined the workings of the forced labor regime and designed a public-private system to police the peasantry. Peons convicted of running away from an estate, even of falling behind in their labor obligations, were subjected to two punitive regimes: first, under the auspices of municipal officials, second, under the rules of their patrón. The officially prescribed punishment for first offenders was hard labor; third-time offenders were dragooned into the army for a period of eighteen months. In both cases, after the "criminal" served his (or her) time, he was returned to his patrón, who was allowed to inflict whatever further punishment he saw fit: in the words of the law, "according to the practices and customs of the patrón."[12]

Allowing employers to exercise private, arbitrary power over their workers ran counter to classic liberal principles that the market, possibly along with the nation-state, should regulate and discipline workers. Nevertheless, Nicaragua's 1862 law not only allowed, but encouraged planters to implement their own punitive practices. It stated: "Landlords and entrepreneurs have the duty to use *whatever means necessary* to ensure that no disturbances occur on their fincas, including those resulting from drunkenness. If peons commit a crime, the landlord should arrest the offenders."[13] Patróns' authority to use "whatever means necessary" to maintain order on their fincas, to arrest peons, and to punish workers according to customary practices indicates that lawmakers and planters anticipated resistance to the labor regime. Consequently, to preempt opposition from below, the law fortified landlords' class control over the peasantry.

In another negation of the tenets of classical European liberalism, the government made no pretence that landlord and peasant were equal before the law. The 1862 decree stated that in disputes between planters and peons, judges "should presume peons are guilty unless there is manifest evidence to the contrary." Although planters' power was extensive, their legal authority was not unlimited. The labor law penalized planters who defrauded workers and established a schedule of fines to punish planters who knowingly hired peasants who had prior contractual commitments.[14]

If Nicaraguan lawmakers left little to the imagination with regard to how to put the poor to work, they were vague about who exactly was subject to the labor regime. In contrast to provisions spelling out property requirements for officials charged with implementing the labor law, the alcalde municipal and juez de agricultura, the law was silent on two key issues: how much "work" or "means of subsistence" would be enough to secure an exemption from the labor regime.[15] This interesting absence probably was an act of commission, not omission, as it allowed local planters to cut and shape the law to suit their needs. This absence contrasts with exemptions of another sort. The law explicitly released "administrators, foremen, overseers, *llaveros* [turnkeys, custodians], and guards," in short, planters' entire supervisory corps, from all public obligations, including the army and the labor draft.[16] Finally, and this time in keeping with liberal precepts of the times, the law made no reference to race or ethnicity. Formally, the government treated forced labor as a class question: property ownership and professional standing determined who was and was not subject to the labor regime.

The 1862 law lacked specificity on a second critical issue: how the enforcement apparatus would be financed. Beyond the magistrate and his constable (*alguacil*), whose salaries derived mainly from the fines they collected from delinquent peons, lawmakers made no provisions to fund a rural police.[17] The law loosely instructed alcaldes municipales "to enlist men to help maintain law and order whenever necessary." In tacit recognition of the scarcity of public funds, the law signaled official intention to place the burden of law enforcement largely in the private realm.

The 1862 labor law was written on the eve of social upheaval in the countryside, as the government was moving to abolish customary land rights. Under these circumstances, the elite feared opposition to the labor law and attempted to obfuscate its coercive character. The law described peasants' obligation to work for planters as "their duty to render public service." Apparently, the planter class held out some hope that peasants might accept the legitimacy of unfree labor if it was called "public service" and seen as promoting the national interest. Significantly, long after a host of new labor laws came into effect, Granada's planters continued to refer to the 1862 law as the fundamental charter of the labor regime.

Between 1865 and 1925, the government enacted more than fifty labor laws.[18] The mountain of legislation created a confusing regulatory framework for planters and peons. Even officials charged with implementing the labor laws complained that they were unable to keep track of the complicated legislation.[19] With new laws piled on top of old, the legal structure for forced labor became a maze of contradictory provisions. While the state long remained committed to forced labor, peasant resistance pushed successive governments to devise new ways of pressing the peasantry into plantation labor.[20] However, the incompatibility of subsistence production and plantation labor did not go away. Struggling to resolve this contradiction, the government passed increasingly coercive labor laws.

The Liberal government of President José Santos Zelaya (1893–1909) moved aggressively to expand the scope of draft labor. His administration enacted various laws compelling vagrants to work on coffee plantations and defined vagrancy so broadly that it embraced most of the population. For example, Article 1 of the 1899 vagrancy law stated:

Anyone is considered a vagrant who:

1. does not have a profession, income from property, salary, trade, or legal means of subsistence,

2. having a profession, trade, or employment, is not regularly engaged in performing those activities,

3. has an income, but not enough for subsistence; is not engaged in a legal trade, and who regularly frequents bars and pool halls.[21]

The 1899 law purposefully exempted only men of substantial property or a profession from the labor regime. In addition, the last provision is particularly invidious, as it all but criminalized leisure pursuits enjoyed by the vast majority of plebeian men.

Just two years later, lawmakers abandoned any pretence that the forced labor regime applied only to vagrants, the poor, and men who loitered outside the boundaries of home and church. The 1901 labor law decreed, "All persons above the age of sixteen, male or female, who possess property or income valued at less than 500 pesos are required to support themselves by working and they must obtain a laborer's workbook [*libreta de trabajadores*]."[22] With this stroke, the government unambiguously expanded the coverage of the labor regime to encompass virtually the entire population, including females. Significantly, the property ceiling of 500 pesos exempted only the wealthy from forced labor. Everyone else in the population had to carry a passbook to demonstrate that they had worked in the plantation sector and thereby were in compliance with the labor law.

In addition to broadening the sweep of the labor draft, officials in Zelaya's administration decided to centralize the repressive apparatus to improve the enforcement of the labor laws. To that end, his government created a national agency with branches throughout the coffee districts to coordinate the capture of runaway peons.[23] Officials boasted that the combination of a central police apparatus, additional funding for law enforcement, and regulation of peasants' workbooks would effectively solve the labor shortage on the coffee plantations. But their optimism was exaggerated. Government funding for the repressive apparatus remained scarce, and a national rural police force was not created until 1904.[24] With national law enforcement agencies chronically starved of funds, compliance with the labor laws was left in the hands of planters, local officials, and civilian patrols made up of peasant volunteers.

Lawmakers attempted to complement the labor draft by regulating debt peonage, which in practice was an integral part of the production regime. Nicaraguan peonage was of the classic kind; coffee planters gave peasants a cash advance, which they had to work off (*desquitar*) by laboring on the landlord's plantation. Intricate laws stipulated levels of cash advances, debt ceilings, repayment periods, and prison terms for peons who failed to repay their adelanto (cash advance) with labor. The government established a cumbersome system of affidavits designed both to prevent peons from evading debts and to ensure that planters recorded peasants' labor. The affidavit system proved unworkable, however. Opponents of forced labor claimed that instead of protecting peons, affidavits and the mountain of paperwork generated by the labor regime had the opposite effect: they fortified planters' control over the peasantry.[25]

In the first decade of the twentieth century, the planter class was divided over how best to organize rural labor. Most Granada coffee growers believed that some combination of debt peonage and draft labor was needed to ensure that they had a steady supply of workers for the sector.[26] Other planters advocated reform; they held that the labor laws did more harm than good because coercion drove peasants to flee from plantation labor. The labor debate filled the country's leading newspapers; one Matagalpan grower wrote, "Faced with the necessity of complying with labor obligations, bonded workers flee from persecution and take refuge outside the country's borders. This practice is prejudicial to agriculture; however, until the oppressive system that now prevails is abolished, there is no remedy [for the problems of agriculture]."[27] Another writer agreed: "Labor should be entirely free . . . It is an urgent necessity to repeal all labor laws because they only perpetuate servitude [which is] contrary to our republican institutions."[28]

However, officials in President Zelaya's government dismissed those who called for abolition of forced labor as high-minded idealists who were out of touch with conditions in the countryside. Managua's jefe político wrote:

Free labor is a noble principle that plays an important role in the advanced ideas of pure liberalism. But notwithstanding the spirit of great deeds that promotes the common good, there are certain realities that we must respect, rules to which we must adapt, laws we must preserve. Our current labor laws, in particular workbooks, are necessary because some people who dwell in miserable hovels in the backwoods and who sustain themselves on the produce of their own communities flee from work and fall prey to petty criminality.[29]

In support of the government position, the editor of El Comercio wrote, "Laborers' workbooks will break the traditional custom of the Nicaraguan people to shy away from work. There is no shortage of workers in this country, rather an abundance of laziness."[30]

Historians commonly state that Zelaya's Liberal administration sealed Nicaragua's transformation to capitalism.[31] But his government ruled that virtually the entire population was subject to the forced labor regime. Furthermore, it introduced the passbook system and the first national enforcement agency to ensure that the rural poor complied with the labor laws. After Zelaya was overthrown in 1909, with the complicity of the U.S. government, Nicaraguan administrations moved to curtail forced labor. Jeffrey Gould found evidence that when the United States was putting in place its occupation of Nicaragua (1911–1933), Washington put pressure on its client state to eliminate what one U.S. official called "the country's illegal slavery in peons."[32] To contain the excesses of bonded servitude, the Nicaraguan Congress established a ceiling for peasant indebtedness and outlawed prison sentences for debt peonage.[33] In 1923, the government abolished debt peonage and all forms of forced labor. But although abolition was a milestone, it did not end unfree labor. The character of debt peonage gradually changed on the coffee estates of Granada, but it remained the cornerstone of the plantation labor system into the 1960s.[34]

The Labor Regime from Below

To solve the shortage of labor in the coffee sector the national government largely devoted its attention to the design and legal regulation of labor drafts. But in Diriomo draft labor was the exception rather than the rule. Although occasionally the rural magistrate sent out a posse to round up peasants, town officials simply lacked the manpower and the financial resources to commandeer peasants on a regular basis.[35] As a consequence, Mombacho's coffee planters relied on debt peonage to mobilize labor. Peonage rested on two legal principles: peasants were required to work on the fincas, and peasant indebtedness gave planters control over peons' labor. These legal features underpinned the coercive character of peonage. Notwithstanding the system's coercive foundation, social conditions in rural Granada mitigated the use of force. Both planters and local officials gradually recognized the limits to their capacity to compel peasants to work in plantation labor. In addition, poorer peasants endeavored to link themselves to a patrón who might help them resolve the mounting difficulties of subsistence production. Consequently, peonage endured for almost a century in the Granada coffee sector because it combined coercion and consent.

From the first decades of the coffee boom, planter-peon relations in Diriomo were formalized in contracts (*matrículas*) ratified by local officials. The contract between General Agustín Avilés and the Flores family is in many ways typical:

In the presence of the rural magistrate, Señor Aristarco Carcache, stood Valetín Flores, who is married and twenty-six years of age. [Flores is] five feet two inches tall, dark wheat-skinned [*trigueño oscuro*], and of delicate constitution. [He has] a round face, flat forehead, sparse eyebrows, a wound above [his] left eyebrow, a bulbous nose, protruding mouth, yellowish eyes of which the left one is cloudy, straight chestnut-colored hair, a beard and moustache, a face scarred by small pox, a wound on his right hand and a crippled middle finger. [Flores] declared that jointly with his two sons, Ascención and Perfecto, he accepts the obligation to pick coffee for Don General Agustín Avilés on his haciendas Progreso and Cutierres, located on the Mombacho Volcano. The family will be paid one real for six boxes [of coffee cherries], plus two meals per day, and must begin work as soon as they are needed. [Flores] received an advance of four ordinary pesos, and the peons [*mozos*] are obligated to work throughout the entire harvest, as well as in subsequent years, until they repay the entire debt with labor. The peons will submit themselves to the practices and customs that govern their patrón's estates.[36]

The ritual of contracting was a theater of landlord domination and peasant subordination. Peons pledged allegiance to their patrón before a panel comprising the rural magistrate and two hombres de bien representing Diriomo's planter elite. Three features of contracting underscore the coercive character of peonage. First, labor contracts contained detailed physical descriptions of peasants to facilitate the identification and capture of runaway workers. Second, contracts explicitly recognized the planters' authority to mobilize peasants whenever their labor was needed and required peons to remain on the plantation throughout the harvest. Third, contracts regularly included the requirement that peons submit themselves to whatever practices and customs governed their patrón's estate. In sum, the process of labor contracting formalized planters' control over the peasantry and peons' subordination to the authority of the planter class.

Around the turn of the twentieth century, the wording of labor contracts began to change. A number of contracts included the planter's pledge "to protect [*socorrer*] laborers and servants on the hacienda."[37] At first, only a minority of planters promised protection, but because some did, an idiom of reciprocity came to be associated with debt peonage. Yet promises of protection often came at a price, quite literally, as planters obliged peons to repay with labor (desquitar) the cash advance as well as "all other assistance [socorro] he [or she] receives."[38] Consequently, socorro and other material manifestations of patriarchy were double-sided: they generated a culture of reciprocity, while at the same time they tightened the bonds of unfreedom.

In Diriomo, peonage was a family labor system. Its class and gender composition reflected the imperatives of peasant subsistence and the exigencies of large-scale coffee production. Planters endeavoured to contract extended families, both to garner more laborers and to perpetuate their control over the peasantry. This clause from a family's contract demonstrates how planters manipulated indebtedness: "If one operario dies, is injured, or for whatever reason is absent from work, the repayment in labor [el desquite] will be assumed by those [in the family] who are fit to work. If the family defaults on the obligation, it will be fined 30 pesos, which will be added to its advance and to whatever other monies it received. [The grandfather], Eusebio Gaitan, will guarantee the loan [with his labor]."[39]

Because of the importance of household production, the peasantry often deployed family labor in a manner that clashed with planters' drive to bond entire families. Male peasants frequently contracted their wife and children into servitude, freeing themselves to cultivate the milpa, the mainstay of subsistence.[40] This gender division of household labor gave rise to a peonage regime that involved large numbers of women and children. Consequently, in Granada, debt servitude was less male-dominated than we might expect from reading the Latin American literature on peonage.[41]

In the period between 1880 and 1915, on average 55 percent of Diriomeños between the ages of ten and fifty-five worked in peonage.[42] Many peasants signed themselves, their wife, their children, even their grandchildren into servitude to complement household production. Paraphrasing David McCreery, their willingness to work was strengthened by the coercive apparatus.[43] Although cash advances coaxed peasants into peonage and coercion was less in evidence in contracting, the everyday regulation of labor arrangements almost always involved an element of force.

Diriomo's peasants attempted to participate in the labor regime on their own terms, what Eric Hobsbawm famously called working the system to minimize its disadvantages.[44] However, when expanding coffee production intensified planters' need for labor, peasants' ability to work the system diminished. In the 1890s, Granada's planters dispensed with some of the contractual formalities of peonage and deployed new ways of bonding labor. Notwithstanding the symbolic value, and the legal requirement, of peasants' consent to servitude, many large planters bypassed the ritual of labor contracting. In 1890 several planters sent Diriomo's magistrate lists of their debt peons. General Avilés, for one, did not mince words. He wrote, "When the harvest ended all of the mozos remained in debt to me, therefore all are compelled to work for me when I need them . . . If any of the mozos claim they have fulfilled their obligation to me, they are lying."[45] The very title of Avilés's declaration—"List of mozos who belong to the hacienda"—suggests that Avilés considered the peons part of his private property. And they were, in a manner of speaking: peons' labor debts figured among an estate's financial assets, along with land, machinery, and coffee trees.

Avilés had a notorious reputation for using coercive tactics to tie laborers to his estates. Following his latest attempt to evade the labor regulations, peons on his plantations contested the new method of bonding labor. Helped by a local scribe, they argued that unilateral renewal of labor contracts contravened the law and that Avilés regularly fabricated debts to tie laborers to his fincas. On the first issue, Diriomo's magistrate ruled that although the practice of automatically prolonging peons' contracts was new to the region, it was not against the law. However, after Avilés refused to allow members of the agrarian tribunal to examine his ledgers, the judge declared that the planter "showed blatant disregard for the law." Yet despite this denunciation, the magistrate proceeded to appease Avilés, who, after all, wielded considerable political clout throughout the region. The judge declared, "I do not doubt the honor of Don General Avilés, but this is a bad precedent and would encourage other coffee growers to do likewise. As a friend of the General, I am ready to render whatever services he needs except those that are an affront to and contravene the authority that I represent."[46]

Before the mozos had time to celebrate their victory, the magistrate's high moral stand was swept aside—not on juridical grounds, but through the deployment of political influence. After General Avilés complained, the governor of the Department of Granada, Juan Urtecho, dispatched this letter to Diriomo: "General Don Agustín Avilés personally visited me at the Prefectura. He explained that on various occasions he appealed to your authority, asking you to renew the matrículas of mozos who are indebted agricultural laborers. You refused his request, presenting a series of difficulties that you could easily have resolved. I order you to proceed as quickly as possible to satisfy the wishes of General Avilés so that his agricultural enterprise is not put in jeopardy for lack of efficient support from this authority."[47]

Soon other planters copied Avilés's method of bonding labor, just as Diriomo's magistrate had predicted.[48] Avilés's move away from a form of labor recruitment that included a measure of peasant consent to one that rested largely on the planters' class domination anticipated changes at the national level. About a decade later, the government expanded the coverage of forced labor and required all peasants to carry workbooks.

The success of debt peonage rested on the dual nature of cash advances: they attracted peasants into the labor regime, and at the same time they extended a planter's control over a person's labor. In a word, cash advances provided the means of eliciting consent, as well as the justification for exercising coercion. Testimony in a case between General Avilés and one of his peons traces the fine line separating consent and coercion. It reveals, too, how planters manipulated the bureaucratic machinery to perpetuate servitude. In 1882 Hijinos Muños told Diriomo's labor tribunal:

> Last February I signed up with General Avilés for six months to work at assorted tasks on his coffee finca El Progreso. I received an advance of four pesos and was promised a salary of four reales plus two meals per day. I have worked for more than six months and have a right to be paid. Notwithstanding many requests, General Avilés never paid me. Instead, using vile language which people say is habitual with this señor, he extended the duration of my contract. Finally, I left the estate without my pay and without an affidavit proving I was not in debt [*una solvencia*]. On General Avilés's orders, the rural magistrate issued a warrant for my arrest. First, I was hunted down and captured by the police; subsequently, I was put in chains and thrown into jail, where I remained for about four days. The magistrate ordered me to pay a fine of one peso per day of imprisonment. I can no longer endure this extreme suffering and ask the authorities to order General Avilés to pay me for my work.[49]

The judge ordered Avilés to pay, but Muños's victory came at a high price. His pain and humiliation were part of the world that landlords made. Muños's testimony demonstrates that planters' abuses were widely tolerated and that peons were presumed guilty unless proven innocent by a tribunal composed of men representing the town's elite.

In Diriomo, the role of cash advances varied, depending on, among other things, the debtor's social standing. Poorer peasants sought cash advances to help sustain their subsistence household economy. Fifty years after coffee first transformed landscape and society in Diriomo, Víctor Granera eloquently explained, "Owing to the poverty that always holds me in the grip of pecuniary difficulties and seeking improvements for my family, whose numerous members I must of necessity feed and support, I consign my legitimate son Eusebio Granera, of about eleven years of age, to work as a debt peon on the finca San Diego . . . My son's contribution to household labor has helped me to provide my family's necessities. But despite his youth and good behavior, he is imprisoned by my poverty."[50] Many poor Diriomeños, like Granera, embarked on debt peonage with their eyes wide open. Fully cognizant of its evils, they hoped indebted labor would mitigate the family's economic difficulties. Other peasants calculated that peonage was preferable to recruitment into the labor draft.[51]

In contrast to poorer peasants, richer peasants frequently found themselves unintentionally drawn into the juggernaut of the labor regime. Rich and middle peasants sometimes borrowed money from planters to expand cash crop farming. However, instead of ascending the social ladder, frequently they found themselves caught in a spiral of downward mobility. José Jesus Nororis told a story that was heard many times in Diriomo's courtroom. Nororis accused one of Diriomo's leading planters, Feliz Castillo, of converting an ordinary loan of 12 pesos into a labor debt. Nororis testified, "When Don Feliz began to treat me like a laborer with a cash advance, I repaid the loan to avoid servitude. Regardless, Don Feliz arranged for my capture and forced me to work." Castillo confirmed Nororis's version of events and frankly stated, "I did not want his cash, I wanted his labor." Castillo's matter-of-fact admission that he loaned money in order to secure control over labor provoked an outcry from Nororis, who declared, "Such abuse is widespread in this region and is tolerated by our officials." Fortunately for Nororis, the judge ruled that Castillo had contravened the law.[52]

Many historians have concluded that peons' debts represent, in Alan Knight's words, a type of peasant credit facility. Under conditions of labor scarcity, peons have been able to exercise a certain bargaining power vis-à-vis planters by ratcheting up loans, which de facto increases the cost of labor.[53] I found little evidence that Granada's planters willingly or unwillingly operated proto–credit agencies. Supervisors on fincas — administrators, foremen, and guards — sometimes received sizable adelantos, but by and large peasants' advances were modest. Between 1876 and 1895, cash advances in Diriomo clustered between 5 and 20 pesos, with almost half below 11 pesos per household.[54] Indebtedness at the conclusion of the harvest was only slightly higher. According to planters' annual declarations, almost one-third of families carried debts between 11 and 20 pesos, and just over half had debts below 11 pesos.[55] In a community where a sombrero cost 6 pesos, a machete 4, and both a day in jail and a Mass for the dead 1 peso, peasants' debts did not represent large sums. Evidence from Diriomo does not support the thesis that peasants exercised power over planters by extracting substantial cash advances. To Granada's planters, debt did not represent one of the problems of peonage; rather, they deployed indebtedness to solve the scarcity of labor. Their major problem with peonage was peasant resistance.

Resistance

Diriomo's peasants endeavored to diminish the oppressive effects of forced labor. One means of defying planters' control over their labor was flight, which was endemic throughout the region: almost 25 percent of peons ran away from the fincas every year.[56] In 1884 Diriomo's alcalde wrote to the prefect explaining the difficulties enforcing the labor regime: "The rural police rarely receive their annual stipend, which undermines morale. Whereas the police are adept at capturing fugitives, frequently peons escape before they are locked up in the town jail for want of proper firearms. The police use their own rifles which often are old and broken, and making matters worse, they are expected to supply their own ammunition."[57] To remedy the situation, the mayor asked the prefect to station professional soldiers on Mombacho. The prefect replied, "Although I do everything in my power to support coffee planters, this office simply does not have sufficient funds to patrol the countryside."[58]

Despite the scarcity of resources, Diriomo's rural police captured the majority of runaway peons. From 1880 to 1905, between 65 and 75 percent of fugitives were apprehended.[59] As in Guatemala and El Salvador, the Nicaraguan security forces were chronically underfunded, yet they were highly effective. This is one of the conundrums of Central American history.[60] Several factors explain the effectiveness of Diriomo's rural police. Municipal patrols arrested many deserters in their own cottages (chozas) or tending their milpas. As Diriomo's agricultural magistrate explained, "Even though Solomon Mayorga fled the finca in order to harvest his milpa, he should be regarded as a work-breaker [*quebrador del trabajo*]. Considering that the worker Mayorga did not offer an explanation that might justify his absence from the finca . . . I condemn him to eight days of labor on public works."[61]

Mayorga was one of hundreds of peons who, year in and year out, fled the fincas during prime coffee-picking time to harvest their milpa.[62] In Managua, Carazo, and Granada, the coffee harvest overlapped with peasants' second harvest of beans and corn, the *postrera*. From early December to the end of January, when planters most needed workers, peasants' highest priority was to harvest food to feed the family. The clash between peasant production and plantation labor drove many peons to break the labor laws. I estimate that 65 percent of Diriomo's runaway peons did so to cultivate their milpa; most of the rest abandoned one finca to work on another, where they hoped to find better working conditions and a good patrón.[63] This pattern of resistance underlines the importance of subsistence production.

Paradoxically, Diriomo's police were adept at capturing peons precisely because they were not professionals. The magistrate handpicked local peasants to carry out rural patrols. In theory, municipal police received a small annual stipend; in practice, they were paid per head for each fugitive captured. In Diriomo, rich peasants who collaborated with public officials to police their neighbors were the eyes and ears of officialdom. In 1887 Diriomo's magistrate explained to the junta municipal just how he maintained law and order in the countryside: "I select agricultores [rich peasants] to patrol the municipality in pursuit of runaway peons. The patrols maintain constant surveillance in the rural hamlets and make my authority felt everywhere in the township. This is the way I succeed in keeping order and preventing work stoppages during the highly sensitive period of the coffee harvest."[64] Practices of peasant policing resulted in high levels of intracommunity violence. Armed vigilantes often clashed with runaway peons, who used their machetes to fight off arrest.[65] With Diriomo's rural police drawn mainly from the township's wealthier families, civilian patrols gave a violent edge to the social differentiation of the peasantry.

In Diriomo, individual acts of sabotage and resistance were common. Frequently peons destroyed estate property; very infrequently they murdered planters, mayordomos, or peasants who served in the rural police.[66] Although the sprinkling of violent incidents alarmed planters, the ruling classes' greatest fear was collective resistance. In 1889 Diriomo's rural magistrate wrote to the jefe político, "There have been several serious occupations on Mombacho carried out by operarios who work in different coffee enterprises."[67] Over and over again, Diriomo's alcalde asked the government to install a guard post on Mombacho, but Granada's prefect always responded that he would if he could, but funds simply were not available. The day after Christmas 1889, the alcalde wrote with a new urgency:

In light of the discord that is evident among the operarios who work in the coffee enterprises on Mombacho, in light of the need to prosecute those who commit various crimes including the destruction of property, the contraband sale of *aguardiente* [alcohol], and the theft of tools and coffee seedlings, and in order to prevent further unrest, the Junta Municipal of Diriomo together with Mombacho's planters urgently request the appointment of a police agent to reside permanently on the volcano. He will capture operarios and fulfill all other functions of the rural police. If the Prefect of Granada is unable to comply with this request, we will immediately take our petition to the Supreme Government [in Managua].[68]

The prefect replied quickly, but again his answer was disappointing. Instead of promising to station guards on Mombacho, he mobilized the militia, a slightly grander version of Diriomo's own rural police.[69] However, before the alcalde had time to take the matter to Managua, events overtook him. In January 1890, when the coffee harvest was just getting underway on the volcano, scores of peons refused to work, and they plundered a number of coffee estates. Almost two days elapsed before soldiers arrived and restored order. In the meantime, peons had destroyed coffee trees, tools, machinery, and two plantation headquarters.[70]

The government responded by arresting thirty-seven peons.[71] Although Diriomo's magistrate and a judge from Granada who sat in on the case endeavored to identify the leaders and the immediate causes of the disturbance, they were unsuccessful. Possibly because premeditated crimes tended to be punished more harshly than incidents sparked in the heat of anger, the peasant defendants insisted that the riot had erupted spontaneously. In the end, the tribunal concluded that the riot was incited by "criminals and habitual troublemakers." Although the transcript throws little light on the events or their causes, it displays a rush to judgment. Local officials tried, convicted, and sentenced to prison eleven men who previously had been convicted of minor crimes against the labor regime. Soon after the riot, the government acceded to the planters' demands and established a small national police post on Mombacho.[72] With the police presence on the volcano more closely felt, peons abandoned collective resistance in favor of covert forms of struggle.

In Nicaragua, the telegraph centralized the repressive apparatus perhaps more effectively than any other instrument of state. It tied together the local policing operations in towns and cities across the country and gave law enforcement a national reach. Rural magistrates throughout Nicaragua communicated daily, sometimes hourly, with their counterparts in other parts of the country to track fugitive peons.[73] Once runaway peons were captured, magistrates argued over the wires about which jurisdiction would press charges, which planter had first rights to the deserter, and which municipality would defray the costs of returning the fugitive to his or her patrón. The telegraph was not installed in Diriomo and the neighboring pueblos until 1898, in part because peasants repeatedly cut the lines.[74] Yet despite continuing sabotage, resistance to the telegraph never escalated into major rebellion in the southern coffee district, as it did in Matagalpa in 1881.[75] Nevertheless, as Diriomo's peasants evidently feared, when the telegraph office finally opened for business in the township, the rural magistrate was its best customer.

Constructing Consent in the Courtroom

Poor peasants generally resisted the labor regime by illegal means, mostly by running away from the coffee fincas. In contrast, richer peasants often contested planters' abuses via the court system. To take a landlord to court, peasants needed both the chutzpah to challenge planters in the public sphere, and the wherewithal to pay a legal advisor. Between 1876 and 1905, Diriomo's magistrates arbitrated on average eighty disputes per year between planters and peons; about 20 percent were filed by peasants, the rest by planters.[76]

Poor peasants often found themselves in court against their will, defending themselves against accusations of breaking the labor laws. However, a number of richer peasants pressed charges against planters for having foisted debt peonage on them. These cases are particularly interesting as they tend to reveal corrupt practices frequently hidden behind a veil of legality. In 1880 Mercedes Pérez, a well-to-do peasant, explained to Diriomo's tribunal just how he became trapped in debt peonage:

> I bought an old, broken-down sugar mill from Alejandro Mejía for which I agreed to pay 35 pesos after the harvest. Señor Mejía forced me to guarantee the loan with a promise to work. I planted twelve manzanas of sugar cane but the harvest was poor and I could not repay 15 pesos of the loan. I asked Mejía to renew the loan but he refused, and instead forced me to work on his finca La Flor as a debt peon. I am a simple man without any schooling in arithmetic whatsoever. However, I kept a record of my work. Like many other peons, I worked for Mejía much more than was

necessary, but this señor kept claiming I was still in debt. He demanded either that I continue working, or give him a mozo to work off the debt. It is widely known that Mejía habitually invents loans and fails to record peons' labor.[77]

Pérez's legal advisor asked the judge to subpoena Mejía's ledgers, even though, as he said, "They are a work of fiction." Pérez ended his testimony by declaring that although he supported debt peonage in principle, he condemned the planters who regularly broke the law and the judges who allowed them to get away with it. Like many other coffee growers before him, Mejía refused to permit members of the tribunal to scrutinize his ledgers; consequently, the judge ruled in Pérez's favor.

Although Mercedes Pérez won a modest victory, peons with fewer resources at their command were rarely so successful. Andrés Marcia, ex-alcalde of Diriomo and one of the town's commercial planters, accused two young peons of "do[ing] all they could to avoid honoring the labor obligations of their deceased father."[78] To free her sons from servitude, the boys' mother, Atanancia Antón, enlisted a schoolteacher to argue her case. Antón charged Marcia with manipulating her sons' debts; she claimed that although the boys worked on Marcia's finca for more than two years, the amount they owed was greater than when her husband died. Her defiant counsel declared to the tribunal, "Marcia's account books are riddled with arithmetic errors and fail to satisfy minimal legal requirements. They make a mockery of the labor system, which proves Marcia is corrupt."

However, the magistrate offered another, far more generous interpretation of the many discrepancies in Marcia's accounts: "We are all susceptible of making arithmetic errors. It is well known that when carrying out operations in which one has to enter numbers, the mind thinks of one number while the hand writes another. Therefore, it is wrong to call Marcia malicious for having made such natural errors."[79] After this finely wrought exculpation, Marcia himself took the stand and brazenly declared, "My clean and exacting accounts demonstrate that I am honorable and of good name. Never would I sell my reputation for manly decency [hombria de bien] for such an insignificant sum." In the end, the judge dismissed the case, saying that, so far as he was able to determine, Marcia's books simply were "not well kept." Evidently, he was unwilling to pass judgment against another member of the fraternity that governed the township.

Diriomo's agricultural tribunal helped to legitimate the labor regime among the upper stratum of the peasantry. Notwithstanding planters' political clout, when richer peasants presented well-documented evidence of abuse, Diriomo's magistrates often ruled in their favor. Peasants won about 30 percent of their suits against planters, many brought by men and women of the upper reaches of the peasantry.[80] In a township where richer peasants carried out police patrols and worked as supervisors on coffee estates, officials recognized that Diriomo's court of law needed to be seen as upholding the administration of justice.

However, when planters filed charges against peons, the scales of justice tended to tip in favor of the growers. Peons in the dock generally were from the poorer strata, and their testimonies, usually delivered without benefit of legal counsel, reveal the brutal underbelly of the labor regime. Many peasants said they were frequently stopped and made to show their passbook in the normal course of a day's activities. Others told of the routine violence used by armed guards sent out to capture poor peasants during the coffee harvest. They recounted how they were roped together and marched off to the municipal jail, where they were put in shackles while awaiting trial. For his part, the rural magistrate explained to Diriomo's junta municipal how he financed his law enforcement operations: "Each prisoner pays one [*peso*] to cover the cost of capture, another for each day of imprisonment, and an additional twenty centavos for administrative fees. Planters advance the sum which they add to their peon's debt."[81]

The social differentiation of justice approximated stratification within the peasantry. When planters pressed charges against fugitive peons, magistrates sided with the growers about 75 percent of the time.[82] Even so, the court did not, for the most part, crudely railroad peasants into a life of perpetual servitude. Significantly, after witnesses were called and testimony heard, tribunals acquitted peasants in almost 25 percent of cases brought by planters.[83] In addition, Diriomo's magistrates sometimes gave shorter sentences for first-time "labor breakers" than those prescribed by national law and often went to lengths to explain the reasons for their leniency.[84]

Judges reserved harsher punishments for peons accused of destroying property, fleeing repeatedly, and rioting. After completing their official sentences, peons known for insubordination frequently were victims of double indemnity, as their patrón meted out a second round of punishment on the hacienda. Hoping to deter resistance, some coffee growers had serial offenders flogged and subjected to a range of grisly ordeals that were carried out under the gaze of the other peons.[85] The private administration of justice, or more accurately, of injustice, occupied a contradictory position as laws obligated planters to maintain order on their estates "by whatever means necessary," at the same time that their punitive regime was largely beyond the reach of the law.

Notwithstanding the occasional extremity of the planters' justice, Diriomo's courts played a role in constructing consent, especially among the upper peasantry. As a number of historians have argued, the judiciary can be an effective tool in legitimating an exploitative system, thereby reinforcing the power of ruling classes. If subordinate classes believe they can achieve justice through the courts, it is more likely they will petition for redress and stay within the boundaries of the legal system, and less likely they will turn to violence to fundamentally change the social order.[86] In other words, if the state can persuade the lower classes to seek reform through a legal system created by, and largely for, the ruling elites, it may stave off radical challenges to the status quo.[87] In rural Granada, peasant participation in the court system played a role in consolidating the emerging nation-state, in particular its fledgling mechanisms of social and ideological control. To the extent that the administration of justice encouraged peasants to accept the legitimacy of the labor regime, and the wider social order, planters consolidated their class power.

Diriomo's peasants sought to use the legal system to their advantage. Many learned to "talk the talk": to present their motivations and actions in the idiom of the elite ladinos who sat in judgment. Peons might defend themselves against a planter's charges by describing their patrón's breach of the rules of debt peonage. Fugitive peons frequently justified flight from one finca to work on another by explaining that because their patrón failed to provide protection and assistance, they decided to run away in search of a good patrón. For example, Concepción Reyes told the magistrate, "Not only did my patrón refuse to pay me, he refused to provide a promise of assistance in exchange for my obligation to labor, so I left the estate."[88] In a similar vein, peons testified that because their patrón did not supply soup with meat, a decent place to hang their hammock, or, more ambiguously, "protection," they left the finca.[89] Peons' testimonies may be self-serving and designed to justify their defiance of the labor laws; nevertheless, they demonstrate that patriarchal practices and ideologies played a part in constructing consent.

Diriomo's courtroom was an arena of contention among planters as well as between planters and peons. Planters frequently poached peons from other estates, leading to all manner of litigation among and between planters and peons. One of the most interesting cases involved Granada's jefe político, General Juan Bodán, charged with enticing peons from other estates with promises that he would permanently exempt them from military service.[90] In Diriomo, contention among planters frequently surfaced along party lines. With few exceptions, Diriomo's commercial planters were Liberal Party members, while Granada's large coffee growers included among their ranks the country's foremost Conservative politicians. Partisan tensions between the two groups frequently spilled over into the courtroom. Luis Felípe Tifer was Diriomo's magistrate and head of the local Liberal Party when Zelaya was president and Liberals held national power. Tifer frequently used his official position in the pueblo to denounce Granada's planters. In one standoff with General Avilés, Tifer declared:

> In common with all supporters of the Conservative Party, the General thinks nothing of violating the inalienable rights of man. Under the enlightened Liberal government of President Zelaya, peasants are bound to provide labor by virtue of the support they owe to the country's agriculture. However, peons enjoy the inalienable right to fulfill that obligation under the terms spelled out in the labor laws. Some of the authorities in Granada trample the laws with serious disregard for society and for the inalienable rights of man. If the General persists in violating peons' rights, I will inform the President of the Republic so that he can remedy this evil.[91]

With these words, in particular the ritualized homage to the inalienable rights of man, Tifer encapsulated the contradictions at the heart of liberalism. Like their counterparts across Latin America, Nicaraguan Liberals advocated coerced labor on the grounds that the poor should be compelled to contribute to the nation's progress. Yet being a good Liberal, Tifer upheld the principle that peons enjoy the inalienable right to render forced labor in strict accordance with the laws of the land.

Like other town officials, when siding with local peasants against a planter from Granada's oligarchy, Tifer often worked into his rulings declarations about the common interests tying together Diriomo's landlords and peasants. Such rhetorical moves to bridge the class divide in the township can be read on several levels. With competition for labor fierce, planters from the pueblo wanted to lay claim to "their" peasants. On top of this, planter rivalry was accentuated by the country's endemic partisan struggles. Finally, racism was another facet of the deep rift that divided Diriomo's planters from Granada's elite.

Hunting Indians

Enigmatically, two major social issues of the day, forced labor and abolition of comunidades indígenas, seemed disconnected in the public imagination. Newspaper articles about the pros and cons of forced labor eschewed direct reference to the Indian question, and decrees abolishing comunidades indígenas made no mention of the need to mobilize plantation labor. Apparently, national figures rarely spoke out about Indians—except, that is, to call for assimilating them.

Under the rule of President Zelaya, liberal officials striving to eliminate Indians through assimilation, on the one hand, and to toughen up the labor draft, on the other, regularly denounced vagrants, the lazy, petty criminals, and peasants who fled from work.[92] I suspect that these derogatory terms may have been code words for Indian. When Managua's jefe político raised the specter of "people who . . . flee from work and fall prey to petty criminality" in a report justifying forced labor, it is likely that politicians, planters, and peasants understood his statement not only as a defense of Zelaya's policy of expanding the compulsory labor regime, but as a condemnation of the Indian way of life. Similarly, newspaper attacks on Nicaraguans with "an abundance of laziness" who "shy away from work" may have been veiled manifestos in favor of force-marching the country's poor, predominantly Indian, peasantry into modernity.

Consistent with the policy of eschewing any formal connection between forced labor and Indian abolition, compulsory labor laws did not discriminate on the basis of ethnicity—nor, surprisingly, of gender. The labor regime was, ostensibly, a class-based system in which property, wealth, and professional standing were the criteria that determined who was subject to forced labor. Unsurprisingly, the absence of explicit references to Indians in the national discourse was replicated in Diriomo's labor records. Municipal reports on labor drafts and debt peonage almost never referred to the township's Indians. The silence is particularly striking given that according to the 1883 census, 73 percent of Diriomo's population was Indian and Indian leaders continued to play a role in the pueblo.[93]

In the rare instances when Indians do appear qua Indians in local labor records, it would appear that Diriomo's officials used ethnicity as a criterion in applying the labor laws—at least some of the time. Two petitions relating to grievances about the labor regime suggest that the formal policy of racial equality in forced labor was violated in practice. In 1885, Diriomeños who titled themselves *priostes y mayordomos indígenas*, or officeholders in the indigenous community, wrote to Granada's jefe político, complaining, "The rural magistrate does not leave us in peace. Every time we go into town to carry out tasks for the community, he arrests us. Citing the authority of various labor decrees, he levies a fine of 50 centavos and orders us to work on the haciendas. The magistrate knows that each of us has sufficient property to be exempt from the labor draft. We beg of you to put an end to this abuse."[94] These petitions lay bare the oppression of Indians in the workings of a labor system that, in theory, was blind to ethnicity and race.

One hundred years later, the patriarch of one of Diriomo's leading families, Noé Campos Carcache, described the past in ways that echoed those earlier petitions. He recalled that his father frequently told him that, "when Zelaya was president, Granadan coffee planters came to Diriomo only for one purpose: to hunt for Indians [*cazar a indios* for their coffee plantations]."[95] Campos's story provides further evidence that in practice the labor system was not blind to race and ethnicity. It also highlights the contradictions of ethnicity in Diriomo and the wider region. Campos described himself and his ancestors as mestizo, and he told me that when, as a boy, he went into Granada with his father, people always called them Indian. With bitterness, he said that Granadans believed that everyone in Diriomo was Indian: rich and poor, planter and peasant, Indian and ladino.

In the piles of paperwork generated by the labor regime over the course of fifty years, Diriomo's officials noted ethnicity, or raza, only in rare circumstances: when a peon was, in their words, an "Indio blanco" or "Indio, color claro."[96] Keeping in mind that physical descriptions were included in labor contracts to facilitate the capture of runaway peons, it appears that magistrates broke the taboo and used the word Indian only when a person's physical characteristics, specifically skin tone, jarred with elite Diriomeños' notion of what Indians looked like. Otherwise, code words for Indian served the purpose, "trigueño oscuro" (dark wheat-skinned) being the most common.

Ethnic difference was part of the social divide that separated Diriomo's poor, mostly Indian peasantry and the town's ladino elite. However, what I loosely call racism also created tensions within the planter class. Memories of ethnic oppression suffered in the early decades of the twentieth century continued to fester among the town's leading families. According to oral histories with Diriomeños from all walks of life, in the early twentieth century larger landowners, whether from Granada or Diriomo, considered themselves mestizo—with the exception of Alejandro Mejía.[97] Yet, according to Luis Felipe Tifer's granddaughter, "at that time, rich Granadans considered all of us [Diriomo's local elite] to be Indian. To them, we were all Indians with little capacity and less culture."[98]

These memories underscore the relativity of ethnic identity.[99] Diriomo's public officials and commercial planters—and the two were virtually the same group—considered themselves mestizo and on that basis superior to the Indians. In their eyes the divide between Indian and non-Indian was a key feature of Diriomo's social hierarchy. But Granada's oligarchs were blind to the ethnic divide in the neighboring township. To them, all Diriomeños, whether planters or peons, were Indian.

In contrast to Granadans' geographic criteria for determining ethnic identity, national officials in charge of the 1883 census espoused biological criteria, and they feared their underlings in the Department of Granada would not be able to decipher people's race. Therefore, along with the census forms, they sent detailed instructions about how to code a person's race (raza). I quote from the official instruction manual:

> I believe it is necessary to call your utmost attention to the difficulties you might encounter filling in some of the boxes [on the forms], so that you do not inadvertently make errors. While the categories age, sex, legitimacy or illegitimacy of birth, civil status (single, married, widowed), political qualifications [capacidades], religion, physical and moral defects, and vaccination should not present difficulties, the same cannot be said for race . . . You must take great care in noting this category in order not to make errors.
>
> The races of people that populate Nicaragua fall into six types which are more or less easily distinguishable. These are: pure White, pure Indian, pure Black [negro], mestizo, mulatto and zambo. The first three are well defined and distinguishing between them will not pose any difficulties. As for mestizo, this is the result of the mixture of Indian and White; for mulatto, of White and Black; and for zambo, of Black and Indian. The fractions of these mixtures can be seen in the skin and hair.
>
> I must insist on the issue of race. I believe it is indispensable that you convey these explanations to the local agents [census takers], keeping in mind their low capacity and understanding, owing to their lack of culture.

For instance, you should explain in detail various examples: a person who is light black, with very frizzy hair, who is fat and short, is clearly a zambo: the hair reveals pure Negro [ancestry], and skin color and stature, that of the Indian . . .

Signed: Your very attentive servant, M Bravo.[100]

Race, according to the Nicaraguan Census Bureau, was in the genes. Señor Bravo was confident that local census takers, despite "their lack of culture," would be able to determine race, provided they had enough training and they carefully assessed a person's skin color, hair texture, and stature. Nicaraguan officials were not alone in believing that racial categories could be readily observed. This was the prevailing viewpoint endorsed by most scientists and pseudo-scientists, and it remained the orthodoxy until the turn of the twenty-first century.[101]

To Granadans race was a function of residence; to census officials race was in the genes. However, evidence from Diriomo demonstrates that, at the turn of the twentieth century, the meanings of Indian were highly fluid and relational; people from different social groups understood race differently. To most Diriomeños, Indianness implied, more than anything else, common land rights administered by the Indian community. After Diriomeños' land was privatized, there was little benefit to identifying oneself as Indian. What remained was forced labor and the stigmas associated with Indianness.

Correspondence between Granada's jefe político and Diriomo's alcalde municipal in 1911 contain the last references to Indians I found in local records. The jefe político wrote, "I will not recognize the authority or even the existence of the Indian mayor [alcalde del pueblo] because the post was legally abolished and should cease to exist." To which Diriomo's alcalde municipal replied, "The alcalde del pueblo is one of my agents, I rely on his efforts."[102] We can only surmise what services the Indian leader performed that made him indispensable to the town's mayor. In the tradition of his forebears, he probably rounded up the poor to clean the plaza, clear pathways, and toil in other public works. Possibly, he made himself felt in other ways: checking passbooks and capturing Diriomeños who ran away from the fincas.

I conducted oral histories with thirty-odd Diriomeños who themselves were or were descended from poor peasants. Only four admitted (I choose the word purposefully) that their ancestors were, or might have been, Indian; three of the four were well into their eighties.[103] Teófilo Cano, a veteran activist and an organic intellectual, to use Gramsci's term,[104] said that his grandfather, José Ana Cano, who died in 1936, had been Diriomo's last *alcalde de vara*. According to Cano, "My grandfather said, with shame, that for many, many decades the alcaldes de vara have been allies, even servants, of the municipal mayor, not representatives of the interests of indigenous people. They were appointed by the municipal mayor, not by the people, and they collected taxes, tribute really, from their own people." He continued, "Whereas in the distant past, the alcaldes de vara carried out political as well as religious functions, by the time my grandfather assumed the post in the 1920s, only the religious functions remained. My grandfather was one of the patrons of the Virgen de Candelaría. His job was to ensure that people provided firewood and food for the fiesta, and that they kept the church clean."

Carmen Ramírez Pérez continued to make and sell traditional rolls until she was about eighty years old. I frequently joined her in the early hours of the morning when she tended her large adobe oven, and she recounted her life history. Doña Carmen said her adoptive parents had told her that once most people in Diriomo had been Indian, and some women wore *huipiles* (traditional dress).[105] But she advised me to stop asking people about the town's Indian past because people were complaining that I was going around "accusing" Diriomeños of being Indian. "In my lifetime, Indian has meant only one thing: ignorant, dirty, poor, and backward. People don't like you suggesting that one hundred years ago almost everyone in Diriomo was an Indian, and that we're all descendants of Indians."

The other Diriomeños I interviewed said they had no knowledge of Diriomo's Indian past; most asserted, in fact, that there had never been a comunidad indígena in Diriomo. When I asked about the coffee planter Alejandro Mejía, who figures as the villain in Diriomo's folk history, most said that Mejía was one of the few Indians in the township, and for that reason he was called el indio. Following Doña Carmen's advice, I stopped questioning people about the pueblo's Indian past, but I continued to ask why Diriomo was "el Pueblo de los Brujos." Although I imagined there might be some connection between the indigenous legacy and the witchcraft, or *brujería*, traditionally practiced by men in the township, no one drew a link between the two.

At the close of the twentieth century, Diriomo's Indian past was overwhelmingly denied, if not forgotten, by the people of the pueblo. I suggest that a complex of factors combined to suppress Diriomo's Indian history: land privatization, abolition of the comunidad indígena, a labor system that

4. Fiesta de la Virgen de la Candelaría, patron saint of Diriomo, 1995.

5. Domingo Dávila, 1993.

6. Doroteo Flores Pérez, 1995.

7. Teófilo Cano surrounded by his sister and brother, with Enrique Rodríguez Ramírez on right, 1995.

8. Carmen Ramírez
Pérez, 1991.

9. Pedro Pablo Cano and wife, 1991.

10. Diriomeña with grandchildren, 1995.

11. Teófilo Cano (second from right), family, and neighbors in front of his home, 1995.

12. Leticia Salazar Castillo, 1995.

in principle ignored ethnicity and divided people along class lines, the persistence of racism, discrimination, shame, and state policy to assimilate Indians.

Late Capitalist Development

International coffee prices crashed in the early 1930s to one-third of their predepression value.[106] Although planters' incomes declined precipitously, the level of coffee production in Granada remained remarkably steady during the depression years. Large coffee growers contracted more or less the same number of peons after the crash as before, and the worldwide upheaval had a minimal impact on the rhythms of peasant life in Diriomo.[107] Precisely because labor was not a commodity there was a certain social continuity in the region. Ironically, debt peonage served to blunt planters' ability to reduce their workforce because labor contracts tied peasants to planters and vice versa from one year to another.[108]

Debt peonage remained the prevailing labor system on Granada's coffee estates for several decades following the depression. However, beneath strong societal continuities, landlord-peasant relations were changing. After the government abolished forced labor and dismantled national enforcement agencies, debt peonage in rural Granada was less formal and less regulated.

Official labor contracts declined in number and planter-peon arrangements tended to be based on verbal understandings. In addition, public officials played a diminished role in policing the labor regime.[109] Nevertheless, Diriomo's alcaldes occasionally fell back on their old ways. In 1930, with a shortage of coffee pickers threatening the harvest, Alcalde Francisco Carcache ordered the police commander to round up peasants in the usual way: "Faced with the urgency of recruiting laborers for the coffee estates, I need the support of your authority. I request that next Monday, February 24, under your direction two members of the National Guard along with the municipal police capture vagrants and drunks who you find walking in the pueblo during working hours. I authorize you to put them to work as I have indicated."[110] But despite the tenacity of local traditions, overt coercion was less prominent in the day-to-day workings of the labor regime during the depression and even less significant thereafter.

Patriarchal relations of unequal reciprocity gradually supplanted coercion. Peonage came to be known as *trabajo al empeño*, literally "pawned labor," from the 1930s until it died out in the 1960s. Many Diriomeños explained that they pawned their labor to the same planter year after year: if they needed help "peleando la tierra [fighting for survival]," they hoped that a long-standing patrón might give them some assistance.[111]

The labor regime on Granada's coffee estates rested on debt peonage for almost a century. Although overt coercion gave way to patriarchal measures eliciting consent, market forces remained marginal to the labor regime. In Granada, debt peonage conformed closely to the noncapitalist labor regimes Polanyi describes.[112] Diriomo's history both supports and contradicts Brenner's model of landlord-peasant relations in export economies. Debt peonage in Diriomo was a generally coercive labor regime, thereby supporting Brenner's view that coercion is a necessary part of labor discipline in nonmarket economies. However, peonage in Diriomo endured not because of coercion, but because patriarchy played a part in mitigating the use of force and in constructing consent. This runs counter to Brenner's hypothesis that coercion is the sole bulwark of landlord power. To my mind, Brenner fails to recognize that frequently extraeconomic coercion is accompanied by measures to elicit extraeconomic consent.

In Diriomo, coercion was necessary but not sufficient to sustain the peonage system. As described in the next chapter, patriarchal practices and ideologies diminished peasants' resistance to the forced labor regime. Debt peonage prevailed for close to a century because both the exploiting and the exploited classes came to regard the system as necessary for their survival.[113] In short, debt peonage was more a fetter than an agent of capitalist development in rural Granada, where the mix of cash advances, wage payments, and patriarchy facilitated more than undermined the continuation of the peasants' way of life.[114] One of the great strengths of the literature on colonialism and postcolonialism is its exploration of the diversity of capitalist transitions.[115] The history of rural Granada suggests that in Nicaragua, capitalism developed late.

Gould proposed that in the Matagalpan coffee sector, the longevity of labor coercion and the intensity of violence surrounding it can be explained by Indian oppression.[116] To my mind, in the Granadan coffee sector, the historical dynamic was somewhat different. Ethnic oppression probably played a role in the forced labor regime, but Indian oppression was not the underlying cause of coercion. Debt peonage developed and endured because rural Granada was a society with markets, not a market society. The coffee sector required a production system built on extraeconomic coercion because the subsistence household economy remained the mainstay of peasant life long after coffee cultivation revolutionized land and labor.

Debt Peonage Debates Revisited

The 1980s was a turning point in historical scholarship about debt peonage in Latin America. An older interpretation of peonage as a coercive labor regime that exemplified Latin American "feudalism" was turned upside down.[117] According to the new paradigm, not only was peonage a largely consensual system, but it accelerated the development of agrarian capitalism. The writings of Arnold Bauer and Alan Knight were pivotal to this conceptual shift. Convinced that the older literature had flattened out the complexities of unfree labor, Bauer argued that the contradictions of debt peonage gave rise to free wage labor. Drawing on Polanyi's theory of the great transformation, Bauer proposed that similar upheavals occurred between 1870 and 1930 in Latin America.[118] In his view, planters deployed debt as a market incentive to coax peasants out of subsistence production and into the wage labor force of the region's expanding capitalist economies. He concluded that on the whole, debt peonage undermined nonmarket relations throughout the countryside and gave rise to societies ruled by market mechanisms.

Widening the temporal and conceptual reach of Bauer's model, Knight developed a typology that sorted peonage into three categories. In type I, debts represented salary advances in an incipient system of free wage labor; in type II, debts were derivative of voluntary and mainly market relations between landlords and peons; in type III, debts were coercive measures, "an excuse for servitude."[119] Knight argued that in Mexico, type II was probably the most common form of peonage from the colonial period until the early nineteenth century, when proto–free wage labor (type I) came to prevail. In recognition of its ubiquity, he called type II "traditional peonage" and proposed that in most circumstances debt was a "peasant credit facility," a benefit rather than a bond. Overall, Knight emphasized the long-standing predominance of market relations in Latin American rural labor systems, stating, "In general terms . . . peonage rested on non-coercive foundations."[120] These reinterpretations of debt peonage cracked open the monolithic model inherited from earlier generations and largely redefined debt peonage as a labor system governed not by coercion, but by market forces.[121] Following in the footsteps of Bauer and Knight, subsequent accounts of peonage have tended to emphasize its consensual character and its market mechanisms.[122]

The history of rural labor in Granada does not fit the orthodox stand that peonage ushered in the capitalist transition.[123] In Diriomo, debt peonage gave rise neither to a labor market nor to a rural proletariat. In the social upheaval set in motion by the coffee boom, the state destroyed old social forms that inhibited the expansion of buying and selling, in particular, the Indian communities and their common rights to land. But the new society did not generate the conditions to make labor a commodity freely bought and sold. In the new rural order, social forms emerged that restricted the development of a market in labor, although not in the old way. The new Nicaragua was a patriarchal society where planters and the state controlled peasants' labor by deploying coercion and eliciting consent.[124]

Planter-peon relations were not those of buyers and sellers of labor, where buying and selling takes on a life of its own and regulates labor relations and society more generally. Planter-peon relations were those of patrons and clients, where powers of the patriarch to command allegiance, protect dependents, and punish disobedience underpinned labor relations and the social order.[125] Nicaragua had no labor market in the capitalist sense that regulated the supply and demand for seasonal workers for the coffee fincas. In its absence, the state relied almost exclusively on the direct exercise of coercion: private armed guards, laws of forced labor, patriarchal rights to discipline peons, and on negotiated forms of consent. Labor relations had none of the anonymity that develops with capitalist labor markets. From their origin in the 1870s until their demise in the 1960s, patrón-peon relations in Diriomo changed substantially, but remained at their core personal arrangements between planters and peasants. Debt peonage in rural Granada did not mark the transition to capitalism.[126] The great contradiction of Nicaraguan liberalism was that it revolutionized land and labor but gave rise to systems of landowning and labor exploitation that impeded more than promoted capitalist development.

Postscript

Debt peonage endured in Diriomo into the 1960s. However, over time it lost its overtly coercive character. Forced labor was outlawed piecemeal when Nicaragua was under U.S. occupation in the 1920s and 1930s, apparently owing in part to Washington's pressure to end "semi-servitude."[127] In addition, when demand for labor declined following the Great Depression and the collapse of international coffee prices, debt peonage inhibited planters' freedom to dismiss workers. Finally, in the 1950s and 1960s, cotton production transformed landscape and society on the western plains of León and Chinandega. Cotton planters expropriated the peasantry and the state moved to consolidate conditions for capitalist agriculture. Repercussions from upheavals in León and Chinandega reached Diriomo, where poor peasants migrated to labor in the cotton fields. Diriomeños continued to work as debt peons on local coffee estates, but less because of compulsion by planters and town officials. Increasingly, poor peasants needed to supplement their household subsistence production with waged labor, and many preferred to indebt or pawn their labor (*empeñarse*) to a local grandee who might lend their family some support or a bit of land, rather than join the ranks of the migrant labor force. Debt peonage prevailed in Diriomo until modern times, and planter-peon relations retained some of their traditional trappings; however, the labor system changed fundamentally. Without coerced labor laws and state regulation, peonage in Diriomo rested on the economics of necessity and the culture of patriarchy.

Labor relations in coffee districts changed in the decades after coffee cultivation revolutionized rural Nicaragua. In Granada the direction of change was not for the most part to capitalism, except in the sense that market relations eventually transformed land, labor, and the state throughout Nicaragua. When market relations finally transformed local society, they emerged neither out of debt peonage nor the coffee sector. Capitalism arose in a different region of the country and in association with the cultivation of a different crop. The cotton boom of the 1950s and 1960s all but destroyed peasant self-provisioning on the country's western coastal plains. In León and Chinandega, planters and the state dispossessed the peasantry and created hothouse conditions for the buying and selling of rural labor.[128] This social revolution spread to other parts of the country and in time undermined debt peonage.[129]

CHAPTER SEVEN

Patriarchy and Peonage

Latin American governance long rested on the principle of patriarchal authority. This chapter argues that patriarchy was central to the longevity of debt peonage in Diriomo and that planters' control over the peasantry and peons' acceptance of their authority were conditioned by gendered understandings of patriarchal privileges and responsibilities. I examine, in particular, how the patriarchal powers of planters and of male peasants shaped labor relations. The former I call patriarchy from above, the latter, patriarchy from below. I investigate the double-sided class character of patriarchy and how the two interacted in the making of debt peonage in Diriomo.[1] Patriarchy was double-sided in a second sense: it coupled senior male control over female and male subordinates with responsibilities to protect them. I examine how the double-sided character of patriarchy, understood in both senses, gave rise to conflicts in Diriomo. Gender analysis is virtually absent from the Latin American literature on peonage. I hope this examination of the gendered character of Diriomo's plantation labor system convinces readers that analysis of gender does not simply add missing pieces to the historical puzzle; it fundamentally changes our understanding of the past.

Reworking Patriarchy

Nicaraguan politicians reshaped long-standing patriarchal laws and practices to the needs of plantation labor in the late nineteenth century. In colonial and postcolonial Latin America, senior male authority over females and younger males was codified in law and regulated daily life. The state invested male heads of household, from the highest to the most humble (excepting the enslaved), with wide-ranging powers over female and male dependents. The legal principle of patria potestad, loosely translated as senior men's authority, regulated male governance of subordinates in and well beyond the domestic domain.² Patria potestad codified unequal reciprocity: it obligated the wife and children to obey the senior male, and it required patriarchs to rule and protect their dependents.

With the rise of a new agrarian order, Nicaraguan jurists purposefully expanded the reach of patriarchal authority to the plantation sector. Previous chapters treated the nature of patriarchal law; my purpose here is to rehearse its main features and demonstrate that politicians in concert with planters reworked the tradition of senior male privilege to fit the needs of the new plantation labor system. As the public expression of the household, patriarchs signed contracts, administered property, and allocated the labor of dependents. Additionally, the state empowered patriarchs to maintain discipline within their sphere, and to this end, senior males were legally bound to punish subordinates as they saw fit. However, patriarchs' power to govern was conjoined with responsibility, as the laws of patria potestad spelled out senior males' obligations to provide for and protect their subordinates.

As land privatization, export growth, and incipient industrialization altered the face of Latin American societies in the late nineteenth century, jurists in a number of countries shied away from measures that would expand women's rights and authority, especially wives'.³ One might say that women's emancipation was sacrificed by politicians anxious to reinforce patriarchal power in an atmosphere of social change. As I have argued elsewhere, at a time when liberal ideas were gaining strength and liberals taking national office, paradoxically patriarchal laws and practices tended to assume more absolutist forms.⁴ In Nicaragua, civil codes reinforced a husband's control over his wife's body, labor, wages, and property. In contrast to a certain relaxation of patriarchal power over adult sons, unmarried daughters remained subordinated to paternal authority throughout their father's lifetime unless legally "emancipated," that is, granted independence by their father. However, the stipulation that adult sons and daughters obey their father was incorporated into revised versions of the civil code, and the state expanded its reach to regulate patriarchal authority both in the public arena and the domestic domain.⁵

Nicaraguan liberals expected that the private property revolution would accelerate the development of export agriculture and economic growth. They were under no illusion, however, that market mechanisms would generate a labor force sufficient for the coffee plantations. Liberal politicians from Managua's governor down to Diriomo's agrarian magistrates publicly declared that in the interests of national development, the state needed to compel the rural poor to work. To that end, Nicaraguan jurists drew on the patriarchal tradition, and explicitly on patria potestad, to structure authority in the coffee sector. To enhance planters' power over their peons, labor laws granted planters authorities customarily exercised by fathers and husbands over family members. Of particular significance, labor laws explicitly borrowed from the patriarchal tradition of senior male responsibility to discipline subordinates and endowed planters with similar powers. For example, the 1862 labor law spelled out a planter's responsibility to punish workers as he saw fit and his obligation to maintain order within his enterprise "by whatever means necessary."[6] In a word, when designing the legal framework that regulated planters' disciplinary powers, lawmakers drew on the principles of senior male privilege. Historians famously call this "inventing tradition."[7]

One of the modernizing principles of classical European liberalism is that the public administration of justice should supersede the private exercise of power. However, Nicaraguan jurists turned that liberal ideal upside down and granted landowners the right to exercise private, arbitrary power. Furthermore, instead of seeking to extend workers' rights and the inviolability of their bodies, lawmakers reworked patriarchal privileges to allow planters to punish delinquent peons much as if they were disobedient children. In short, Nicaragua's statesmen took steps to ensure that the gender hierarchy of patriarchy fortified labor relations in the new plantation sector. In the Hispanic legal tradition, the senior male's authority was twinned with responsibility to dependents. Yet, labor laws were silent on that issue. Nevertheless, evoking the patriarchal tradition, Diriomo's peasants frequently demanded that landlords extend a measure of protection to indebted peons, and some planters implicitly accepted the legitimacy of their claim.

Patriarchy from Above

Nicaraguan politicians purposefully adapted long-standing gendered norms to enhance planters' power over the peasantry. In Diriomo, planters' gendered power, patriarchy from above, was institutionalized in debt peonage. Planters' authority over peasants, in particular their right to command obedience, was codified in the formalities of labor contracts (matrículas) between planters and peons. The gendered hierarchy associated with patria potestad was reproduced in the contractual language of forced labor. Peons swore "to subjugate themselves to all of the practices and customs established by their patrón [que se somete a todo los usos y costumbres establecidos por su patrón]." The rituals of labor contracting reveal that gendered traditions governing household patriarchy acquired new powers and meanings in the context of plantation labor. Much like sons and daughters promising to obey their father, peasants pledged to submit themselves to the authority of their patrón. In keeping with the double-sided nature of patriarchy, some planters, though not all, promised "to provide succor to the peons and servants on their hacienda [socorrer operarios y sirvientes de la hacienda]," thereby reproducing the unequal reciprocity of domestic patriarchy.[8] Labor contracts adhered to an established template, and their language reveals how planters and officials perceived patriarchy from above.

By contrast, transcripts of court cases between planters and peons provide a window on peasants' understandings of the ways patriarchy governed peonage. These frequently document contests that in some measure involved conflicting interpretations of the morality of forced labor. Peasants would invoke the principle that planters' protection was an intrinsic part of the peonage system. Planters, on the contrary, commonly insisted that assistance to peons was a manifestation of charity and benevolence; consequently, patriarchal protection was discretionary, not obligatory. When debt peonage first took hold in the region, in the ritual of labor contracting only a minority of planters pledged to assist their peons. Nevertheless, in litigation between planters and peons, peons routinely claimed that they expected their patrón would provide assistance (socorro). In the courtroom, appeals to patriarchy tended to be marshaled in self-defense by both sides: by peons to justify their lawbreaking, and by planters to illustrate compliance with the spirit, if not the letter, of the law. From a reading of peasants' testimonies, it is impossible to disentangle their aspirations, expectations, and justifications; the same can be said of planters' declarations. However, the very fact that planters and peons appealed in different ways and for different reasons to the provision of assistance indicates that patriarchal protection was widely accepted but at the same time highly contested.

In Diriomo's courtroom, peons accused of failing to pay off debts with labor or of running away from an estate frequently argued that they broke the law only after their patrón violated the principles underlying planters' power and peasants' submission. Peons often maintained that they fled from the clutches of a patrón who had failed to provide assistance to their family to seek another who would. Julio Telles explained to the magistrate, "Not only did my patrón Don Julio Castillo refuse to pay me; he did not even provide succor in exchange for my promise of labor. So I took up servitude with another patrón [No es solamente que el patrón negó a liquidarme, ni mucho menos que me diera socorro a cuenta del mismo compromiso]."⁹ In 1883, Alejandro Mejía ordered Diriomo's rural magistrate to arrest fifteen peons who absconded from his finca at the peak of the harvest. One of the fugitives, Tiburcio Ríos, was captured on a neighboring finca. After several days in the town jail, Ríos appeared before the agrarian tribunal and admitted that he had left Mejía's hacienda without permission. Ríos justified his escape by explaining that several times he had asked his patrón for assistance, but Mejía ignored his plea. Consequently, he fled in hopes of "pawning his labor [empeñando su trabajo] to a patrón who would assist his family."¹⁰

Similar stories were repeated over the years by peons accused of breaking labor laws. In 1900, Don Joaquín Cuadra, one of Mombacho's larger planters, ordered Diriomo's rural magistrate to capture about fifty runaway peons. Mercedes Ayala was among the men and women rounded up in the dragnet operation. Diriomo's rural police arrested Ayala in his milpa harvesting beans. After spending two days in jail, Ayala explained to the judge that he fled because Cuadra reneged on his promise to pay debts incurred by his wife's sickness and death. Ayala's defense rested on the claim that Cuadra had violated the morality implicit in planter-peon relations. However, Diriomo's agrarian magistrate did not accept Ayala's defense. He ruled that Ayala was a "labor breaker" and sentenced him to join a work gang building roads in the municipality.¹¹

Taken together, peons' testimonies are a manifestation of peasant politics. Debt peons sought to establish the principle that compliance with the labor regime was conditional on patriarchal protection. Their claim rested not on law, but, I argue, on gendered understandings of the double-sided nature of patriarchy. Court transcripts reveal that peons believed planters' disciplinary powers should be coupled with protection. However, there is little evidence that the two were, in fact, linked in practice. Diriomo's judges never accepted peasants' defense that planters' violation of the patriarchal bargain justified lawbreaking.

On their side, planters accused by peons of violating labor laws often defended their *hombría de bien* — meaning both patriarchal generosity and manliness — by emphasizing their charity. Before a tribunal of their peers, planters and their agents regularly recited lists of their benevolent practices. When Agapito Fernández, foreman on the hacienda El Progreso, was accused of not paying peons, he attempted to clear his name by arguing, "I give the mozos food and money for cane liquor [guaro], and I give them charity [*limosnas*] if their families are suffering from sickness or death."[12] Fernández's testimony suggests that in his mind, charity and assistance were more important than wages. Others made similar declarations, demonstrating that planters believed it was important to cultivate a reputation as a charitable patrón.[13]

Many planters emphasized their patriarchal qualities, especially when answering charges of malfeasance. Alejandro Mejía, the planter most frequently accused of violating labor laws, routinely declared to Diriomo's agrarian tribunal that he was a generous patrón. When charged with failing to pay peons, Mejía countered that his accounts demonstrated his charity. Responding to charges by Casimiro Ramírez of withholding wages and generally fiddling his payroll, Mejía explained that he paid his peons according to a complicated formula that set cash advances and additional debts against the quantity and quality of the coffee they picked. In addition, he gave his peons warm clothing if it was cold on the volcano.[14] Furthermore, he paid a priest, a pharmacist, and a doctor to provide services to the peons that "belonged to his hacienda." Mejía concluded his testimony insisting he was a "good patrón who provided charity to the mozos." However, after Mejía extolled his own goodness, Ramírez's legal advisor declared that "[because] Mejía is known to be a habitual liar . . . the court should believe neither what he says, nor the figures that appear in his ledgers." Similarly, when General Augustín Avilés was accused of cheating on wages, he told the court, "My account books give a false sense of my mozos' remuneration . . . I give them plenty of guaro, food, assistance and charity."[15] In the same vein, when inviting Diriomo's rural magistrate to his annual fiesta, Don Celedino Borge wrote, "At the culmination of festivities, my wife and I personally give guaro, food, and gifts to the men, women and children who work as mozos . . . I am like a father to them, and I know each and every one of my mozos."[16] Diriomeños who had worked on the fincas years before frequently recalled the great festivals at the end of the harvest, when planters and their wives gave gifts to the peons.[17] In a similar vein, but from a different class position, Diriomeñas descended from leading coffee planters told me that fiestas provided an opportunity for the planters to demonstrate their generosity and the peons to show their gratitude.[18] Peons and planters shared an expectation that planters would protect peons, but they viewed the morality of peonage differently. Planters referred to assistance as charity and emphasized its contingent character. Acts of charity demonstrated their benevolence, their noblesse oblige, and several planters indicated that they expected generosity would elicit loyalty. Peons, for their part, argued that planters' assistance was an obligation. They upheld the principle that landlords had a responsibility to help them in times of need. Significantly, peons accused of breaking the labor laws frequently attempted to persuade Diriomo's magistrates that compliance with the labor regime should be conditional on planters' upholding the patriarchal principle that power incurred responsibility.

Contradictions of Charity

In the contested world of forced labor, planters' charity was double-edged. Sometimes charity increased indebtedness, thereby extending planters' control over the peasantry. Peons' contention that protection was obligatory, and planters' that it was discretionary, frequently was played out in courtroom dramas. The complicated and often contradictory regulations governing advances and repayment of labor debts, combined with planters' illegal practices, obscured the whole business of paying wages. A series of cases involving claims that planters failed to pay fair wages shows that disputes over patronal assistance contributed to the mystery of wage payments. Put simply, some planters added the cost of assistance to peons' debts, thereby manipulating patriarchal protection to tighten the bonds of unfreedom. Peasants regularly contested this version of patriarchal morality, claiming that protection formed part of the unequal reciprocity of debt peonage.[19]

However, other planters made no secret of the fact that they added the cost of food and assistance to peons' debts. Srs. Eisenstuck and Bahlcke, whose estates constituted the largest coffee enterprise in the country, were the first in the vicinity to use printed forms for labor contracting. In 1905, the firm sent a batch of forms to Diriomo's agrarian magistrate, asking him to sign up responsible peasants on their behalf to work in the coffee harvest. The form included the proviso "All assistance, help [ayuda], food and provisions will be charged to the laborers' accounts."[20] In 1905, Ramona Zambrano's husband signed her up to work on the Hacienda Alemania, owned by Eisenstuck and Bahlcke. Although he signed the contract, thereby authorizing his wife to work for wages, the matrícula reads, "Zambrano swears that she assumes the obligation to repay with labor the entire sum plus whatever might be added to it representing the cost of all assistance, help, food and provisions."[21] Testimony heard in Diriomo's courtroom suggests that planters' charity, cum assistance, played a triple role. Depending on circumstances, patronal assistance might have been a means of bestowing favors and eliciting loyalty, a covert mechanism deployed to augment peasants' debts, or an open and aboveboard means of calculating debts and payments.

Judicial transcripts, with their contrapuntal testimonies, reveal a measure of shared belief regarding patriarchy. In Diriomo, rich and poor, planter and peon subscribed to a morality in which planters bore some responsibility to protect peons, and peons had some grounds to expect patriarchal protection. However, in everyday practice, planters negotiated patriarchy to tie laborers to their estates and to elicit loyalty, while peons negotiated patriarchy to minimize the disadvantages of forced labor and to secure a measure of protection against the vagaries of subsistence farming.

In Diriomo, many planters attempted to generate some acceptance of peonage by deploying consensual practices. Yet court transcripts show a systematic gap between planters' promises and peons' expectations of patriarchal protection. Often this gap was filled by another aspect of patriarchal privilege: violence. Planters' patriarchal right to discipline peasants was enshrined in agricultural labor laws and played a role in the workings of debt peonage in Diriomo.[22] Some peons told Diriomo's magistrate about inhumane treatment on the fincas. Pedro Mercado declared that Alejandro Mejía "caused me extreme suffering."[23] However, like Mercado, peasants in the dock only alluded to excessive disciplinary measures. Perhaps they shied away from recounting the details of their indignities because Diriomo's courtroom was, in effect, the pueblo's public theater.

In marked contrast to the subdued tenor of court transcripts, latter-day Diriomeños provided graphic details about corporal discipline on the fincas. Oral histories I recorded in the 1990s are replete with grisly accounts of sanguinary punishments, and these stories form a vital core of peasants' historical memory of the era when coffee was king. Men and women who had worked as debt peons recounted the ordeals peasants suffered at the hands of planters. Diriomeños described humiliating punishments which, they said, were standard fare on the plantations. Yet the majority of stories about arbitrary justice focused on the brutality of just a few planters, foremost among them, Alejandro Mejía, the infamous "indio rico."[24]

Diriomeños who had worked on the coffee fincas in the first half of the twentieth century said they and their cohorts believed planters had the right to punish peons. Orlando Salazar Castillo and Emilio Vásquez contended that the planters' personal administration of justice was a detested but widely accepted feature of the labor regime. Significantly, notwithstand-

13. Emilio Vásquez and Orlando Salazar Castillo, 1995.

ing vivid historical memories about planter brutality, I found no court cases where peons accused their patróns of imposing cruel and unusual punishments. The reticence found in written records, juxtaposed with Diriomeños' oral histories, suggests two contrasting interpretations of planter violence. Either, as contemporary Diriomeños contend, brutality was routine and peons accepted that sanguinary measures were a legitimate part of planters' patriarchal practices, or planters inflicted brutal punishments rarely, generally only for flagrant offenders and as a means of deterring peasant resistance. But whether private violence was habitual or exceptional, it was inherent in the system of arbitrary justice whereby planters ruled the peasantry. The legal and customary basis of planters' authority to punish peons as they saw fit represented a reworking of long-standing patriarchal traditions. In Diriomo the patriarchal power to punish contributed to the class and gendered nature of peonage.

In addition to the gendered relationships of patriarchy and peonage codified in labor laws, landlords exercised another form of patriarchal right. Remembering the past, Diriomeñas and Diriomeños explained that some coffee planters expected females on their plantations to regularly provide sexual services to men from the upper echelons of the estate hierarchy.[25] However, as with corporal punishment, sexual abuse on the fincas was only hinted at in court transcripts. Understandably, peasant men may have been reluctant to describe their wife's and daughters' experiences of rape and sexual violation.[26] Nonetheless, the few veiled references I found, the hidden transcripts, take on a significance beyond their number, especially in light of the very public nature of Diriomo's courthouse. Litigation required witnesses, testimonies, and all manner of revelations that husbands and fathers might well have wanted to avoid in the town's close quarters. Also, let us not forget, few women were permitted to speak in the courtroom. Only widows and "spinsters" could speak out for themselves; other females were represented before the tribunal by the family patriarch.

Patriarchy from Below

Patriarchy from above was shored up in important ways by patriarchy from below. Senior male power over the labor, bodies, and property of subordinate females and males allowed peasant men to consign their wife and children to servitude. This possibility turned into a reality in part because Nicaragua's rural labor laws did not discriminate against women. On the contrary, rural labor legislation stated explicitly, "All persons above the age of sixteen, male and female, who possess property or income valued at less than 500 pesos are required to support themselves by working for a patrón."[27] The gendered character of legislation contributed to normalizing female labor in the plantation sector.

Paradoxically, gender blindness inscribed in labor law collided with the spirit of patriarchal authority. Patria potestad institutionalized gender *inequality* for the purported objective of protecting women and children. This contrasted with agrarian labor laws that ratified gendered *equality* in forced labor. By establishing gender equality in the forced labor regime agrarian laws stood one of the objectives of patria potestad on its head. Instead of facilitating male protection of women and children, labor laws in combination with patriarchal authority allowed peasant men to consign their dependents to peonage. In Diriomo, the practical consequences of peasant men's control over the bodies and labor of subordinates pushed women and children into, rather than out of, the workforce for the burgeoning coffee sector.

The stark contrast between gendered equality in Nicaragua's rural labor laws and gendered inequality in family law supports a central hypothesis of feminist theory: historically, the significance of patriarchal protection varied according to social class. In Nicaragua, although patriarchal law required senior males to protect as well as to control their female and male dependents, the protective side of patriarchy was more in evidence, and more feasible, in the higher reaches of society than in the lower. Despite or, in this case, because of the laws of patria potestad, Diriomo's poor peasant women were subjected to the harsh realities of debt peonage alongside their partner as well as on their own.

In Diriomo, the majority of peasants who willingly or unwillingly enlisted in the labor regime did so jointly with household members. The peasant family, both male- and female-headed, was the typical labor unit for harvesting coffee.[28] Family peonage brought large numbers of women and children into the labor regime. This hidden history of peonage expands the scope of the classic model of peasant production. Usually the peasant household as a unit of production and consumption is formulated in terms of self-provisioning and subsistence agriculture. Debt peonage extended the activities of peasant household production to encompass deployment of family labor in the plantation sector.

Frequently peasant men in Diriomo contracted their wife and children into peonage. This allowed men to dedicate their labor largely to subsistence production. Labor contracts demonstrate that many men received a cash advance in return for signing up dependents for servitude. This was a routine feature of patriarchy from below in the township. For example, in 1893 the husband of Señora Felicia Acevedo pledged that she would work for Don Feliz Castillo as a servant (*sirvienta*) on his hacienda. Her husband signed the labor contract, took a cash advance of 8 pesos, and swore that his wife, "under my authorization, is obligated to repay with labor the entire sum plus whatever might be added to it."[29] In common with all married women, Felicia Acevedo was not permitted to sign contracts or receive wages without her husband's permission. Similarly, José María Marcía received a cash advance of 34 pesos and a sombrero worth 6 pesos from Don Alejandro Mejía. For this substantial sum, Marcía pledged that his wife and six-year-old daughter would pick coffee in successive coffee harvests until the debt was repaid.[30]

The dynamics of peonage in Diriomo cannot be understood without an analysis of gender. In Nicaragua, as in Latin America more widely, peasant patriarchs represented all members of their family in the public sphere. As a consequence, because peasant men pledged not only their own labor but that of their dependents, in Diriomo males appeared in lists of plantation peons in greater numbers than their actual participation rate in the labor regime.[31] Although on a first reading, men seem to predominate in lists of peons, a closer reading, a gendered reading, reveals that many women and children were consigned by the male head of household to plantation labor. Their presence was obscured by patriarchy from below.

Labor contracts allow us to count the number of women and children consigned to working in plantation labor but reveal nothing about their willingness to participate in debt peonage. By contrast, Diriomo's court records are replete with stories of wives, sons, and daughters who contested the patriarchal right to consign them to servitude. Margarita Aguilar, for one, challenged her father's control over her labor. The roots of the conflict between father and daughter began in 1878, when Enrique Aguilar took an advance from Don Vicente Cuadra and pledged that Margarita, his thirteen-year-old daughter, would work off the debt. Ten years later, and still indebted to Cuadra, Margarita petitioned the judge to annul the arrangement. Her counsel argued that "since [she] is an adult and free from her father's authority [patria potestad], no longer should the court force her to work off her father's debt." Unfortunately for Margarita, and other women in similar circumstances, Cuadra's savvy lawyer reminded the court that unmarried daughters remained subjected to their father's authority unless legally emancipated.

Consequently, Margarita remained subordinated to her father's patriarchal authority and locked into the labor regime.[32]

The popular stereotype of male breadwinner/female housewife entirely misrepresents the gendered allocation of labor in Diriomo's poor peasant households. That paradigm was based on an urban, mostly middle-class model of the division of household labor in the United States and Western Europe in the 1950s. The model is more ideal than real even for the time and place it was designed to fit; family patterns among Diriomo's peasantry demonstrate an entirely different gender and generational distribution of labor. When families sought to supplement self-provisioning, women and children were often the first to work "off-farm" or, more precisely, outside the boundaries of the peasant economy. The family model most in evidence among Diriomo's peasantry turns the 1950s model on its head. In Diriomo, peasant men often dedicated themselves to what might be called the domestic sphere of self-provisioning, while women and children worked in what passed for the formal sector, debt peonage.

The manner in which Diriomo's peasantry supplemented subsistence production was similar to the ways many Latin American rural households have tried to sustain their peasant livelihood. Fieldwork repeatedly demonstrates that when peasant household production is threatened, daughters frequently are the first to seek outside employment, usually in domestic service and sweatshops (*maquiladoras*).[33] However, social scientists often overlooked the patriarchal roots of this practice: that senior males had the legal and customary authority to allocate the labor of their dependents. Consequently, women's work outside the home was determined not by what wives and daughters wanted but by men's exercise of authority.

In Diriomo, women and children composed, on average, about two-thirds of the labor force that harvested coffee.[34] The high participation rate of women and children in debt peonage in Diriomo seems to have been the product of four factors: (1) agrarian laws that codified sexual equality for the rural poor in the forced labor regime; (2) patriarchal laws and customs that gave peasant men the authority to consign their wife and children to servitude; (3) the custom of women and children working in the coffee harvest while senior males were responsible for self-provisioning; and (4) the high incidence of female-headed households in Diriomo.

Against the grain, I found one tantalizing example of a wife who enrolled her husband in the labor regime. In 1882 Vicenta López pledged the labor of her husband, Fernando Acevedo, and received an advance of 13 pesos.[35]

This apparently unique case stands in stark contrast to the patriarchal tradition and is compelling for what it does and does not reveal about the gender order. It indicates that the patriarchal system was not cut from whole cloth. But beyond that, this enigmatic labor contract underlines the need for further research on the gendered nature of debt peonage.

The Endurance of Peonage and Patriarchy

Oral histories underscored the contradictory nature of the labor regime. Thinking back over my fieldwork in Diriomo, I conclude that archival and oral sources, if studied separately, would each have given a false view of the plantation system. I started my research in the municipal archives, reading labor laws, peonage contracts, court transcripts, and reports filed by rural magistrates detailing policing of the labor regime. These sources emphasized the violence and coercion of debt peonage. However, memories of people who had worked as peons portrayed a somewhat different picture of the plantation system. Many Diriomeños and Diriomeñas described how planters combined the power to appropriate peasants' labor with manifestations, however partial, of patriarchal protection.

Listening to former debt peons tell their life stories persuaded me that patriarchy contributed to the development and endurance of debt peonage in Diriomo. Domingo Dávila best explained the contradictions of patriarchy and peonage. Dávila recalled more vividly than most the coercive character of peonage, at the same time lauding planters' benevolence more than others did. When he was young, Dávila began working with his family as a coffee picker on La Chuzcada, a hacienda on the slopes of the volcano owned by the widow Doña Saula Echaverri. After many years, he was hired on permanently to supervise coffee pickers. "My hard work and loyalty were rewarded when Doña Saula lent me a small plot of about two manzanas on the far edge of the finca." Dávila and his family worked for the same patróna on the same finca for more than fifty years. He described labor drafts in the 1930s, when the rural police sent peasants to work on "his" finca. Dávila was the only Diriomeño who could recite chapter and verse from the labor laws. He explained that because of his job he had to know the rules governing the plantation labor system. To his way of thinking, the advantages of debt peonage outweighed the disadvantages. "If the mozos were obedient and worked hard, Doña Saula paid them and gave them good food, and if they returned year after year la Doña would help them out." Dávila stressed the benevolent side of the patriarchal, in this case matriarchal, social relations.[36]

Unlike Domingo Dávila, Carmen Ramírez Pérez never formed a patriarchal relationship with a good patrón. Beginning in the 1930s she and her family regularly worked as debt peons. After Ramírez unexpectedly inherited five manzanas of excellent land in the 1950s, her family no longer needed to work as coffee pickers, but they did anyway. As she said, "Life brings unexpected things. It brought me land, and I thought it might also bring poverty. So year after year I signed on to pick coffee because I hoped to cultivate a relationship with an honest and kind planter who, God willing, would help me and my children if someday we needed assistance. Although I pawned my labor to coffee planters for some thirty years, I never found a good patrón."[37]

Most of the Diriomeños I interviewed said that until the 1950s planters retained their power over the peasantry through informal indebtedness combined with promises of protection. Afterward, the character of peonage changed substantially, while maintaining much of its outward form. Peasants continued to "pawn their labor" to planters; however, economic necessity combined with aspirations to establish an enduring clientelist relation with a benevolent patrón drew peasants into seasonal waged labor in the coffee sector.

The history of peonage in Diriomo is not about modernizing patriarchy.[38] In Nicaragua, although patriarchy was reshaped to fit the needs of the coffee barons, it was not part of a modernizing process. Rather than promoting capitalism, the adaptation of household patriarchy to plantation agriculture prolonged the life of nonmarket relations. Karl Polanyi argued that reciprocal relations that establish unequal hierarchical bonds are one of the hallmarks of nonmarket societies, societies not governed by self-regulating markets.[39] This case history from Nicaragua supports his theory. After the rise of coffee production, Diriomo's social order was regulated by the patriarchal duality of coercion and clientelism, not self-regulating markets. Leading historians have argued persuasively that in some Latin American countries the expansion of coffee cultivation simultaneously reinforced patronage and consolidated capitalism.[40] Social development in rural Granada took a different turn. Rather than modernizing society, patriarchy revitalized premodern social relations, which endured throughout the countryside well beyond their time.

The central thesis of this book, its red thread, is that land privatization and peonage did not bring about the capitalist transformation of rural Granada from 1870 to 1930. My argument goes against the prevailing view that the rise of coffee production in Nicaragua consolidated capitalism. In this conclusion, I reassess theories of capitalist development, patriarchy, and mestizaje presented earlier and consider whether the evidence from Diriomo supports their central theses. I compare my findings with other studies of the region to ascertain whether Diriomo's history was typical or atypical of social change in Nicaragua.

On Capitalist Development

A major controversy in Latin American history centers on the nature and timing of the region's transition to capitalism. This study revisits that debate, adding a gender perspective. I conclude that analysis of the gendered character of class relations fundamentally changes our understanding of capitalist and noncapitalist transitions. Arnold Bauer first challenged the prevailing view that Latin American peonage was the antithesis of capitalist labor.[1] Turning that interpretation on its head, he argued that in the nineteenth century debt peonage was an incipient form of free wage labor. Bauer proposed that planters deployed debt to coax peasants out of subsistence production and into the free wage labor force of expanding export economies. In his view, debt was a market mechanism and planters' cash advances a manifestation of the compulsion of the marketplace. In contrast to earlier writers who maintained that peonage perpetuated a type of feudalism, Bauer argued that debt peonage played a pivotal role in the region's great transformation to capitalism by precipitating market relations. His theory was highly influential and became the template against which to measure peonage in nineteenth-century Latin America. Alan Knight expanded the temporal scope of Bauer's theory, proposing that in colonial Mexico peonage sometimes was proto–free wage labor.[2]

The Bauer-Knight thesis became the new orthodoxy. Although their interpretation is persuasive, I conclude that peonage in Diriomo does not fit their model; it did not give birth to capitalism in rural Granada. The structures of power that governed class relations in the countryside rested on extraeconomic compulsion, not coercion of the marketplace. The combination of forced labor laws, rural police who dragooned peasants to participate in the coffee harvest, and planters' private guards ensured that peasants' willingness to work was "strengthened by the repressive apparatus."[3] Alongside coercive measures, cash advances played a part in drawing peasants into peonage. But coercion was not far beneath the surface. Planters used debt to bond peasants to plantation labor over the long term; in addition, peasant men exercised their patriarchal authority to enroll wives and children into servitude. Without a gender analysis of peonage, historians failed to recognize the latter form of labor coercion.

Notwithstanding consensual measures that facilitated peasants' acceptance of peonage, nonmarket coercion remained central to the labor regime in Diriomo into the 1930s. Indebted labor lived on partly because privatization did not generate landlessness in rural Granada. Alienation from land is a necessary precondition for the development of a free wage labor force, a system that relies on coercion of the marketplace, not direct coercion. In the absence of a class of landless workers driven by economic necessity to pick coffee, Granada's coffee planters bonded peasants by coercive as well as consensual means.

Karl Polanyi's classic theory of capitalist transformation underlines the distinction between *societies with markets* and *market societies*. In the former, a k a noncapitalist societies, markets play a marginal role in social relations; in the latter, capitalist societies, markets regulate most social interactions and govern the entire social order. Polanyi's understanding of the great transformation rests on his thesis that the nature and social role of markets are fundamentally different in noncapitalist and capitalist societies. Under capitalism people are compelled by necessity to continually sell their labor in order to buy products they consume. Consequently, markets regulate exchange relations involving labor, land, and products more generally. The key to Polanyi's theory is that as buying and selling permeates everyday life, the entire social order becomes regulated by market forces. However, in noncapitalist societies, exchanges of labor, land, and other products are regulated not by market mechanisms, but by norms and power relations intrinsic to the social system. In these societies, market exchanges are occasional and tangential to the reproduction of the social organization.[4]

Using Polanyi's theory as a template against which to measure evidence from Diriomo, I conclude that market forces did not regulate acquisition of land or planters' control over labor. Land privatization in Diriomo was not driven by the market. At the pinnacle of the social order, Granada's large coffee planters wielded power and influence to consolidate their properties. At the other extreme, Diriomo's peasants worked their way through a maze of bureaucratic steps to title small plots of land. In the period from 1870 to 1930, price mechanisms were not key to the acquisition of private property in land. Nor was labor bought and sold in the capitalist sense. The direct use of force, conjoined with consensual measures, regulated the everyday operation of debt peonage. Diriomo's peasants received wages for their work on the coffee fincas, at least in principle. However, planters' methods of recruiting and disciplining labor bore none of the hallmarks of capitalism. Forced labor laws and the police apparatus underpinned peonage; they were the social structures on which peonage was built. Nevertheless, force was necessary but not sufficient to sustain peonage in rural Granada. Consequently, planters deployed consensual as well as coercive measures to bind peasants to their plantations.

This finding challenges Robert Brenner's theory of the barriers to capitalist development in landlord-peasant societies. Brenner's central thesis is that where production is organized for export, landlords rely exclusively on coercion to subordinate labor.[5] Peasants tend to privilege subsistence production over paid work, as the former is the basis of their livelihood, he argues. Therefore, the planter class is driven to fund a repressive apparatus capable of forcing peasants out of their subsistence economy and into plantation labor, even when to do so reduces profits. Brenner concludes that although coercion is necessary to maintain planters' control over labor, it undermines the economic viability of the export and the peasant sectors. This dilemma is the fundamental contradiction of landlord-peasant societies and prevents capitalism from developing in the interstices of noncapitalist relations. Brenner's theory is the opposite of Bauer's; it can be read as a highly analytical defense of the interpretation Bauer sought to overturn. Both authors agree that planters do their all to coax peasants out of the subsistence economy and into paid labor for the export economy. But Brenner concludes that this process prevents capitalist development, whereas for Bauer it sets capitalism in motion.

On one level it would seem that evidence from Diriomo supports Brenner's theory: peasants favored subsistence production over plantation labor, and planters used force to bond workers. However, Brenner's central tenet does not apply; debt peonage in Diriomo did not rest exclusively on coercion. Coercion was necessary but not sufficient to maintain peonage. Although Brenner's model does not address the limits to coercion, in Diriomo the limits to coercion modified planter-peon relations. Granada planters and the state were unable to adequately fund a repressive apparatus, nor could they eliminate peasant resistance. For these and other reasons, planters partially acquiesced to peasant demands that patriarchal authority implied some acceptance of responsibility to protect peons. Following the legal abolition of indebted labor in the 1920s and 1930s, peonage survived in Diriomo in large measure because of its consensual side. Peasants endeavored to mitigate the vicissitudes of small-scale production by forging patriarchal ties. In sum, although Brenner's and Bauer's theories influenced my thinking, evidence from Diriomo supports neither of them.

James C. Scott's theory of the barriers to capitalist development contradicts both Brenner's and Bauer's views. Unlike them, he stresses the construction of consent in landlord-peasant societies.[6] Whereas Brenner contends that direct coercion blocks capitalist development, and Bauer that market coercion in the form of debt peonage generates capitalism, Scott argues that peasants retard the onslaught of capitalism by everyday forms of resistance. He highlights the ways peasants bring pressure on planters to accede to demands from below and proposes that through this process peasants establish an alternative morality that curbs the intensification of exploitation associated with capitalism. Somewhat along lines Scott describes, Diriomo's peasants struggled to assert a morality in which planters' patriarchal authority over peons was combined with a measure of protection. Although peasants had some success, class relations between planters and peons continued to rest on coercive foundations. My findings support elements of Scott's proposition, but the longevity of peonage and the use of force suggest that his theory, particularly as interpreted by others, may understate the importance of social structures and overstate peasants' ability to minimize planters' class power. In Diriomo, coercive structures underpinned the plantation labor regime. Peasant resistance modified the everyday workings of the system, but did not fundamentally transform its social character.

In the Central American literature, my portrayal of late capitalist development and the significance of coercion largely coincides with David McCreery's interpretation of Guatemalan history. Indeed, I was influenced by his theoretical approach. In the Nicaraguan historiography, my finding that land privatization in the context of the coffee revolution did not, for the most part, dispossess the peasantry corroborates the new orthodoxy. Studies by Jeffrey Gould on the western highlands and by Julie Charlip on Carazo reach similar conclusions.[7]

In other respects, my findings go against the grain of the Nicaraguan historical literature. My conclusion that land privatization and forced labor set in motion by the coffee boom postponed more than promoted capitalism is controversial. It challenges the Sandinista historiography and other more recent contributions to the field.[8] Gould stresses the coercive character of labor relations in the coffee-producing zones of Matagalpa and Jinotega but does not treat the issue of capitalist transition. Charlip paints a very different picture of rural society from the one presented here. In Carazo, the department contiguous with Granada, she finds a society of prosperous small and medium farmers who produced coffee along with other crops, had plentiful land and access to financing sufficient to their needs. Finding no evidence of labor coercion, Charlip suggests that people may have worked on coffee plantations because high wages attracted them.[9] The contrast between the world Charlip describes and Diriomo's history is intriguing. The economic power and political influence of Granada's oligarchy, combined with Diriomo's Indian heritage, might explain some of the disparity.

On Gender and Patriarchy

The constitution of political power and social upheavals set in motion by the coffee boom cannot be understood without analyzing gender. Following Independence, with a vacuum of power at the national level, local state making in Nicaragua was to a remarkable degree gender politics. Before the advent of land privatization and forced labor, Diriomo's ladino elite, its rich peasantry, accumulated political power in large part by regulating sexual and domestic arrangements. Court records show that in deciding cases concerning sexual mores, violence, and parental authority, Diriomo's town fathers attempted to establish a double morality, one for the town's upper ladino peasantry, another for the poorer, mostly Indian population of the pueblo. Furthermore, within the double morality, different codes of conduct applied for men and women.

In similar measure, gender analysis provides new insights into the great legislative reforms of the postcolonial era, especially land privatization and modernization of the inheritance regime. Although it has been argued that the liberal project that swept Latin America in the nineteenth century ushered in progress for women, evidence presented here shows that the reforms had regressive as well as progressive effects. On the progressive side, elimination of the common property regime extended property rights to Indian women, formerly excluded from direct access to land in Indian communities. This change may have contributed to the high incidence of female household headship and the substantial presence of women proprietors in the lower ranks of Diriomo's peasantry in the early twentieth century. On the regressive side, reforms rolled back women's guarantees to an equal portion of inherited property and wealth. The rollback may explain the absence of women in the higher echelons of Diriomo's landed proprietors.

Gender analysis also underpins one of the central conclusions of this study: that peonage rested on coercion but relied on consent. My analysis of the consensual side of peonage was influenced by Steve Stern's theoretical interpretation of patriarchy, particularly his argument that gendered understandings of patriarchal rights condition peasants' acceptance of authority.[10] However, where Stern focuses on gender culture, defined as languages of argument, I attempt to uncover the gendered character of political and social structures. Key to my analysis is that planter-peon relations were sustained by patriarchal traditions of governance long codified in the Hispanic legal tradition. With the rise of coffee production, Nicaraguan jurists expanded the reach of patriarchal authority, thereby fortifying planters' control over labor. Of particular significance, labor laws explicitly extended patriarchs' disciplinary powers from the domestic to the plantation domain. Diriomeños' and Diriomeñas' acceptance of planters' right to discipline peons lends support to Stern's thesis that gendered understandings of patriarchy play a role in sustaining authority. Similarly, pressure on planters to assume a measure of responsibility for subordinates chimes with Stern's argument that gender relations can also undermine authority. In rural Granada, coffee planters' power, as well as peasants' resistance to the labor regime, drew strength from the principles and practices of patriarchal governance.

In Diriomo, the gender and generational bias within the plantation labor force is striking: women and children made up a large proportion of coffee pickers. Analysis of patriarchy partly explains the preponderance of female and child labor. Senior males' broad legal authority over wives and children enabled peasant men to contract wives and children into peonage. In Granada, coffee and basic grains are harvested simultaneously, exacerbating contradictions between peasant and plantation production. To resolve this dilemma, adult males often labored in the subsistence economy, enlisting their wife and children to work on the fincas. One of the central conclusions of this study is that planters' patriarchal authority, *patriarchy from above*, and male peasants' patriarchal privileges, *patriarchy from below*, prolonged the life of peonage in Diriomo beyond its time, retarding capitalist development in the Granada countryside.

On Ethnicity and Mestizaje

In *To Die in This Way: Nicaraguan Indians and the Myth of Mestizaje*, Jeffrey Gould describes how Indians resisted forced mestizaje and the violent expropriation of their land and labor. Historical evidence from Diriomo reveals a different story. There Indians did little to resist official abolition of their community or privatization of the commons. Rather than collectively opposing state policy, Diriomeños and Diriomeñas individually turned their attention to acquiring title to land. Paradoxically, in the Granada region voices opposing Indian assimilation came from unlikely quarters. Some ladino politicians took a stand against abolition of indigenous communities because, as they argued, the Indian leaders had served the state well. The contrast between Gould's findings and my own suggest that the character of intra-ethnic politics strongly conditions the continuation, and the destruction, of community.

Demographic collapse and centuries of social dislocation eroded the distinguishing markers of Indianness in the pueblos surrounding Granada. After Independence, the Indian-ladino divide rested primarily on differential land rights and the coexistence of Indian and ladino authorities in the communities, the former increasingly subjugated to the latter. In the nineteenth century, Indian leaders regularly collaborated with ladino elites to privatize land, quell unrest, and mobilize labor. I argue that this undermined Indians' allegiance to community. Following land privatization and abolition of the Indian community, Indian identity in Diriomo all but disappeared. Some writers propose that class and proto-class antagonisms within an ethnic group weaken the ties that bind;[11] evidence from Diriomo lends some support to this thesis. In Diriomo, abolition, land privatization, and ultimately the demise of Indian identity may have been facilitated by widening disparities in access to land. However, it seems that Indian leaders' collaboration with ladino officials played the greater role in the destruction of community.

Joan Vincent writes, "Ethnicity in operation is like all else social, a tool in the hands of men; it is not a mystic force in itself. Ethnicity is a mask of confrontation."[12] Vincent seems to be suggesting that because ethnicity is social, not biological, it can be deployed more easily for political ends. For instance, to mobilize a following politicians might paper over social differences by appealing to ethnic traditions and identities. Notwithstanding Vincent's thesis, I found little evidence that ethnic identity served as a mask of confrontation uniting Diriomo's Indians against ladinos inside or outside the pueblo. However, on a number of occasions, Diriomo's ladino politicians appropriated the discourse of Indian rights to their own ends. For example, town elites mobilized Indians to oppose an attempt by Granada's municipal council to expand its boundaries to take in the coffee zone on the Mombacho Volcano. Cynically, Diriomo's politicians claimed they were acting in defense of Diriomeños' common interests, when in fact they were engaged in privatizing the Indians' common lands. Aside from spurious appeals to community by ladino leaders engaged in destroying the material basis of the Indian community, I found remarkably little evidence of ethnic struggles from below. Again, the absence may be explained by Indian leaders' long collaboration with ladino politicians. Recalling the words of Diriomo's mayor, "The Indian mayor is one of my agents, I rely on his efforts."[13]

Finally, one of the principal conclusions I draw from this study of class, gender, and ethnic upheavals in Diriomo in the era routinely described as Nicaragua's capitalist transition is that history is not linear. Social transformations in the modern era are not all steps on the capitalist road.

History Matters—The Sandinistas' Myth of Modernity

The past is never dead. It's not even past.
—William Faulkner

All political movements create historical myths, usually to demonstrate that they alone embody the nation's destiny.[1] Referring to leaders of the French Revolution, Edmund Burke declared, "Re-writing history is a matter not of choice, but of necessity."[2] In each epoch the call for change adopts the radical rhetoric of the time. In the nineteenth century, Latin American liberal elites employed a discourse of modernity, invoking democracy and the rights of man, though they had no intention of fundamentally democratizing society. Similarly, in the twentieth century, Marxism was the language of modernity throughout the developing world, whether or not its exponents sought to overthrow capitalism. In the case of the FSLN, this language had particular appeal, for it represented the antithesis of the ideology of the U.S. government, which played a crucial role in maintaining the Somoza dictatorship they struggled to defeat.[3] The Sandinistas led an antidictatorial and anti-imperialist struggle, yet they portrayed themselves not merely as a national liberation movement, but as socialists.[4] Not only did the Sandinistas call themselves Marxists, but they reinterpreted the past to justify this definition of themselves.

The Sandinistas rewrote history to convince partisans of the FSLN that Nicaraguan capitalism was mature, and their country ripe for socialist revolution. Jaime Wheelock and his followers argued that the nineteenth-century coffee boom marked Nicaragua's transition to capitalism. Thereafter, the rural social order was divided into a haute bourgeoisie and landless laborers.

Table 4. Land Tenure in Nicaragua, Percentage Distribution of Land:
1978, 1982, 1988, 1990

Form of Tenure[1]	1978	1982	1988	1990
Large producers[2] (over 200 mzs.)	52	29	15	15
Medium producers (50–200 mzs.)	30	30	17	17
Small producers[3] (1–49 mzs.)	18	16	37	41
Production cooperatives[4]	—	2	11	11
State farms	—	23	12	8
Abandoned[5]	—	—	6	6
Communal[6]	—	—	2	2

Notes:

1. There were an estimated 8 million manzanas of arable land in Nicaragua. Figures for 1990 represent land distribution prior to the inauguration of the UNO government in April.

2. 1 manzana = 1.72 acres, or 0.7 hectares.

3. For 1982, 1988, and 1990 figures include the traditional peasant sector that had access to land prior to 1979, beneficiaries of the Sandinista Agrarian Reform whose land was incorporated into cooperatives that legally were associations of individual producers, that is, Cooperativos de Crédito y Servicios, peasants who received titles to land they claimed prior to 1979 ("Titulación Especial"), and lands distributed to individual peasant households.

4. Cooperativas Agrícolas Sandinistas (CAS). Although laws stipulated that the land in CAS be farmed collectively, most cooperative land was not worked in common.

5. Most abandoned land was in the war zones.

6. Land titled to comunidades indígenas on the Atlantic Coast.

Sources: Computed from data presented in Centro de Investigación y Estudios de la Reforma Agraria, *La reforma agraria en Nicaragua, 1979–1989*, 9:39–61, tables 1–23; INRA-MERA, *Marco estratégico de la reforma agraria* vol. 2.

Derivative from this analysis was Sandinista leaders' contention that the primary demand of the rural poor was not land, but improved wages and working conditions. After the FSLN came to power in 1979, the government confiscated the large agrarian enterprises belonging to the Somoza family and its close associates; most were converted into state farms.[5] Rural workers became employees of state farms. Most peasants affected by the reform were organized into production cooperatives directly regulated by the Ministry of Agriculture; almost none received individual land titles. Table 4 shows that between 1978 and the end of 1983 control over land by large private producers decreased substantially, primarily as a result of the confiscation of the somocistas immediately after the Revolution's triumph in 1979. These properties, almost one-quarter of the nation's agricultural land, came into the state sector. Small producers' direct control over land declined slightly from 1978 to 1983, reflecting government policy of encouraging or imposing cooperative over individual ownership. Peasant access to land, credit, and technical assistance became contingent on cooperativization. Thus, from 1979 to 1984, government policy strongly favored large production units, both private and public, and strongly discouraged peasant agriculture. In addition, the government forced peasants to sell basic grains, especially corn and beans, to the state at prices that, according to the producers, fell below the costs of production.[6]

In Diriomo, medium-size fincas belonging to somocista politicians were confiscated and reconstituted as production cooperatives. Some coffee fincas on Mombacho became state farms; others were turned into production cooperatives managed, in effect, by the Ministry of Agriculture. However, some large fincas that belonged to Granada families that supported the FSLN remained in private hands.

Policies favoring state farms rested partly on the Sandinistas' view of history.[7] The Sandinistas held that the peasantry had long ceased to be a significant social force, and in the main peasants no longer demanded land. But events proved them wrong. Though a substantial portion of the rural population was landless or land-poor in the 1970s, landlessness on an extended scale dated only from the 1950s and 1960s, when cotton production gave rise to widespread peasant expropriation.[8] According to official statistics, a third of the rural population was landless by 1979, in the sense that they did not enjoy ownership. But it did not necessarily follow that they lacked access to land for subsistence purposes, nor that their class consciousness derived principally from working as seasonal wage laborers.[9] Many households classified as landless obtained access to land through traditional forms of tenancy. In Diriomo, some landless families gained access to land via patron-client relations with commercial planters. Furthermore, whether or not most of the monetary income, or most of the working time, of rural families derived from wages did not necessarily determine their class consciousness. As the Sandinistas later recognized, the rural poor maintained a strong peasant consciousness forged over the long term by efforts to sustain household self-sufficiency.[10]

Following the triumph of the Revolution and creation of the first state farms, peasants called for the Sandinistas to fulfill their promises and distribute land to the rural poor.[11] In response to demonstrations across the country in 1980 and 1981, the government agreed to lease land to peasants, but only in the short term. The National Union of Farmers and Ranchers (Unión Nacional de Agricultores y Ganaderos), created by the Sandinistas to represent medium and small producers, opposed many aspects of agrarian policy, including promotion of state farms, preference for cooperativization over individual ownership, low producer prices, and the politics of state grain procurement. Under the leadership of veteran campaigner Teófilo Cano, peasants in Diriomo joined the clamor for land. Uniting with thousands of others, they marched in Masaya in 1981 calling for land distribution. For his resistance to agrarian policy, Cano was jailed briefly by the FSLN. But despite pressure from below, before 1985 the government refused to give land to individual households.

Large state farms appealed to different groups within the Frente for a variety of reasons. Leading Sandinista officials held that large-scale agriculture was the most efficient form of production and argued that breaking enterprises into smaller units would lower productivity and output. Policymakers resisted cooperativization of large enterprises for the same reasons. Some Sandinistas opposed redistributive measures, arguing that peasantization, or expanding the peasantry, would mark a retreat from the modern agrarian class structure that prevailed since the nineteenth century. The propertied allies of the Frente also opposed giving land to the peasantry, fearing that following land distribution, fewer people would seek seasonal wage labor. Officials in the Ministry of Agriculture were sympathetic to this view.[12] Sandinista policymakers, some drawing on a classical socialist critique, argued that the formation of a class of independent farmers would lead inevitably to social differentiation in the countryside and to the re-creation of a rural bourgeoisie and agrarian capitalism. In addition, they maintained that rural small producers were inherently reactionary, and, like the propertied classes (though from the opposite perspective), they were wary of a large group of small farmers independent of the state. As the elections of 1990 were to prove, there appeared to be some truth to this last view. But whatever the merits of these arguments, the analysis that most of the rural population had a working-class perspective and did not demand land would be refuted by events.

Agrarian policy changed dramatically in 1985, not from analytical reassessment, but from necessity. The war against the contras, the counterrevolutionary army funded by the U.S. government to overthrow the FSLN, proved so expensive that the state could no longer afford the huge subsidies required to maintain state farms. More important were the political consequences of agrarian policy. By 1984 it became apparent that opposition to the government led increasing numbers of peasants to support the contras, particularly in the war zones. And the contra war provoked further resistance to the FSLN because people objected to the military draft. To assuage the rural poor, the government finally yielded to pressure and began to distribute land to households. Property that belonged to state farms and to enterprises abandoned by their owners passed to cooperatives and, for the first time since the triumph, directly to those who worked the land. Between 1982 and 1990, the proportion of the nation's agricultural and grazing land held by state farms declined dramatically, from 23 to 8 percent. Land on large private estates declined from 29 to 15 percent, and the proportion held by medium-size farms dropped from 30 to 17 percent (Table 4). This shift in the social structure of the countryside was associated, from 1985 to 1990, with an extensive government program that assigned land titles to smallholders: 20 percent of the country's farm land was titled under this program (Table 5). In the end, most rural families gained land by virtue of the Sandinista agrarian reform.

By 1990, Nicaragua was a country radically different from what it had been a decade before, but the transformation was contrary to the intentions of the Sandinista leadership. Control of land by the propertied classes had drastically declined, both because of and despite state policy. By abandoning their property and maneuvering to subvert the government the landed bourgeoisie forfeited the measure of economic power the Sandinistas had been willing to grant them. At the same time, a new political force emerged: small farmers, freed from the servile and patriarchal relations of production that underpinned the class structure of rural society before the revolution (Table 5). These changes created the potential for a major political transformation, which would find expression in the electoral defeat of the Sandinistas.

The Fall of the Sandinistas

International pressure organized largely by the U.S. government pushed the Sandinistas to hold presidential elections in 1990. The FSLN lost the vote, not least because of illegal operations organized by Ronald Reagan and George H.W. Bush to bring about the downfall of a government that refused to take orders from Washington. However, external intervention interacted with in-

Table 5. Changes in Landholding by Small Producer Households, Nicaragua, 1978–1990

Peasant/Small Producer Households (× 1,000)	Number	Percentage[1]
I. Small Producer Households[2]	160	100
A. Households in need of land in 1978[3]	120	75
B. Households receiving land under SAR[4]	48	33
C. Households acquiring title to land they occupied/ cultivated prior to SAR	38	24
D. Households gaining land (B+C)	86	54
Arable Land (in manzanas)[5] (× 1,000)		
II. Land in use for grazing and agriculture[6] (as percentage of arable land)	8,000	100
A. Acquired by small producer households through SAR (1979–1990)	1,398	17
B. Titled to small producer households that previously occupied/cultivated same land (1979–1990)	1,598	20
C. "Land to the tiller" through SAR (A+B)	2,996	37

Notes:

1. As percentage of small producer households.
2. Official 1990 estimate by MIDINRA (Ministry of Agrarian Reform in the Sandinista Government) of number of peasant households. Estimate does not vary from 1978 to 1990.
3. Calculated from official statistics, MIDINRA.
4. Distribution and titling of land through Apr. 1990 (the inauguration of the UNO government). SAR = Sandinista Agrarian Reform. Direct access to land in all cooperative farms and lands distributed to individual households.
5. 1 manzana = 1.72 acres, or 0.7 hectares.
6. Official estimate, MIDINRA.

Sources: Computed from data presented in Centro de Investigación y Estudios de la Reforma Agraria, *La reforma agraria en Nicaragua, 1979-1989*, 9:40–61, tables 2–23; Gutierrez, "La política de tierras de la reforma agraria Sandinista"; de Groot, "Reforma Agraria en Nicaragua: una actualización," 106–108, tables 1 and 2.

14. La Luz, coffee cooperative on Mombacho Volcano, 1991.

15. Rustic choza, 1995.

ternal political dynamics. By postponing land distribution to the peasantry, the FSLN had incurred the wrath of large numbers of rural voters, 64 percent of whom cast their ballots against the FSLN, above the national average of 59 percent.[13] The role of smallholders in the vote reflected the contradictory class stand of the petite bourgeoisie and the particular history of the Sandinista Revolution.

Paradoxically, by fulfilling the demand of the peasantry for land, the FSLN may have contributed to its electoral defeat. For a number of reasons the small farmers that the Sandinistas created after 1985 vacillated in their political allegiance. On the one hand, they owed their existence to the Sandinista government and feared that a return to the rule of the traditional elite might threaten their control over land—which it did. On the other hand, land distribution came too late, long after the Sandinistas had rebuffed calls to give land to those who worked it. When the government finally changed course and assigned land titles to peasant households, it gave insufficient attention to the bureaucratic process of titling land. Some who received land were awarded an agrarian reform certificate, whose status in law was not clear, perhaps being valid only under an FSLN government. Further complicating the picture, agrarian reform certificates often indicated only the general location of the land, not its precise boundaries.[14] As a consequence, the reform process generated confusion and hostility. Those peasants who received certificates were among the fortunate, for many nominal beneficiaries received nothing to prove their right to land. Furthermore, the titling program got underway after the government was financially squeezed because of the war. After 1985, the state was unable to provide the loans, technical assistance, and agricultural inputs that small producers required. In principle, the agrarian reform should have provided the Sandinista leadership a large rural clientele. Instead, it perpetuated considerable distrust between the peasantry and the FSLN, which explains why so many of those who in the end benefited from the agrarian reform voted against the party.[15]

The main electoral opposition to the Sandinistas, the Unión Nacional Opositora (UNO), a patchwork of centrist and rightist politicians cobbled together by the U.S. Embassy, attempted to woo the rural electorate. The UNO sought to appeal to the class interests of small rural proprietors with promises to respect the land distribution carried out by the FSLN. At the same time, the UNO pledged to return to owners property that had been confiscated; obviously it was impossible to fulfill the two promises simultaneously. During the campaign the UNO stressed the former, for reasons of expediency, overtly courting the beneficiaries of the Sandinista agrarian reform rather than the traditional propertied classes, which would support the UNO in any case.

The UNO won the election. Even if the Sandinistas had had a different interpretation of the past, one that emphasized the recent and incomplete proletarianization of the peasantry, it may not have altered the vote significantly. The U.S. government was on a path to defeat the Sandinistas by whatever means. But possibly, if the Sandinista leaders had not insisted that capitalism had all but wiped out the peasantry a century ago, they may have listened earlier to voices in the countryside demanding land. Land distribution would not have prevented U.S. intervention, but it might have stopped counterrevolution from turning into civil war.

A major revolution transformed Nicaragua during the rule of the Sandinistas, though largely outside its control; indeed, to an extent, it occurred contrary to the stated goals of the FSLN leadership. At least two interrelated revolutionary changes occurred to alter society: the historically divided dominant classes suffered a major weakening of their economic and political power, such that it took more than a decade for the bourgeoisie to reassert its hegemony over the country; and in the countryside, social relations that subordinated the peasantry were largely destroyed, creating a class of small farmers. Neither of these fundamental changes conformed closely to the design of the leadership of the FSLN; perhaps the first did so to a degree, but certainly not the second.

After the FSLN's defeat, owners of large properties clashed with small farmers as both endeavored to establish their rights to land. Property disputes perpetuated violent struggles in the countryside for more than a decade, preventing successive governments from establishing the rule of law.[16] Large landowners proclaimed that the Sandinistas had violated the sanctity of their private property and demanded that the state force smallholders to relinquish land. But the bourgeoisie turned history upside down. One hundred years earlier, the landlord class and the state destroyed centuries-old common property rights to create conditions for coffee production. Following abolition of Indian communities and widespread land privatization, wealthy Nicaraguans used their economic and political clout to appropriate land to create coffee fincas. Large private property in Nicaragua was rooted in the expropriation of the commons, not the buying and selling of land. But the true history of private property has been suppressed.

Notes

Introduction   Who Controls the Past Controls the Future

1 For analyses of the intersections of class, race, and gender, see, among others, "Raza/Etnia y Género," a special issue of *Política y Cultura*, no. 14 (autumn 2000); Benería and Roldán, *The Crossroads of Class and Gender*; Stephen, *Zapotec Women and Zapata Lives*; Gutmann, *The Meanings of Macho*; de la Cadena, *Indigenous Mestizos*.

2 "Men [and, he should have added, women] make their own history, but they do not make it just as they please; they do not make it under circumstances chosen by themselves, but under circumstances directly found, given and transmitted from the past. The tradition of all the dead generations weighs like a nightmare on the brain of the living." Marx, "The Eighteenth Brumaire of Louis Bonaparte," 595.

3 See Joan W. Scott's caveat: "The point of historical investigation is to disrupt the notion of fixity, to discover the nature of the debate or repression that leads to the appearance of timelessness." "Gender: A Useful Category of Historical Analysis," 1068.

4 Eric Hobsbawm famously wrote, "The most submissive peasantry is not only capable of 'working the system to its advantage'—or rather to its minimum disadvantage—but also of resisting and, where appropriate, of counterattack." See "Peasants and Politics."

5 For essays emphasizing women's exclusion from peasant proprietorship, see Deere and León, *Rural Women and State Policy*; León and Deere, *La mujer y la política agraria en américa latina*.

6 I have adapted the terminology Terence J. Byres develops for a different purpose; see *Capitalism from Above and Capitalism from Below*.

7 See, among others, Tinsman, *Partners in Conflict*; Stern, *The Secret History of Gender*; Vaughan, *Cultural Politics in Revolution*; Besse, *Restructuring Patriarchy*; Arrom, *The Women of Mexico City*; Lavrin, "Women in Spanish American Colonial Society" and *Women, Feminism and Social Change*; Rodríguez Sáenz, *Hijas, novias y esposas* and *Mujeres, Genero e Historia en América Central*; Nazzari, *Disappearance of the Dowry*; Guy, *Sex and Danger in Buenos Aires*; Klubock, *Contested Communities*; Findlay, *Imposing Decency*; Caulfield, *In Defense of Honor*; Dore and Molyneux, *The Hidden Histories of Gender*; Rosemblatt, *Gendered Compromises*;

Dore, *Gender Politics in Latin America*; and the special issue "Gender and Sexuality in Latin America," *Hispanic American Historical Review* 81, nos. 3–4 (Aug.–Nov. 2001).

8 Steven Topik calls the era when coffee was king Latin America's second conquest in "Coffee." For an excellent overview of the historical literature on Latin America's coffee economies, see Topik, "Coffee Anyone?" For a useful typology of capitalism and the Latin American coffee economies, see Roseberry, "La Falta de Brazos." For country studies, see Yarrington, *A Coffee Frontier*; Dean, *Rio Claro*; Stein, *Vassouras*. For gender and class in Brazil, see Stolcke, *Coffee Planters, Workers and Wives*; Clarence-Smith and Topik, *The Global Coffee Economy*. For studies of capitalist transition in Peru, see Jacobsen, *Mirages of Transition*; Mallon, *The Defense of Community*.

9 Wheelock Román, *Imperialismo y dictadura*; Vargas, *La intervención norteamericana* and *La revolución que inició el progreso*; Vilas, *The Sandinista Revolution*; Barahona, *Estudio sobre la historia de Nicaragua*; Lanuza, "La formación del estado nacional en Nicaragua"; Blas Real Espinales and Marco Valle Martínez, "Consideraciones sobre la producción del café y sus incidencias en la estructura agraria en Nicaragua (1900–1945)," paper presented at the seminar "Estructura Social Rural y Análisis Regional en Centro América y Panamá," San José, Costa Rica, 1975.

10 See Thomson, *Puebla de Los Angeles*, for local history.

11 The literature on capitalist development in Central America includes McCreery, *Rural Guatemala*; Lauria-Santiago, *An Agrarian Republic*; Gould, *To Die in This Way* and *To Lead as Equals*; Charlip, *Cultivating Coffee*; Grandin, *The Blood of Guatemala*; Roseberry, Gudmundson, and Samper Kutschbach, *Coffee, Society, and Power*; Weeks, "An Interpretation of the Central American Crisis"; R. Williams, *States and Social Evolution*; Baumeister, *Estructura y reforma agraria en Nicaragua*; Paige, *Coffee and Power*; Molina Jiménez, *Costa Rica*; Acuña Ortega and Molina Jiménez, *Historia económica y social de Costa Rica* and *El desarrollo económico y social de Costa Rica*; Carolyn Hall, *Costa Rica*; Cardoso and Pérez Brignoli, *Centro América y la economía occidental* and *Historia económica de América Latina*; Pérez Brignoli, *A Brief History of Central America*, 66–97; Torres-Rivas, *Interpretación del desarrollo social centroamericano*; Samper, *Generations of Settlers*; Gudmundson, *Costa Rica before Coffee* and "Lord and Peasant in the Making of Modern Central America."

12 See, among others, Dunkerley, *Power in the Isthmus*; Booth, *The End and the Beginning*; Pearce, *Under the Eagle*; Bermann, *Under the Big Stick*; LaFeber, *Inevitable Revolutions*.

13 My analysis of capitalism is drawn from the Marxist tradition. Marx, *Capital*, vol. 1, pt. 8, chaps. 26–33, pp. 667–724; Polanyi, *The Great Transformation*.

14 Utting, *Economic Adjustment under the Sandinistas* and *Economic Reform and Third World Socialism*; Spoor, *The State and Domestic Agricultural Markets in Nicaragua*;

Dore, "La Respuesta Campesina"; MICOIN, *Sistemas de Comercialización*, vol. 1; Biondi-Morra, *Revolución y política alimentaria*.

15 Enríquez, *Harvesting Change*; Baumeister, "The Structure of Nicaraguan Agriculture"; Núñez Soto, *Transición y lucha de clases en Nicaragua*; Centro de Investigación y Estudios de la Reforma Agraria (CIERA), *La Reforma Agraria en Nicaragua*.

16 Fagan, Deere, and Coraggio, *Transition and Development*, especially chapters by Deere, Baumeister and Neira, and Fagan; Rubén and De Groot, *El Debate Sobre la Reforma Agraria en Nicaragua*; Dore, "Nicaragua."

17 Wheelock Román, *Imperialismo y dictadura*, 12.

18 Ibid., 190.

19 Orwell, *Nineteen-Eighty Four*, 31.

20 For debates about peasant versus proletarian consciousness, see Goodman and Redclift, *From Peasant to Proletarian*; Byres, *Capitalism from Above*. Classics in the field include Lenin, "The Development of Capitalism in Russia" and "A Characterization of Economic Romanticism"; Chayanov, *The Theory of Peasant Economy*.

21 John Negroponte and Elliott Abrams were President Ronald Reagan's operatives charged with secretly channeling funds to the contra raised through illegal arms sales to Iran. At the time of writing, Negroponte is U.S. Director of National Intelligence and Abrams serves on President George W. Bush's National Security Council as the top Middle East advisor. *Plus ça change, plus c'est la même chose* (The more things change, the more they are the same).

22 Vargas, *Adonde Va Nicaragua*; Vilas, "Nicaragua: A Revolution That Fell from the Grace of the People" and *Between Earthquakes and Volcanos*.

23 Gould, *To Die in This Way*.

24 Population data from interview with Diriomo's *alcalde municipal* (municipal mayor), Francisco Campos Carcache, Diriomo, 12 July 1998. Brujo, the masculine form, suggests that both men and women practiced witchery and sorcery.

25 I gratefully thank Licenciado Alfredo González Vílchez for telling me about Diriomo's archive. At the time, González was chief archivist at the Instituto de Estudios de Sandinismo; later he became the director of the Archivo General de la Nación. I call Diriomo's collection of municipal documents the Archivo Municipal de Diriomo (hereafter cited as AMD).

26 In four letters (1896, 1904, 1914, 1926) spanning twenty years, officials higher up ordered Diriomo's alcaldes municipales to send the municipality's historical documents to the Archivo General de la República. See, in particular, Señor Jefe Político de Granada al Sr. Alcalde Municipal de Diriomo, Granada, 24 Dec. 1904, Correspondencia, Ramo Alcaldía Municipal, AMD.

27 See, among others, Tonkin, *Narrating our Pasts*; James, "Listening in the Cold"; P. Thompson, *The Voice of the Past*; Portelli, *The Death of Luigi Trastulli and Other Stories*; Passerini, *Autobiography of a Generation*; Grele, *Envelopes of Sound*; Frisch,

"Oral History and Hard Times." For an analysis of the use of oral history sources, see Tinsman, *Partners in Conflict*, 17–18.

28 I borrow the analogy to deafness from James, "Listening in the Cold," 128–33.

29 Stern, *Secret History*, 131.

30 Gould, *To Die in This Way*.

31 Censo de la población: Diriomo, Año 1883, caja 191, leg. x7, fol. 152, Archivo Municipal de la Prefectura de Granada (hereafter cited as AMPG). Copy kindly given to author by Justin Wolfe. For analysis of ethnicity in the department of Granada, see Wolfe, "Rising from the Ashes."

32 Gámez, *Historia Moderna de Nicaragua* and *Historia de Nicaragua*; Ayón, *Historia de Nicaragua*, 3:344–45; Coronel Urtecho, *Reflexiones sobre la Historia de Nicaragua*.

33 Gould, *To Die in This Way*, 17–19.

34 For historical analysis of Nicaragua's Atlantic Coast, see C. R. Hale, *Resistance and Contradiction*; Freeland, *A Special Place in History*.

Chapter One   Capitalism, Class, Gender, and Ethnicity

1 I elaborate this argument in Dore, "Understanding Third World Capitalism."

2 Brenner, "The Origins of Capitalist Development"; Weeks and Dore, "International Exchange and the Causes of Backwardness"; Kay, *Latin American Theories of Development and Underdevelopment*; Sunkel and Paz, *El subdesarrollo latinoamericano*.

3 For a contemporary Marxist revision of this theory, see Weeks, "Epochs of Capitalism." For a heterodox interpretation, see Thomas, *Dependence and Transformation*. For refutation, see Anderson, *Arguments within English Marxism*, 131–56.

4 For the classic Marxist debate on the transition from feudalism to capitalism between those who emphasize class and those who emphasize trade, see Hilton, *The Transition from Feudalism to Capitalism*.

5 For key articles in the paradigm shift, see Stavenhagen, "Seven Fallacies about Latin America"; Vitale, "Latin America."

6 Marx, *Capital*, vol. 1, pt. 8, chaps. 26–33.

7 For classic dependency theory, see Gunther Frank, *Capitalism and Underdevelopment in Latin America*; for world systems theory, see Wallerstein, *The Modern World-System*. For a critical synthesis and application to Latin America, see Stern, "Feudalism, Capitalism, and the World-System."

8 Marx's classic and widely accepted definition of mode of production (which, incidentally, does not use the term) is this: "[A mode of production is] the specific economic form in which surplus labor is pumped out of direct producers. This determines the relationship of rulers and ruled, as it grows directly out of production itself and in turn reacts upon it as a determining element. Upon this . . . is founded the entire formation of the economic community which grows up out

of production relations themselves, thereby simultaneously its specific political form. It is always the direct relationship of the owners of the conditions of production to the direct producers—a relation always naturally corresponding to a definite stage in the development of the methods of labor and thereby its social productivity—which reveals the innermost secret, the hidden basis of the entire social structure." *Capital*, vol. 3, chap. 47, sect. 2, pp. 791–92. For different interpretations of Marx's meaning, see Fine and Harris, *Re-Reading Capital*; Althusser and Balibar, *Reading Capital*.

9   For analysis of articulation of modes of production, see Foster-Carter, "The Modes of Production Controversy."

10 See James C. Scott, *Weapons of the Weak*; Mallon, *The Defense of Community*, 5–7.

11 For this interpretation, see Wolpe, *The Articulation of Modes of Production*.

12 Banaji, "Modes of Production in a Materialist Conception of History."

13 For contributions to this debate, see Cooper et al., *Confronting Historical Paradigms*. In European historiography, see Holmes, *Cultural Disenchantments*. Ironically, unlike these authors, André Gunther Frank argues that Marx got it completely wrong, that capitalism never existed except as an ideology. See *ReOrient*.

14 Weeks, "Epochs of Capitalism"; Wood, *The Origin of Capitalism*; and McCreery, who writes, "Instead of being a sort of pre-history of capitalism, primitive accumulation proved to be an ongoing and self-reproducing historical process" (*Rural Guatemala*, 3). For a similar argument, see Jacobsen, *Mirages of Transition*.

15 Marx, *Capital*, 1:667–724. See also Perelman, *The Invention of Capitalism*.

16 Weeks, *Capital and Exploitation*; Fine and Saad Fihlo, *Marx's Capital*.

17 Ibid.

18 Mauss, *The Gift*; Lapavitsas, "Commodities versus Gifts."

19 Polanyi, *The Great Transformation* (2001 ed.), vii.

20 Ibid., 43–75.

21 Marx, *Capital*, vol. 1, pt. 8: "The So-Called Primitive Accumulation."

22 Mintz, *Caribbean Transformations*, 35.

23 Polanyi, *The Great Transformation*, 59–70.

24 Ibid., 47. Ellen Meiksins Wood develops a complementary argument in *The Origin of Capitalism* and *The Origin of Capitalism: A Longer View*.

25 Lenin, "Development of Capitalism in Russia"; Moore, *Social Origins of Dictatorship and Democracy*; Huber, introduction. For an excellent analytical review of Marxist debates on the Latin American peasantry and the development of capitalism, see Harris, "Marxism and the Agrarian Question in Latin America."

26 Byres, *Capitalism from Above*.

27 Brenner's "The Social Basis of Economic Development" develops issues treated in "The Origins of Capitalist Development: A Critique of Neo-Smithian Marxism," *New Left Review* 104 (July–Aug. 1977): 25–92. Brenner's earlier and better-known work includes "Agrarian Class Structure and Economic Development in Pre-Industrial Europe," which led to Aston and Philpin, *The Brenner Debate*.

28 James C. Scott, *The Moral Economy of the Peasant* and *Weapons of the Weak*.

29 James C. Scott, *Weapons of the Weak*, 304–50.

30 For literature placing gender at the center of social transformation, see Goldman, *Women at the Gates*. I adapted Goldman's metaphor of the puzzle, 30–31. See also Deere, *Household and Class Relations*; Cooper and Stoler, *Tensions of Empire*; Stoler, *Race and the Education of Desire* and *Carnal Knowledge and Imperial Power*; Mallon, "Exploring the Origins of Democratic Patriarchy in Mexico"; Fowler-Salamini, "Gender, Work and Coffee"; Chassen-Lopez, "Cheaper Than Machines."

31 Classics in the field include Eisenstein, *Capitalist Patriarchy and the Case for Socialist Feminism*; Kelly, *Women, History, and Theory*. For a review of the debates, see Dore, "Introduction: Controversies in Gender Politics"; Tinsman, *Partners in Conflict*, 8–14.

32 Rose, "Introduction to Dialogue."

33 Joan W. Scott, "Gender: A Useful Category of Historical Analysis."

34 This definition draws on Phillips, *Divided Loyalties* and *Which Equalities Matter?*; Vaughan, "Modernizing Patriarchy"; Kandiyoti, "Bargaining with Patriarchy"; Tinsman, *Partners in Conflict*.

35 Exceptions to the theoretical division include Canning and Rose, *Gender, Citizenship and Subjectivities*; Rose, *Limited Livelihoods* and *Which People's War?*

36 Tinsman, "Reviving Patriarchy" and *Partners in Conflict*; Vaughan, *Cultural Politics in Revolution*; Mallon, "Exploring the Origins of Democratic Patriarchy"; Besse, *Restructuring Patriarchy*; Stern, *Secret History*; Arrom, *Women of Mexico City*; Lavrin, "Women in Spanish American Colonial Society"; Klubock, *Contested Communities*; Valdés, *Mujer, trabajo, y medio ambiente*; Valdés, Rebolledo, and Willson, *Masculino y feminino en la hacienda chilena*.

37 Hartmann, "The Unhappy Marriage of Marxism and Feminism." Hartmann's essay sparked broad debate, some of which was included in Sargent, *Women and Revolution*.

38 Marx, *Capital*, 3:597, 804.

39 Weber, *The Theory of Economic and Social Organization* and *Economy and Society*.

40 E. P. Thompson, *Customs in Common*, 189–212 and "Patrician Society: Plebian Culture." For a contrasting approach, see Bennett, "Feminism and History."

41 There are no references to Thompson in Stern's *Secret History*. However, Stern cites James C. Scott, *Weapons of the Weak* and *Domination and the Arts of Resistance*, which draw directly on Thompson.

42 Stern, *Secret History*, 19–20.

43 Ibid., 320–30.

44 Vincent, "The Structuring of Ethnicity," 377.

45 Larson, *Trials of Nation Making*.

46 Ibid., 17.

47 Knight, "Racism, Revolution and Indigenismo."

48 Grandin, *The Blood of Guatemala*; McCreery, *Rural Guatemala*; Arias, "Changing Indian Identity."

49 Molina Jiménez and Palmer, *The Costa Rica Reader*.

50 Alvarenga, *Cultura y etica de la violencia*; Gould and Santiago, "They Call Us Thieves and Steal Our Wages"; Kinloch Tijerino, *Nicaragua en busca de su identidad*; Field, *The Grimace of Macho Raton*; C. R. Hale, *Resistance and Contradiction*; Edelman, "Don Chico y el Diablo."

51 Alonso, "The Politics of Space, Time and Substance"; Martínez Echazabal, "Mestizaje and the Discourse of National/Cultural Identity"; Field, "Who Are the Indians?"

52 Wade, *Race and Ethnicity in Latin America*.

53 Adams, "Ethnic Images and Strategies in 1944," 13–31.

54 Stephen, "The Creation and Re-Creation of Ethnicity"; de la Cadena, *Indigenous Mestizos*.

55 Oral histories with Gloria Tifer Figueroa and Noé Campos Carcache, Diriomo, Feb. 1991.

56 Vincent, "The Structuring of Ethnicity."

57 Gilroy, *Against Race*.

58 Gould, *To Die in This Way*, 15.

59 B. Williams, "A Class Act."

60 Comaroff, "Of Totemism and Ethnicity."

61 B. Williams, "A Class Act."

Chapter Two   Colonialism and Postcolonialism

1 Newson, *Indian Survival in Colonial Nicaragua*, 336, table 31.

2 11 Mar. 1550, AI.23, leg. 1511, fol. 137, Archivo General de Centro América (hereafter cited as AGCA), Guatemala City.

3 Ibid.

4 6 Sept. 1579, AI.22, leg. 1513, fol. 565, AGCA.

5 25 Mar. 1633, AI.23, leg. 4579, fol. 61, AGCA.

6 McLeod, *Spanish Central America*, 96–106.

7 For economic and trade relations in colonial Latin America, see Fisher, *The Economic Aspects of Spanish Imperialism in America, 1492–1810*.

8 Letter from bishop of Nicaragua to judge of the Real Hacienda, 12 May 1649, AI.24, leg. 1560, exp. 10204, fol. 174, AGCA.

9 Guatemala: Razón de las Cuidades, villas y lugares, vecindarios y tributarios de que componen las Privincias del Distrito de esta Audiencia. Contaduria 815 (1682), Archivo General de Indias (hereafter cited as AGI), Sevilla, Spain. The calculation of tribute was based on the number of adults resident in the pueblo and their marital status.

10 28 Apr. 1655, AI.24, leg. 1561, exp. 10205, fol. 107, AGCA.

11 3 Nov. 1694, A3.14.4, leg. 495, exp. 3792, AGCA. For similar censuses for pueblos of the region, see AGCA for Nindirí, A3.1, leg. 2724, exp. 39048 (1724); for Masaya, A3.16.3, leg. 499, exp. 3838 (1733).

12 Newson estimates the Indian population totaled 21,500 (*Indian Survival*, 336, table 31).

13 12 Feb. 1649, A1.24, leg. 1560, exp. 10204, fol. 68, AGCA.

14 9 Feb. 1649, A1.24, leg. 1560, exp. 10204, fol. 48, AGCA.

15 11 Aug. 1676, A1.23, leg. 4586, fol. 47, AGCA.

16 One caballería = 105 acres.

17 23 Mar. 1694, A1.24. leg. 1569, exp. 10213, fol. 105, 127, AGCA.

18 Stern, *Peru's Indian Peoples*, 114–37.

19 Romero Vargas, *Las Estructuras Sociales de Nicaragua*, 88–94.

20 Bula de la Santa Cruzada, 3 July 1776, A.39 (5), leg. 1749, exp. 28130, AGCA.

21 Petición del cabildo y regimiento de la Cuidad de Granada al Audiencia del Gobierno Supremo, Guatemala, 12 Oct. 1776. A1.15, leg. 4128, exp. 32705, AGCA. Earlier, the mayor of Nueva Segovia reported on ethnic mixing and passing, "In the city there are people who are taken for and known commonly [*vulgarmente*] as Spaniards." He goes on to suggest that the city's mestizos were Indians who had fled their pueblos, "but here they are known as mestizos." Guatemala: Razón de las Cuidades, villas y lugares, vecindarios y tributarios de que componen las Privincias del Distrito de esta Audiencia. Contaduria 815 (1682), AGI.

22 A3.16 (5), leg. 152, exp. 1078, 1094 (1817, 1818), AGCA.

23 10 Feb. 1733, A3.30, leg. 2575, exp. 37805, AGCA.

24 23 Sept. 1808, Guatemala, 650, AGI.

25 21 Nov. 1808, A1.11.50, leg. 76, exp. 613, AGCA.

26 11 May 1649, A1.24, leg. 1560, exp. 10204, fol. 173, AGCA.

27 Relación de la Visita de la Diocesis de Nicaragua hecha por el Licenciado Don Pedro Agustín Morel de Santa Cruz, Obispo de Nicaragua (1751), Guatemala, 950, and Visita de Francisco de la Vega (1761), Guatemala, 593, AGI.

28 4 Sept. 1796, 21 Mar. 1798, A1.11.47, leg. 81, exp. 619; 10 Oct. 1800, A3.12, leg. 491, exp. 3740, AGCA.

29 Visita de Francisco de la Vega (1761), Guatemala, 593, AGI.

30 In 1776 Diriomo's population included 1,027 Indians (97 percent); the rest were Spaniards, mulattos, and mestizos. Bula de la Santa Cruzada, A3.29, leg. 1749, exp. 28130, AGCA.

31 Relación de la Visita de la Diocesis de Nicaragua hecha por el Licenciado Don Pedro Agustín Morel de Santa Cruz, Obispo de Nicaragua (1751), Guatemala, 950, AGI.

32 28 June 1844, Libro de Terminaciones Verbales, Ramo Alcaldía Constitucional, AMD.

33 Entre los indios principales de Masaya y Don Francisco Alvarado, 28 Mar. 1811, A1.57, leg. 468, exp. 3353; 28 May 1807, A1.45.7, leg. 446, exp. 2939, AGCA.

34 30 Apr. 1811, A1.57, leg. 468, exp. 3353, AGCA.

35 18 July 1810, A1.15, leg. 171, exp. 1226, AGCA. The judges who tried the ringleaders of the 1810 riot failed to determine the causes of the uprising. They concluded that the Indians of Masaya were rebellious and their leaders disposed to challenge royal authority.

36 Lynch, *The Spanish American Revolutions* and "The Origins of Spanish American Independence."

37 Burns, *Patriarch and Folk*, 35–65; for an analytical synthesis, see Carmagnani, *Estado y Sociedad en América Latina 1850–1930*.

38 10 Dec. 1843, Libro de Actas Municipales, AMD.

39 28 Oct. 1844, Libro de Actas Municipales, AMD.

40 5 Aug. 1845, Libro de Actas Municipales, AMD.

41 23 July 1847, Libro de Actas Municipales, AMD.

42 28 June 1844, Libro de Terminaciones Verbales, Ramo Alcaldía Constitucional, AMD.

43 Kinloch Tijerino, in *Nicaragua: Identidad y cultura política*, argues that intraelite warfare primarily reflected an ideological divide within Nicaragua's dominant groups about the system of governance. Disagreements about the nature of citizenship, political centralization versus decentralization, and institutionalization of the armed forces fueled partisan struggles that mired the country in long-term internecine wars.

44 Gámez, *Historia Moderna de Nicaragua* and *Historia de Nicaragua desde los tiempos prehistóricos hasta 1860*; Ayón, *Historia de Nicaragua desde los tiempos más remotos hasta el año de 1852*, 3:344–45; Cuadra Downing, *Bernabé Somoza (1815–1849)*.

45 Burns, *Patriarch and Folk*, 145–59; Casanova Fuertes, "¿Heroes o Bandidos?" and "Hacia una nueva valoración de las luchas políticas del periodo de la anarquía" and "Orden o anarquía."

46 José María Valle, "A los pueblos del Jeneral en Jefe libertador del mismo Jose Maria Valle," *La Gaceta de Guatemala*, no. 15, 28 Aug. 1845, cited in Casanova, "¿Heroes o Bandidos?," 23.

47 Manuel Pasos Arana, "Granada y sus arroyos," *Revista de la Academia de Geografía y Historia de Nicaragua* 6, no. 2 (Managua, Aug. 1994): 116–22, cited in Casanova, "¿Heroes o Bandidos?," 18.

48 Ibid., 11.

49 J. Hale, *Six Months' Residence and Travels in Central America*, 30; Scherzer, *Travels in the Free States of Central America*; Byam, *Wild Life in the Interior of Central America*.

50 3, 8 June 1849, Correspondencia, Ramo Alcaldía Municipal, AMD.

51 5, 11, 23 June 1849, Correspondencia, Ramo Alcaldía Municipal, AMD.

52 J. Ferrar, Prefectura Departmental de Granada, al Alcalde Constitucional de Diriomo, 26 July 1849, Correspondencia, Ramo Alcaldía Municipal, AMD.

53 11 July, 12 Aug. 1849, Correspondencia, Ramo Alcaldía Municipal, AMD.

54 Ley de Agricultura, Decreto de 18 de Febrero 1862, Archivo Nacional de Nicaragua (hereafter cited as ANN). Typescript of document given to author by director of the ANN, Alfredo González, before it was catalogued. Hereafter cited as Ley de Agricultura, 1862.

55 7 May 1853, and 23 Feb. 1860, Libro de Actas Municipales, AMD.

56 Jefe Político de Granada al Alcalde Constitucional de Diriomo, 31 Apr. 1856, Correspondencia, Ramo Alcaldía Municipal, AMD.

57 4 May 1856, Libro de Actas Municipales, AMD.

58 3 Jan. 1862, Libro de Actas Municipales, AMD.

59 2 Jan. 1865, Libro de Actas Municipales, AMD. Similar cases are described by Justin Wolfe in "Becoming Mestizo: Ethnicity, Culture, and Nation in Nicaragua, 1850–1900," paper presented at the Tercero Congreso Centroamericano de Historia, San José, Costa Rica, 15–18 July 1996, 11–14.

60 3 Apr. 1876, Libro de Actas Municipales, AMD.

61 Jefe Político de Granada al Alcalde Constitucional de Diriomo, 21 Apr. 1864, Correspondencia, Ramo Alcaldía Municipal, AMD.

62 Jefe de la Prefectura de Granada al Alcalde Constitucional de Diriomo, 20 Feb. 1867, Correspondencia, Ramo Alcaldía Municipal, AMD.

63 Jefe de la Prefectura de Granada al Alcalde Constitucional de Diriomo, 26 July 1849, Correspondencia, Ramo Alcaldía Municipal, AMD.

64 Jefe de la Prefectura de Granada al Alcalde Constitucional de Diriomo, 30 Sept. 1863, Correspondencia, Ramo Alcaldía Municipal, AMD.

Chapter Three   Patriarchal Power in the Pueblos

1 In "An Introduction," William Roseberry describes the state's many activities as taking place within the "field of power" of the dominant classes.

2 Corrigan and Sayer, *The Great Arch*.

3 On gender and state making, see Joan W. Scott, *Gender and the Politics of History*; Dore and Molyneux, *Hidden Histories*, in particular Molyneux, "Twentieth-Century State Formations in Latin America" and Vaughan, "Modernizing Patriarchy"; Rosemblatt, *Gendered Compromises*; Tinsman, *Partners in Conflict*; Stern, *Secret History*.

4 Silvia Marina Arrom was the first to use the term "corporate patriarchy" (*Women of Mexico City*, 76).

5 Colonial law was based on the Siete Partidas compiled under King Alfonso X of Castile in the thirteenth century, the Leyes de Toro, and the Council of Trent, which date from the fifteenth and sixteenth centuries.

6 Arrom, *Women of Mexico City*, 95; Seed, *To Love, Honor and Obey in Colonial Mexico*, 61–108.

7 For elaboration of this argument, see Dore, "One Step Forward, Two Steps Back."

8 Although the Nicaraguan Code does not explicitly refer to "the womb" as such, it

was not uncommon to do so at this time in Latin America. The Rio Branco Law of 1871 in Brazil was called "the Law of the Free Womb." It decreed that children born of slave mothers would be free upon reaching the age of majority.

9 The 1904 Civil Code stated that a wife could be granted a divorce on the following grounds: "[Si] el concubinato del marido, siempre que tenga a la mujer en su propia casa, o notoriamente en otro sitio, o cuando en el hecho concurren tales circunstancias que constituyan una injuria grave para la esposa y finalmente el abandono manifesto." Zuñiga Osorio, "Patria Potestad," 40.

10 "One would expect people to remember the past and imagine the future. But in fact when discoursing or writing about history, they imagine it in terms of their own experience, and when trying to gauge the future, they cite supposed analogies from the past: till, by a double process of repetition, they imagine the past and remember the future." Namier, *Conflicts*, 11.

11 For the former, see Lamas, "Scenes from a Mexican Battlefield"; for a critique of the latter view, see Kandiyoti, "End of Empire."

12 Lyndal Roper makes a similar argument for the effects of the Reformation in Western Europe, in *Oedipus and the Devil*.

13 Rodríguez, "Civilizing Domestic Life"; Guy, "Parents before Tribunals"; Varley, "Women and the Home in Mexican Family Law."

14 Diego Cano pide al Alcalde Municipal, 18 May 1868, Tierras Ejidales, Ramo Alcaldía Municipal, AMD. Similar male property systems have been found in Indian peasant communities in Chihuahua, Mexico, and the Central Highlands of Peru. For Mexico, see Nugent and Alonso, "Multiple Selective Traditions in Agrarian Reform and Agrarian Struggle." For Peru, see Mallon, "Patriarchy in the Transition to Capitalism."

15 Prefectura Departamental al Alcalde Constitucional de Diriomo, 3 Mar., 6 May, 11 June, 26 July 1849, Correspondencia, AMD. In response to requests from the prefectura departamental in Granada for information about individual wealth for the purposes of levying a war tax, the alcalde of Diriomo sent lists of owners of property and mejoras, which included members of the Indian community.

16 Entre Josefa Ramírez y Víctor Ayala por la compra de una huerta, 19 July 1867, 19 Oct. 1864, 8 Dec. 1865, 9 Mar. 1865, Tierras, Libro de Demandas Verbales, Ramo Alcaldía Municipal, AMD.

17 We cannot generalize about gender relations in Latin American Indian communities from one or two cases. Nevertheless, there may be a certain romanticism in the so-called theories of pre-Western or precapitalist gender equality. For the first, see Etienne and Leacock, *Women and Colonization*, v–vi; for the second, Engels, *The Origin of the Family*.

18 Peña Torres, "Las cofradías indígenas en Nicaragua."

19 Documents from the nearby Indian communities of Masaya and Nindirí indicate the practice of collective male decision making. For the former, see Entre los indios principales de Masaya y Don Francisco Alvarado, 28 Mar. 1811, A1.57, leg.

468, exp. 3353; 28 May 1807, AI.45.7, leg. 446, exp. 2939, AGCA. For the latter, Deliberaciones: Comunidad Indígena de Nindirí, 18 Feb. 1878, Ramo Agricultura, AMD.

20 Frances Kinloch Tijerino analyzes early republican debates about voting qualifications and argues that they significantly fueled partisan differences and perpetuated political instability. See *Nicaragua*, chap. 3. See also Burns, *Patriarch and Folk*, 133.

21 Until the 1860s property transactions in Diriomo involved the buying and selling of mejoras, improvements to the land, not land itself. This system of ownership is apparent in bills of sale, wills, and disputes over property, which recorded frequent transactions involving animals and crops, none involving land. See, for example, El Sr. Tiffer intentando la prohibatoria a Don Vicente Espinosa sobre una huerta . . . , 23 Jan. 1864, Juzgado Unico Constitucional de Diriomo, AMD. For taxation of carts and a distillery owned by Sr. Florencio Fernández, see La Prefectura de Granada al Alcalde Constitucional de Diriomo, 5 Nov. 1849, Correspondencia, Ramo Alcaldía Municipal, AMD.

22 For details on gender differentiation in Nicaraguan property law, see Zúñiga Osorio, "Patria Potestad," 32–38.

23 Demanda verbal motivada por Juana Carballo y Olaya Vásquez por difamación de delito, 14 Nov. 1865, Juzgado Municipal de Diriomo (hereafter cited as JMD), AMD. For a similar case, see Demanda motivada por La Sra. Juana Isabel López, 14 Mar. 1843, Libro de Conciliaciones, JMD, AMD.

24 Libros de Terminaciones Verbales, 1851–1873, AMD.

25 Gertrudis Banegas expona que el Sr. Tómas Vasconcelos ha perpetrado los delitos de rapto y estrupo en mi hija . . . 11 June 1869, Libro de Terminaciones Verbales, AMD.

26 Salinas, *Las chilenas de la colonia*; Montesinos, *Madres y huachos*.

27 In the case of Costa Rica, Rodríguez, "Civilizing Domestic Life," suggests that the creation of municipal tribunals might have effected a certain democratization of power, especially in the regulation of gender relations.

28 Sr. Marcelino Cano contra el cura de almas de este pueblo Parroco Don Aureliano Gutierres, 18 Feb. 1869, Libro de Terminaciones Verbales, AMD.

29 Burns, *Patriarch and Folk*, 78; Guy, "Parents before Tribunals."

30 Burns, *Patriarch and Folk*, 80.

31 Agustín Vijil, "Datos de Curia de la Ciudad de Granada durante el Año de 1846. Granada, 1 Jan. 1847," *Revista del Archivo General de la Nacion* (Managua) (Jan.–Mar. 1964): 5–7, cited in ibid., 77–78.

32 Burns, *Patriarch and Folk*, 66–67. My interpretation draws on and corroborates Burns's argument.

33 Ibid., 47.

34 For elaboration of this argument, see ibid., 80; Dore, "The Holy Family"; Szurchman, *Order, Family and Community in Buenos Aires*, 225–36.

35 Bula de la Santa Cruzada, 3 July 1776, A.39 (5), leg. 1749, exp. 28130, AGCA. This population count was administered by ecclesiastical authorities for the purpose of selling indulgences. According to the Bula, in Diriomo 64 percent of the adult Indian population was married, 31 percent was single, and 4 percent widowed. It is not apparent what the categories "married" and "single" meant, for instance, whether people in consensual unions were considered married or single. Also, it is unclear whether the data refer only to the town center or whether they include rural hamlets.

36 For analysis of the Latin American historical literature on female household heads in the eighteenth and nineteenth centuries, see Arrom, *Women of Mexico City*; Dore, "The Holy Family."

37 Censo de la población: Diriomo, Año 1883, caja 191, leg. X7, fol. 152, AMPG.

38 Cubitt and Greenslade, "Public and Private Spheres."

39 La Sra. Bermúdez contra el Sr. Eufreciano Alfaro, 30 Apr. 1866, JMD, AMD.

40 Reclamo de Santiago López, 18 June 1860, Libro de Conciliaciones, AMD.

41 Luiza Vallecío contra Andrés Marcía por alimentos, 21 Mar. 1874, Libro de Terminaciones Verbales, AMD. Child support cases in the previous decade spelled out that pasar alimentos meant providing food and firewood. Although the language of this case referred to pasar alimentos, the judge said that support in this instance should take the form of money payments. This may have reflected a certain monetization of the economy associated with the coffee revolution, or the fact that Marcía was one of the richest men in the pueblo, one of the first to participate in the regional cash economy.

42 Legally neither single mothers nor widows exercised *patria potestad* (paternal authority over children). They had legal responsibility to support their offspring but not the authority that, for fathers, accompanied it.

43 For analysis of state control over gender and sexual practices, see Connell, "The State, Gender and Sexual Politics."

Chapter Four The Private Property Revolution

1 For a typology of capitalism and the Latin American coffee economies, see Roseberry, "La Falta de Brazos"; Topik, "Coffee" and "Coffee Anyone?"; Yarrington, *A Coffee Frontier*; Dean, *Rio Claro*; Cardoso and Pérez Brignoli, *Historia económica de América Latina*.

2 Wheelock Román, *Imperialismo y dictadura*; Vargas, *La intervención norteamericana y sus consecuencias*; Barahona, *Estudio sobre la historia de Nicaragua*; Lanuza, "La formación del estado nacional en Nicaragua"; and Real Espinales and Valle Martínez, "Consideraciones sobre la producción del café." Prior to the 1870s, large swaths of unoccupied land, or tierras baldías, were technically owned by the state.

3 See Gould, *To Die in This Way*, for Indian resistance to land privatization in Sutiava and Matagalpa.

4 For analysis of Mexican liberalism, see Charles A. Hale, *The Transformation of Liberalism in Late Nineteenth-Century Mexico*; for popular liberalism, see Mallon, *Peasant and Nation*; for a local study, see Thomson, "Agrarian Conflict in the Municipality of Cuetzalan (Sierra de Puebla)"; for liberalism in Latin America, see Escobar Ohmstede, Falcón, and Buve, *Pueblos, comunidades y municipios*.

5 Colonial land grants ordinarily stipulated the duration of the lease and placed restrictions on land use. See Composicion de Tierras de la Provincia de Granada, 11 Dec. 1769, A1.45.6, leg. 479, exp. 3119, AGCA; Titulo de Confirmacio de el libreado por el Senor Oydor . . . de el Real Derecho de Tierras de 4 Cavallerias . . . , 14 Feb. 1631, A1.24, leg. 1588, exp. 10232, fol. 63, AGCA.

6 *Terrateniente* (land tenant or landholder), the word for "large planter" used in Spanish America throughout the colonial era and into the late nineteenth century, accurately captures the nature of the landed relationship between Crown and grantee: landlords were tenants of the Crown. Another sign of the social relation of landholding in the colonial era is the Spanish word for the measure of large land areas, *caballería*. The king's noblemen, or cavaliers, were *caballeros*, and land granted in this relationship was measured in caballerías, or the amount of land a horseman (a caballero) could traverse in one day. In Nicaragua a caballería was equivalent to 105 acres. Hence, land itself was conceptualized in terms of services rendered to the Crown. Rosobo, "State Formation and Property."

7 For analysis of European, particularly Spanish, liberal political theory, see Labanyi, *Gender and Modernization in the Spanish Realist Novel*, 31–51.

8 For a discussion of European liberal ideologies, see Hobsbawm, *The Age of Revolution 1789–1848*, 277–98. For analysis of liberal state formation, property, and the reorganization of space in Central America, see Rosobo, "State Formation."

9 Kinloch Tijerino, *Nicaragua*, chap. 3.

10 Describing the policies of Guatemala's liberals, McCreery, *Rural Guatemala*, uses the term "aborted liberalism."

11 For European debates and land policies see Polanyi, *The Great Transformation* (2nd ed.), 35–136.

12 Lanuza, "La formacion del estado nacional en Nicaragua"; Burns, *Patriarch and Folk*, 224.

13 Decreto de 15 Febrero 1862, Ley Agraria (draft laws with legislators' comment, typescript document not catalogued in 1999), Archivo General de la Nación (hereafter AGN).

14 Fernández, "Nicaragua."

15 *Decreto legislativo sobre comunidades indígenas y terrenos ejidales.*

16 Analyzing "El Censo Cafetalero de 1909/10," leading scholars have drawn contrasting conclusions as to whether coffee production in different zones was dominated by large, medium, or small producers. The various interpretations principally result from the construction of different typologies designed to illuminate the size distribution of land or output and the different social meanings assigned

to size categories. For elaboration of my argument that large estates dominated in the Managua-Carazo-Granada coffee zone, see Dore, "La Producción Cafetalera Nicaragüense." For similar interpretations, see Paige, *Coffee and Power*, 153–80, and correspondence between the author and Eduardo Baumeister, March 2003. Writing against the grain, Julie Charlip, in *Cultivating Coffee*, argues that the coffee sector in Carazo in the period 1870 to 1930 was dominated by small to medium farmers.

17 5 Dec. 1855, Libro de Actas Municipales, AMD.

18 Buitrago, "El Municipio en Nicaragua."

19 3 Jan. 1854, Libro de Actas Municipales, AMD.

20 9 Nov. 1874, Tierras de Cofrades, Libro de Actas Municipales; 1 June 1875, Libro de Actas Municipales; and Terrenos Comunes, Corporación Municipal, 16 July 1887; 28 Aug. 1896, Tierras Ejidales, Corporación Municipal, AMD.

21 The regional Central American war of 1856–1858 fought between Liberals and Conservatives is called the National War, la Guerra Nacional. However, Nicaraguans refer to the combined forces of Liberals and Conservatives that fought to expel the U.S. filibuster William Walker as the National War.

22 Burns, *Patriarch and Folk*, 93.

23 27 Nov. 1861, Libro de Actas Municipales, AMD.

24 For example, Yo, Don Joaquín Cuadra, denuncia terreno ante la municipalidad . . . 13 Oct. 1865, Ramo Alcaldía Municipal, AMD. Cuadra petitioned for a grant of two hundred manzanas de tierras ejidales, equivalent to 350 acres. Manzana continues to be the common measure of land size in Nicaragua.

25 Entre el Sr. Víctor Ayala, Luciano Torres y Vicente Gómez por la compra de una huerta, 22 Oct. 1866, Libro de Demandas Verbales; 16 Sept. 1863, 30 Dec. 1866, 2 Jan., 5 Mar. 1866; Tierras, Ramo Alcaldía Municipal, AMD.

26 Francisco Básques pide al Alcalde Municipal . . . 9 Jan. 1861, Libro de Terminaciones Verbales, AMD. Subsequent quotes are from this document.

27 21 Oct. 1861, Libro de Terminaciones Verbales, AMD.

28 31 Dec. 1861, Libro de Terminaciones Verbales, AMD.

29 Don Gregorio Cuadra al Sr. Prefecto de Granada y el Subdelegado de Hacienda, caja 174, leg. 465, fol. 10–21, 1882, Denuncia de Tierras, 1882, AMPG. To see the dispute through the eyes of the men who served on Diriomo's junta municipal, see 10 Feb. 1883, Libro de Actas Municipales del Año 1883, AMD.

30 In 1883, 74 percent of the population of the pueblo was Indian. Censo de la población: Diriomo, Año 1883, caja 191, leg. x7, fol. 152, AMPG.

31 The national legislature established the boundary between Diriomo and Granada in 1882. Ibid.

32 Denuncias de Tierra, Año 1874, 1875, 1878, Ramo Alcaldía Municipal; 7 Sept. 1873, Libro de Actas Municipales; 17 May 1879, Libro de Terminaciones Verbales, AMD.

33 2 Dec. 1889, Juez de Agricultura, Ramo Agricultura, AMD.

34 10 Feb. 1873, Plan de Arbitrios, Libro de Actas Municipales del Año 1873, AMD.

35 25 Aug. 1874, Plan de Arbitrios, Libro de Actas Municipales del Año 1874, AMD.

36 Two high-ranking military officers, General Agustín Avilés and Comandante Celendino Borge, received grants in the common lands of Diriomo. Avilés received more than 150 manzanas over the years, and Borge more than forty. In both cases national politicians supported their petitions. For Avilés, see 28 Dec. 1889, Libro de Actas Municipales, AMD. For Borge, see 16 Oct. 1875; 22, 27 Oct.; 2 Nov.; 9 June 1876, Juzgado Civil de Diriomo, AMD.

37 See 4 Apr. 1878, 6 July 1880, 29 Sept. 1881, Tierras Ejidales, Ramo Alcaldía Municipal, AMD.

38 Libro de Matrícula de Fincas, Año 1905, Diriomo, Ramo Agricultura, AMD.

39 25 Aug. 1874, Plan de Arbitrios, Libro de Actas Municipales del Año 1874, AMD. The transaction fee for land was between 1.5 and 2.5 pesos per manzana. This pertained to land grants and land that the junta municipal sold. Denuncia de Tierras, 1882, caja 174, leg. 465, AMPG; Tierras Ejidales, 1875, 1887, 1894, Ramo Agricultura, AMD.

40 25 Aug. 1874, Plan de Arbitrios, Libro de Actas Municipales del Año 1874, AMD.

41 There is an interesting ambiguity regarding which body initiated the meeting. The minutes were taken by the junta's secretary and recorded in the Libro de Actas Municipales, but the text begins, "Reunida la municipalidad a invitacíon del Sr. Alcalde del Pueblo Indígena, Priostes, Mayordomos y demas cofrades de tales comunidades . . ." 13 Oct. 1875, Libro de Actas Municipales, AMD.

42 13 Oct. 1875, Libro de Actas Municipales, AMD. Subsequent quotes are from this document.

43 15 Apr. 1884, Libro de Actas Municipales, AMD. Don Yndalecio Morales had been alcalde municipal for six years and served on the junta for a further four.

44 La Disputa Diriomo-Granada, 28 Nov. 1875, Libro de Actas Municipales, AMD.

45 La Sra. Timotea Amador demanda a Julian del mismo apellido por un terreno, 9 Nov. 1874, Tierras de Cofrades, Libro de Actas Municipales; 23 Mar. 1876, Alcalde Municipal, Ramo Alcaldía Municipal, AMD.

46 18 Jan. 1878, 29 Mar. 1883, Libro de Actas Municipales, AMD.

47 The following documents record the case between Aguirre and Borge: 19 Apr., 16 Oct., 17 Nov. 1875; 22, 27 Oct., 2 Nov., 9 June 1876, Libro de Actas Municipales, AMD.

48 No, Señor Alcalde, ni un hombre del campo puede tragarse pilderas tan deformes sin las tenazas . . . 9 June 1876, Libro de Actas Municipales, AMD.

49 Demanda de Marcos Aguirre contra Joaquín Ybargüen por una liquidación, 24 Dec. 1895, Jueces de Agricultura, Ramo Agricultura, AMD.

50 3 July 1886, Libro de Actas Municipales; and 7 Oct. 1882, 10 Dec. 1884, Juzgado Civil de Diriomo, AMD.

51 9 June 1876, Libro de Actas Municipales, AMD.

52 A good example of the usefulness of Pérez to the junta is drawn from 1860, when,

at its bidding, he collected funds for the junta and put together and supervised a contingent of laborers who repaired roads and wells in the pueblo. 3 Apr. 1876, Libro de Actas Municipales, AMD.

53 17 May 1889, Libro de Actas de la Junta Municipal, AMD.

54 4 July 1889, Libro de Actas de la Junta Municipal, AMD.

55 2 May 1869, 19 Nov. 1876, Juzgado Criminal de Diriomo; 9 May 1876, Alcalde Municipal, Ramo Alcaldía Municipal, AMD.

56 2 Dec. 1889, Juez de Agricultura, Ramo Agricultura, AMD.

57 2 Feb. 1896, Tierras Ejidales, Corporación Municipal, AMD. Two members of the junta put together sizable fincas by buying and appropriating claims of their smaller and less influential neighbors. The junta municipal approved their actions. Doug Yarrington describes a similar process in "Public Land Settlement, Privatization and Peasant Protest in Duaca, Venezuela, 1870–1936."

58 28 Dec. 1899; 5 Jan., 28 Jan. 1900, Actas de la Junta Municipal, AMD.

59 28 Dec., 1899; 5 Jan., 28 Jan. 1900, Actas de la Junta Municipal, AMD.

60 3 Jan. 1894, Actas de la Junta Municipal, Ramo Alcaldía Municipal, AMD.

61 Solicitud de Don Donesio Chamorro, hijo, para que se le vende un terreno ejidal como de 15 manzanas, Diriomo, 17 Mar. 1918, Tierras, terrenos ejidales, Ramo Alcaldía Municipal; and Ministerio de Gobernación, Managua, 2 Dec. 1918, Tierras, terrenos ejidales, Ramo Alcaldía Municipal, AMD.

62 4 Mar. 1894; 7 Feb., 26 May 1895, Tierras Ejidales, Ramo Alcaldía Municipal, AMD.

63 A land dispute between Don Ynocente Malespin, a large coffee planter from Granada, and Diriomo's junta municipal lasted twelve years. Although Malespin declared that he owned land on Mombacho, the junta refused to recognize his claim, maintaining that "the land was part of what little remained of Diriomo's terrenos ejidales." After the jefe político of Granada intervened, Diriomo's junta recognized Malespin's title. Correspondence between Y. Malespin and Diriomo's alcalde municipal, Diriomo, 20 Dec. 1917; Granada, 11 Nov. 1918, Correspondencia, Ramo Alcaldía Municipal, AMD.

64 In 1911, Salvador Serda petitioned the alcalde municipal to regularize title to twenty manzanas "más o menos" (more or less) that he had cultivated continuously for twenty-five years in the tierras ejidales. Salvador Serda al Alcalde Municipal, 21 Feb. 1911, Correspondencia, Ramo Alcaldía Municipal, AMD.

65 4 July 1889, Actas de la Junta Municipal, AMD. Instead of petitioning for land grants, Tifer and Fernandez offered to buy land. As this was unprecedented in Diriomo, they explained that they were anxious to accelerate the bureaucratic process and the difference in the price per manzana was minimal.

66 In 1911, when the United States occupied Nicaragua, Wall Street bankers incorporated the first Banco Nacional de Nicaragua. The bank was registered in Hartford, Connecticut, not in Nicaragua. See Quijano, *Nicaragua*, 37–85. Fruto Obando demanda a Víctor Manuel Aragón, and Don Domingo Calderon demanda a Sil-

verio Flores el cumplimiento de mi contracto, 13 Feb. 1905, 10 July 1902, Jueces Locales, Ramo Judicial, AMD.

67 In 1924, José Luis Pérez filed a petition with Diriomo's corporación municipal asking the town counsellors to help him convert his use rights to twenty-one manzanas in the town's terrenos ejidales to private property. He explained that he began the process (*los tramites*) sixteen years earlier but had been unable to complete the paperwork. José Luis Pérez a la honorable Corporación Municipal, Diriomo, 13 Feb. 1924, Tierras Ejidales, Ramo Alcaldía Municipal, AMD.

68 Libro en que figuran las personas obligadas a pagar el cañon de ley, Diriomo, 1902; and Libro de Matrícula de Fincas, Año 1905, Diriomo, Ramo Agricultura, AMD.

69 Censo de la población: Diriomo, Año 1883, caja 191, leg. x7, fol. 152, AMPG. Copy kindly provided by Justin Wolfe. For analysis of race in the department of Granada, see Wolfe, "Rising from the Ashes." It is noteworthy that in southwestern Nicaragua ladino meant, more than anything else, simply "not Indian," and for census purposes most of Diriomo's ladinos were labeled "mulatto."

70 Oral histories with Virgilio Aguirre, 11 July 1998; Francisco Campos, 15 July 1998; José Esteban Vasconcelos, 12 July 1998, Diriomo.

71 "El Censo Cafetalero de 1909/10." Carried out by the administration of President Zelaya to take stock of the nation's coffee industry, for each of the thirteen thousand coffee fincas in the country the census records the size of holding (in manzanas), number of coffee trees, total output in semiprocessed coffee beans (in *quintales*, or hundredweights), value of production, and type of processing equipment. Other analyses of the 1910 coffee census include Paige, *Coffee and Power*, 53–95 (see in particular his tables 1 and 6, pp. 61, 72); R. Williams, *States and Social Evolution*, 79–91; Charlip, *Cultivating Coffee*.

72 For a statistical analysis of Nicaraguan coffee production in 1910 and 1956 and long-term trends in the industry, see Dore, "La Producción Cafetalera Nicaraguense."

73 "El Censo Cafetalero de 1909/10."

74 Oral Histories with Leticia Salazar Castillo, 17 July 1998; Orlando Salazar Castillo, 26 July 1998; and Carmen Ramírez Pérez, 3 Jan. 1991.

75 Libro en que figuran las Personas Obligadas a Pagar el Canon del Ley, Diriomo, 1902, AMD.

76 Libro de Matrícula de Fincas, Año 1905, Ramo Agricultura, AMD. Although the title of the document suggests it is a list of fincas only, with finca generally meaning agricultural enterprise, the list includes artisans and their workshops and the owners of wells and all of their apparatus, including water tanks and employees.

77 Polanyi, *The Great Transformation*, 56–75.

78 For analysis of the relationship between coffee production and peasant production, see McCreery, *Rural Guatemala*, 218–32, 332–35. McCreery argues that extraeconomic coercion was a mark of the vitality of Mayan communities because

subsistence peasants did not need to work on coffee fincas. See McCreery, "Coffee and Indigenous Labor in Guatemala."

79 In Nicaragua's southern coffee region, the Managua-Carazo-Granada triangle, the coffee harvest clashes with the demands of peasant production. The harvest season, the peak demand for coffee pickers, lasts from November to January. This overlaps with the period when peasants harvest their second planting of corn and beans, known in Nicaragua as *la postrera*.

Chapter Five   Gendered Contradictions of Liberalism

1 For discussions of Latin American liberalism, see Larson, *Trials of Nation Making*; Mallon, *Peasant and Nation*; McCreery, *Rural Guatemala*; Jacobsen, *Mirages of Transition*; R. Williams, *States and Social Evolution*.

2 Burns, *Patriarch and Folk*, 13–50, 210–37.

3 Kinloch Tijerino, *Nicaragua*; Vargas, *Elecciones Presidenciales en Nicaragua*; Vásquez, "Luchas políticas y estado oligárquico"; Vásquez Pereira, *La Formación del Estado en Nicaragua*; Barahona, "Intervención extranjera y dictadura"; Gould, *To Die in This Way* and *To Lead as Equals*; Burns, *Patriarch and Folk*; Walter, *The Regime of Anastasio Somoza*; Field, *The Grimace of Macho Raton*.

4 Patria potestad is a juridical term whose technical meaning in the Hispanic legal tradition refers to fathers' authority over their children.

5 For elaboration of this argument, see Dore, "One Step Forward, Two Steps Back."

6 Mandatory partible inheritance laws required parents to divide assets equally among their heirs, thus guaranteeing equality of inheritance. However, this principle applied to the total value of assets, and not necessarily to the division of landed property. Iván Molina informed me that in Costa Rica, in the mandatory partible inheritance regime, parents tended to bequeath landed property to sons and property in furniture, clothing, jewelry, and household effects to daughters. As he says, this pattern represents a typical case of the inequality of equality. Correspondence with author, 12 Oct. 2004.

7 Carmen Diana Deere and Magdalena León, *Empowering Women* and "Liberalism and Married Women's Property Rights in Nineteenth-Century Latin America."

8 For comparative studies, see Arrom, *Women of Mexico City* and "Changes in Mexican Family Law in the Nineteenth Century."

9 Censo de la población: Diriomo, Año 1883, caja 191, leg. x7, fol. 152, AMPG.

10 Calculated by author from Libro de Matrícula de Fincas, Año 1905, Diriomo; Libro en que figuran las personas obligadas a pagar el cañon de ley, Diriomo, 1902; and Resúmen del Censo Provisional de 1906, Departamento de Granada, Población Diriomo, Ramo Agricultura, AMD.

11 For the demographics of the township, see Censo de la Población: Diriomo, 1883; and Censo del Departamento de Granada, Año 1882, caja 172, leg. 486, fol. 121,

AMPG. Later in this chapter I analyze the demographics of marriage and of household headship.

12 Kandiyoti, "Bargaining with Patriarchy."

13 Nussbaum, "Women's Capabilities and Social Justice"; Molyneux, *Women's Movements in International Perspective*, 169; Molyneux and Razavi, introduction, 9; Deere and León, *Empowering Women*, 338–39. For a discussion of individuation and land rights in contemporary Mexico, see Helga Baitenmann, "Processes of Individuation: Gendered Conceptions of Rights in the New Agrarian Court Rulings," paper presented at Workshop on Law and Gender in Contemporary Mexico, Institute of Latin American Studies, London, Feb. 2004.

14 Republica de Nicaragua, Código Civil de la Republica de Nicaragua aprobado 25 enero 1867 (Managua: Imprenta de El Centro Americano, 1871). Details and citation kindly supplied by Carmen Diana Deere. Correspondence with author, 26 July 2005.

15 Deere and León, "Liberalism and Married Women's Property Rights."

16 Ibid.

17 Anne Phillips, *Which Equalities Matter?*

18 For a historical analysis of the gendered and racial contradictions of liberalism, see Findlay, *Imposing Decency*.

19 "El Censo Cafetalero de 1909/10."

20 Censo de la Población: Diriomo, 1883; and Censo del Departamento de Granada, Año 1882, caja 172, leg. 486, fol. 121, AMPG.

21 For analyses against the grain of peasant studies, see González Montes and Salles, *Relaciones de Género y Transformaciones Agrarias*; for a review of the literature on male and female household headship in nineteenth-century Latin America, see Dore, "The Holy Family."

22 For a critique of the category female household headship, see Varley, "Women Heading Households"; Chant, *Women-Headed Households* and *Women and Survival in Mexican Cities*.

23 16 Jan., 18 Feb. 1873, Plan de Arbitrios, Actas de la Junta Municipal, AMD.

24 Censo de la Población: Diriomo, Año 1883, caja 191, leg. X7, fol. 152, AMPG. Approximately 7 percent of adult women and the same percentage of adult men participated in the cash economy: for women, 48 out of a total of 716; for adult men, 51 out of a total of 676.

25 I found no systematic information about age at the time of marriage of women and men of different social strata. Without these data, the analysis of marriage rates is only indicative.

26 Les Field, in *The Grimace of Macho Raton*, analyzed the work and culture of Indian artisans in other towns on the Meseta de los Pueblos in the late twentieth century.

27 For details on women's participation in the cash economy, see Dore, "Patriarchy and Private Property in Nicaragua."

28 Plan de Arbitrios, Libro de Actas Municipales, Aug. 1885, Aug. 1903, AMD.

29 Entre La Niña Fernández y Sr. Juan de la Cruz Espinoza, demanda verbal, Libro de Demandas Verbales, 1894, Ramo Alcaldía Municipal, AMD.

Chapter Six   Debt Peonage in Diriomo

1 Bauer, "Rural Workers in Spanish America"; Knight, "Mexican Peonage" and "Debt Bondage in Latin America."

2 I am far from alone in arguing that peonage came into its own in the nineteenth century; most Latin American historians take this view. See Tutino, *From Insurrection to Revolution in Mexico*; Van Young, *Hacienda and Market in Eighteenth-Century Mexico*; Wells and Joseph, *Summer of Discontent*. However, most historians see peonage as a predominantly voluntaristic labor system. See the discussion of the Latin American debt peonage debates at the end of this chapter.

3 For a theoretical analysis of European political thought born of the Enlightenment, see Polanyi, *The Great Transformation*, 71–89.

4 *Informe del Jefe Político de Managua*.

5 Bauer, "Rural Workers in Spanish America"; Knight, "Mexican Peonage" and "Debt Bondage in Latin America"; Gonzales, *Plantation Agriculture and Social Control in Northern Peru*.

6 Traven's six-volume *Jungle Novels*, first published in the 1930s, are about the violence of peonage in Mexico. Julian Markels presents an interesting Marxian analysis of social realism as a literary genre in *The Marxian Imagination*.

7 Ley de Agricultura, Decreto de 18 de febrero 1862, AGN. Typescript given to author by director of AGN, Alberto González Vílchez, before document was catalogued. Hereafter cited as Ley de Agricultura, 1862.

8 For time series on the volume and value of Nicaraguan coffee exports, see Dore, "La Producción Cafetalera Nicaragüense."

9 Ley de Agricultura, 1862, Art 7. The law defines operarios as "persons of both sexes with a labor obligation, including for domestic service" (Art. 17), and jornaleros as "persons hired daily" (Art. 33). In turn-of-the-century Diriomo, jornalero was used to mean poor peasant.

10 David Montgomery informed me that laws restricting labor mobility were commonplace in Britain and the United States in the early to mid-nineteenth century. Personal correspondence, May 1999. See also his *Citizen Worker*, 13–51.

11 Ley de Agricultura, 1862, Arts. 32 and 35.

12 Ibid., Arts. 36 and 37.

13 Ibid., Art. 16, emphasis in original. For analysis of planters' private power in other coffee-producing countries of Latin America, see Topik, "Coffee Anyone?"

14 Ley de Agricultura, 1862, Arts. 13 and 34.

15 Ibid., Art. 16. The law required alcaldes municipales and jueces de agricultura to have a "capital" of 500 pesos.

16 Ibid., Arts. 24 and 39.

17 "De todas las multas que conforme a esta ley deben imponerse por el Juez de Agricultura, corresponden a el tres cuartaspartes," ibid., Art. 21.

18 For labor legislation, see Fernández, "Nicaragua," 60–73; Charlip, *Cultivating Coffee*.

19 Juez de Agricultura de Diriomo al Jefe Político de Granada, 18 Feb. 1899, Juzgado de Agricultura, Correspondencia, AMD.

20 Gould, *To Die in This Way*, 42–50.

21 Ley de Vagos, Art. 1, *El Comercio* (Managua), 4 Jan. 1899.

22 Ley de Trabajo, Art. 1, *La Gaceta* (Managua), 3 Oct. 1901.

23 Ley Sobre Agricultura y Trabajadores, *La Gaceta*, 5 Oct. 1894; Ley de Agricultura, *La Gaceta*, 9 Mar. 1898.

24 Decreto de 18 de Abr., 1904, *El Comercio*, 22 Apr. 1904.

25 *El Comercio*, 8 Jan. 1908.

26 *Diario de Granada*, 10 Oct. 1907. In this period, Granada's five newspapers, regardless of partisan loyalty, tended to favor forced labor. Interestingly, *El Diario Nicaragüense*, supporter of the Conservative Party, serialized Booker T. Washington's *De esclavo a catedrático* in 1911. At the same time, it ran articles supporting forced labor (see, e.g., *El Diario*, 22 Aug. 1911).

27 *El Comercio*, 8 Jan. 1908. For Matagalpan planters' views, see Gould, "El café, el trabajo y la comunidad indígena"; see also Gould, *To Die in This Way*, 42–50.

28 *El Comercio*, 19 Jan. 1908.

29 *Informe del Jefe Político de Managua*.

30 *El Comercio*, 25 Sept. 1902. For a similar view, see *El Independiente* (León), 3 Oct. 1899.

31 Wheelock, *Imperialismo y dictadura*, 104–13; Vargas, *La revolución*, 25–46.

32 Report by Admiral Kimball, 12 Mar. 1910, National Archives, U.S. State Department, RG 59, 6369/811, cited in Gould, "El café, el trabajo y la comunidad indígena," 320. For Gould's analysis of these events, see 319–21; see also *To Die in This Way*, 50.

33 *El Comercio*, 2 Dec. 1919 and 8 July 1913. For an analytical chronology of government policies, see Charlip, *Cultivating Coffee*, chap. 6.

34 Oral histories with Domingo Dávila and Isabel Rivera, Vera Cruz, Diriomo, Feb. 1991.

35 For accounts of labor drafts, see Actas de la Junta Municipal, 5 Jan. 1878 and 9 Feb. 1884, Ramo Alcaldía Municipal; Juez de Agricultura de Diriomo al Jefe Político de Granada, 10 Feb. 1892, Correspondencia, Ramo Agricultura, AMD.

36 Partida 233, 30 Sept., Lista de Operarios 1879, Ramo Alcaldía Municipal, AMD.

37 Partidas 278, 17 Sept., 397, 19 Oct., and 422, 2 Nov., Libro de Operarios Comprometidos 1899, Ramo Alcaldía Municipal, AMD.

38 Matrícula 287, 4 Feb. 1905, Operarios de los Señores Eisenstick y Bahlcke, Hacienda Alemania, Ramo Alcaldía Municipal, AMD. In a contract between Ramona

Zambrano's husband and Srs. Eisenstuck and Bahlcke, owners of the largest coffee company in Nicaragua, Zambrano pledged "to pay back this entire sum, and any other assistance my husband receives, by working on the coffee estates that Señores [Eisenstuck and Bahlcke] own in the Republic of Nicaragua."

39 Partida 381, 16 Mar., Matrícula de la familia de José Angel Gaitan con Don Apolinar Marenco, Libro de Matrículas 1886, Juez de Agricultura, Ramo Agricultura, AMD.

40 "José María Marcía autorizó amplias y legalmente a mi esposa y hija en plata y el resto en un sombrero de pita con valor de 6 pesos, a desquitar todo esto por trabajo," Matrícula 357, 28 July, Operarios de Alejandro Mejía, Libro de Operarios Comprometidos 1879, Ramo Alcaldía Municipal, AMD.

41 For discussion of the gendered character of debt peonage, see Dore, "Patriarchy from Above."

42 Calculated by author from *Censo de la población, 1883, Censo Provisional de 1906*, and *Censo general de la República*; Libros de Operarios, 1880–1915, AMD.

43 McCreery, *Rural Guatemala*, 223–28.

44 Hobsbawm, "Peasants and Politics."

45 Lista de los mozos que pertenecen a las haciendas Progreso y Cutierrez, 31 Jan. 1890, Ramo Agricultura, AMD. To underline his intent, General Avilés sent a copy of the list to the rural police with the same instructions.

46 Libro de copiados de notas del Juez de Agricultura de este pueblo, Diriomo 1890, no. 7, 25 Feb. 1890, Ramo Agricultura, AMD.

47 Juan S. Urtecho, Prefecto de Granada, al Juez de Agricultura de Diriomo, Granada, 4 Mar. 1890, Correspondencia Recibida, Ramo Agricultura, AMD.

48 In 1899 fourteen planters sent lists to Diriomo's juez de agricultura. Listas de Mozos Deudores 1899, Ramo Agricultura, AMD.

49 Entre Hijino Muños y Don Gral. Agustín Avilés: una demanda, 18 May 1882, Juzgado, Ramo Agricultura, AMD.

50 Entre José Esteban Sandoval y Marcelino Alguera: una demanda, 28 Apr. 1924, Juzgado, Ramo Agricultura, AMD. This case shows that after abolition debt peonage continued in Diriomo.

51 For an excellent analysis of the interrelationship between draft labor and debt peonage, see McCreery, "An Odious Feudalism."

52 Demanda verbal entre Sr. José Jesus Nororis y Don Feliz Castillo, 18 Apr. 1882, Juzgado, Ramo Agricultura, AMD.

53 Knight, "Mexican Peonage"; Katz, "Labor Conditions on Haciendas in Porfirian Mexico"; Gould, "El café, el trabajo y la comunidad indígena."

54 Calculated by author from a random sample of four thousand matrículas, Libros de Matrículas, 1876–1895, Ramo Agricultura, AMD. Because the complex and sometimes incomplete nature of judicial documentation impedes quantification, I organized cases into broad categories.

55 Calculated by author from a random sample of two hundred planters' declarations sent to Diriomo's *juez de agricultura* between 1890 and 1905. Listas de Mozos Deudores, Ramo Agricultura, AMD. In the absence of reliable statistics on wage rates, in particular how much money a typical family earned in a day, I use indirect indicators, that is, expenses peasants incurred, to support my argument about the low level of peasant indebtedness.

56 Calculated by author from Libros de Condenas, 1880–1905, Juzgado, Ramo Agricultura, AMD.

57 Alcalde Municipal de Diriomo al Jefe Político of Granada, 4 Feb. 1884, Correspondencia, Ramo Alcaldía Municipal, AMD.

58 Jefe Político de Granada al Alcalde Municipal de Diriomo, 24 Mar. 1884, Correspondencia Recibida, Ramo Alcaldía Municipal, AMD.

59 Calculated by author from Libros de Operarios, 1880–1905, and Libros de Condenas, 1880–1905, Ramo Agricultura, AMD. Benjamin Teplitz's figures for the arrest of fugitives in Managua (1897–1900) are considerably lower than in Granada. See "The Political and Economic Foundations of Modernization in Nicaragua," 200. The discrepancy probably lies primarily in the nature of the sources, and secondarily in differences between the regions. Teplitz used data published in *Memoria del Ministerio de Fomento 1899–1900*.

60 Patricia Alvarenga's excellent book *Cultura y ética de la violencia* helped me understand the nature of local policing. For discussions of the conundrum, see McCreery, *Rural Guatemala*, 281–88; Lindo Fuentes, *Weak Foundations*.

61 Entre Don General Terencia Sierra y Obrero Solomón Mayorga, una demanda, 22 Jan. 1906, Juzgado, Ramo Alcaldía Municipal, AMD.

62 For a complementary analysis of indebtedness and labor coercion in Venezuela, see Yarrington, *A Coffee Frontier*, 153–55.

63 Calculated from a sample of 550 court cases between 1880 and 1905. Juzgado, Ramo Agricultura, AMD.

64 Actas de la Junta Municipal, 2 Jan. 1887, Ramo Alcaldía Municipal, AMD.

65 Criminal por atentado contra la autoridad de los jefes de cantón, Bérnabe Marcia y Leónardo Pavón, 27 Aug. 1894, Juzgado Unico de lo Criminal, AMD. For similar cases, see 4 Mar. 1894, 18 Jan. 1897, and 5 Feb. 1899, Juzgado Unico de lo Criminal, AMD.

66 For the assassination of peasants in Diriomo's rural police, see Presidente y Comandante General de la República de Nicaragua, José Santos Zelaya al Alcalde Municipal de Diriomo, 17 July 1896, Correspondencia Recibida, Ramo Alcaldía Municipal, AMD. For cases involving destruction of property, see 13 Sept. 1886, 2 Jan. 1889, and 10 Mar. 1895, Juez Local de lo Criminal, AMD. For the murder of a planter, see Entre Marcelina Rodríguez y José Cano, 2 Dec. 1889, Juez Local de lo Criminal, AMD. For assaults against plantation personnel, see 4 Mar. 1894, 7 Feb. 1895, and 26 May 1895, Juez Local de lo Criminal, AMD.

67 Juez de Agricultura de Diriomo al General Juan Bodán, Jefe Político, Granada, 18 Nov. 1889, Correspondencia, Ramo Agricultura, AMD.

68 Alcalde Municipal de Diriomo al Prefect of Granada, 26 Dec. 1889, Correspondencia, Ramo Alcaldía Municipal, AMD.

69 "All the vecinos of this place should attend in order to register themselves, all without exception . . . It seems necessary to warn you of the urgency of this registration." Mayor de Plaza del Departamento a los Alcaldes Municipales del Departamento: Circular, 2 Jan. 1890, Correspondencia Recibida, Ramo Alcaldía Municipal, AMD.

70 Alcalde Municipal de Diriomo al Prefect of Granada, 4–7 Jan. 1890; Alcalde Municipal de Diriomo al Comandante de Armas de Granada, 4–7 Jan. 1890, Correspondencia, Ramo Alcaldía Municipal, AMD.

71 Criminal entre Don Celendino Borge, Don José Ana Morales, Don General Agustín Avilés . . . y Marcos Pavón, Eugenio Martínez . . . por levantamiento, 23–26 Jan. 1890, Juzgado Criminal de Diriomo, AMD.

72 Jefe Político de Granada al Alcalde Municipal de Diriomo, 18 Feb. 1890, Correspondencia Recibida, Ramo Alcaldía Municipal, AMD.

73 Juez de Agricultura de Diriomo al Juez de Agricultura de Managua, 16 Jan. 1899, also 24 and 29 Jan. 1899; 5 and 8 Feb. 1900; and 24 Dec. 1904, Telégrafos de Nicaragua, Colección de Telegramas Recibidas en la Alcaldía en el Año de 1899, 1900, 1904, AMD.

74 Sr. Comandante de Armas de Granada al Alcalde Municipal de Diriomo, 16 Apr. 1897, 4 Feb. 1899, and 16 Mar. 1903, Correspondencia Recibida, Jueces de Agricultura, AMD.

75 Gould, *To Die in This Way*, 26–38.

76 Juicios, 1876–1905, Ramo Agricultura, AMD.

77 Entre Mercedes Pérez y Don Alejandro Mejía, su liquidación, 7 Sept. 1880, Juicios, Ramo Agricultura, AMD.

78 Don Andrés Marcia a La Sra. Atanancia Antón, una demanda, 16 and 27 Feb. 1879, Juicios, Ramo Agricultura, AMD.

79 Ibid., 28 Feb. 1879.

80 Calculated by author from random sample of eight hundred cases. Juicios, 1876–1905, Ramo Agricultura, AMD.

81 Actas de la Junta Municipal, 16 Jan. 1899, Ramo Alcaldía Municipal, AMD.

82 Calculated by author from random sample of eight hundred cases. Juicios, 1876–1905, Ramo Agricultura, AMD.

83 Ibid.

84 Entre María Rugama y Don Julio Castillo, una demanda, 19 Oct. 1990, Juicios, Ramo Agricultura, AMD.

85 Entre Francisco Tardencilla y Don Alejandro Mejía, demanda por trabajo, 10 Mar. 1902, Juicios, Ramo Agricultura, AMD; oral histories of Pedro Pablo Cano, Di-

riomo, 1 Mar. 1991, Emilio Vásquez, Mombacho, Diriomo, 7 Feb. 1994, Leticia Salazar Castillo, 8 July 1995, and Orlando Salazar Castillo, Diriomo, 16 Aug. 1995.

86 For analysis of the social dynamics of the courtroom, see Wells and Joseph, *Summer of Discontent*, 14–17.

87 Stern, *Peru's Indian Peoples*, 114–37.

88 Entre Concepción Reyes y Don Joaquín Cuadra, una demanda de trabajo, 8 May 1900, Libro de Condenas, Ramo Agricultura, AMD.

89 Entre Senór Peña y Lorenzo Carcache, una demanda, 7 Jan. 1889, and Entre Sunción Suazo y Don Andrés Ayala, una demanda, 8 Apr. 1882, Juicios, Ramo Agricultura, AMD.

90 Entre Don Andrés Marcia y General Juan Bodán, una demanda, 8 May 1900, Libro de Condenas, Ramo Agricultura, AMD. For other disputes between planters, see 16 Jan. 1901 and 22 Dec. 1901, Juicios, Ramo Agricultura, AMD.

91 Juez de Agricultura de Diriomo al Juez de Distrito de Granada, 17 Oct. 1902, Juez de Agricultura, Correspondencia, AMD.

92 For analysis of the meanings of "race," see Wade, "Race, Nature and Culture."

93 Censo de la Población: Diriomo, Año 1883. 27–29 Mar. 1911, Correspondencia, Ramo Alcaldía Municipal, AMD.

94 Agustín Pasos, Jefe Político de Granada al Alcalde Municipal de Diriomo, 26 June 1885, Correspondencia Municipal, AMD.

95 Oral history with Noé Campos Carcache, Diriomo, Feb. 1991.

96 Partida 167, 18 Nov. 1875; Partida 1, Libro de Matrículas, 1889; Partida 399, 9 Dec. 1892; Matrícula 5, 4 Sept. 1902, Libros de Operarios, Ramo Agricultura, AMD.

97 In local oral history and memory, Alejandro Mejía, Diriomeño and owner of two coffee estates on Mombacho, was called "el indio rico," shortened to "el wico." Oral histories of Emilio Vásquez, Mombacho, Diriomo, 7 Feb. 1994, Leticia Salazar Castillo, 8 July 1995, and Orlando Salazar Castillo, Diriomo, 16 Aug. 1995.

98 Oral history with Gloria Tifer Figueroa, Diriomo, Feb. 1991.

99 For meanings of race and ethnicity, see Vincent, "The Structuring of Ethnicity"; B. Williams, "A Class Act"; Knight, "Racism, Revolution, and Indigenismo"; Escobar Ohmstede, *Historia de los pueblos indígenas de México*.

100 Censo, raza, profesion, Circular No. 4, Dirección General de Estadísticas, Managua, 18 May 1883, caja 184, leg. X5, Rama Estadísticas, AMPG. Julie Charlip kindly sent me a copy of this document. I greatly appreciate her generosity.

101 Wade, "Race, Nature and Culture," "La construcción de 'el negro' en América Latina," and *Race and Ethnicity*.

102 Jefe Político de Granada al Alcalde Municipal de Diriomo, 13 Dec. 1911, Corrspondencia Recibida, Ramo Alcaldía Municipal, AMD.

103 Oral histories with Doroteo Flores Pérez and Domingo Dávila, Jan. and July 1991, Carmen Ramírez Pérez, Jan. and July 1991, and Aug. 1992, Teófilo Cano, Jan. and July, 1991, Feb. 1995 and Aug. 1998, Diriomo.

104 Gramsci, *Prison Notebooks*.

105 Doña Carmen was given away at a very young age to one of the well-to-do families in Diriomo.

106 International coffee prices fell by 70 percent from 1929 to 1932. For time series on coffee prices and Nicaraguan production, see Dore, "La Producción Cafetalera Nicaragüense," 388–403.

107 Lista de Jornaleros, Francisco Salinas, 4 Jan. 1933; Lista de Jornaleros, Francisco Sandoval, 8 Feb. 1937; Lista de Jornaleros, Celendino Borge, hijo, 16 Mar. 1937, Ramo Agricultura, AMD; Libros de Matrículas de Fincas y Empresas Agrícolas e Industriales, Años 1929, 1930, and 1931, Diriomo, Ramo Agricultura, AMD.

108 For analyses of coffee production in the depression, see Torres Rivas, *Interpretación del desarrollo social centroamericano*, 79–102, 211–17; Bulmer-Thomas, *The Political Economy of Central America Since 1920*, 48–51. For transformation of rural labor into a commodity, see de Janvry, *The Agrarian Question and Reformism in Latin America*, 94–109; Polanyi, *The Great Transformation*, 71.

109 Libro de Contratos de Jornaleros, 1937, Ramo Alcaldía Municipal, AMD. Oral histories of Doroteo Flores Pérez, Diriomo, Jan. 1991, and Eusebio Mena López, Diriomo, July 1991.

110 Alcalde Municipal Francisco Carcache to Sr. Comandante de Policía, 22 Feb. 1930, Ramo Alcaldía Municipal, AMD.

111 Oral histories of Teófilo Cano, Diriomo, 13 July 1991, and Carmen Ramírez Pérez, Diriomo, 17 July 1991.

112 Polanyi, *The Great Transformation*, 47, 70.

113 Stern makes a similar point; see *Peru's Indian Peoples*, 157.

114 Mallon, *The Defense of Community*, 160–67, 334–48.

115 Cooper et al., *Confronting Historical Paradigms*, especially Cooper, "Africa and the World Economy," 84–201, and Roseberry, "Beyond the Agrarian Question in Latin America," 318–68; Stoler, *Capitalism and Confrontation*; Zeitlin, *The Civil Wars in Chile*.

116 Gould, *To Die in This Way*, 50–56.

117 Historical accounts include Byrd Simpson, *Many Mexicos*, 229–39; Klaren, *Modernization, Dislocation, and Aprismo*, 24–37; Martínez Peláez, *La patria del criollo*, 618–27. Influential novels include Icaza, *Huasipungo*; Traven, *March to the Montería*.

118 Bauer, "Rural Workers in Spanish America"; Polanyi, *The Great Transformation*.

119 Knight, "Mexican Peonage," 41–74. See also Knight, "Debt Bondage in Latin America."

120 Knight, "Mexican Peonage," 45.

121 Contributions to the debate include Loveman, "Critique of Arnold J. Bauer's 'Rural Workers in Spanish America'" and Bauer's "Reply"; Brass, "Unfree Labour and Capitalist Restructuring in the Agrarian Sector" and "The Latin American Enganche System" and the exchange between Brass and Laird W. Bergad in the *Journal of Latin American Studies* 16, no. 1 (1984): 143–56.

122 Bergad, *Coffee and the Growth of Agrarian Capitalism in Nineteenth-Century Puerto Rico*; Gonzales, *Plantation Agriculture*. For comparative essays, see Lal, Munro, and Beechert, *Plantation Workers*.

123 For Marxist interpretations of debt peonage and other forms of unfree labor, see Ramachandran, *Wage Labour and Unfreedom in Agriculture*; Miles, *Capitalism and Unfree Labour*.

124 For patronage and the capitalist state, see Graham, *Patronage and Politics in Nineteenth Century Brazil*, 1–7; Yarrington, *A Coffee Frontier*, 8–9. My point is not that patronage and capitalism cannot coexist, but that they did not in Nicaragua before the middle of the twentieth century.

125 Although Topik does not explicitly address the noncapitalist nature of the Central American coffee revolutions, overall my argument is consistent with his. See "Coffee Anyone?"

126 For accounts of modern-day debt peonage, see Le Breton, *Trapped*; Bales, *Disposable People*.

127 Report by Admiral Kimball, 12 Mar. 1910, National Archives, U.S. State Department, RG 59, 6369/811, cited in Gould, "El café, el trabajo y la comunidad indígena," 320.

128 Gould, *To Lead as Equals*, 85–181.

129 My interpretation draws on Gould, *To Lead as Equals*; Walter, *The Regime of Anastasio Somoza*; and my own research.

Chapter Seven   Patriarchy and Peonage

1 Judith Stacey calls the extension of patriarchal rights to peasant men in socialist China "democratic patriarchy" in *Patriarchy and Socialist Revolution in China*, 12. Although there are similarities between democratic patriarchy and what I call patriarchy from below, to my mind Stacey's term is an oxymoron.

2 For Mexican laws, see Arrom, *Women of Mexico City*, 55–96; for Argentine law, see Guy, "Lower-Class Families." For patriarchy and family relations, see Varley, "Women and the Home"; Guy, "Parents before Tribunals." For patriarchy and nation building, see Szurchman, *Order, Family and Community*, 190.

3 Varley, "Women and the Home."

4 Dore, "One Step Forward, Two Steps Back."

5 Nicaragua's constitution of 1858 suspended a man's rights of citizenship if he suborned his father's authority. Zúñiga Osorio, "Patria Potestad," 47. For implementation of laws, see Burns, *Patriarch and Folk*.

6 Ley de Agricultura, 1862.

7 Hobsbawm, "Inventing Traditions."

8 Libros de Operarios, 1879–1905, Ramo de Agricultura, AMD. See, for example, Contratos de Agricultura, 1905, no. 32, Jorge Cabrera compromete con Sr. Alejandro Mejía, Ramo Alcaldía Municipal, AMD.

9 Julio Telles contra Don Julio Castillo, 21 Mar. 1875, Demandas, Jueces de Agricultura, Ramo Agricultura, AMD.

10 Alejandro Mejía contra Tiburcio Rios, 30 Dec. 1885, Demandas, Jueces de Agricultura, Ramo Agricultura, AMD.

11 Joaquín Cuadra contra Mercedes Ayala, 8 May 1900, Libro de Condenas, Jueces de Agricultura, Ramo Agricultura, AMD.

12 Sr. Agapito Fernández, una demanda, 1886, Jueces de Agricultura, Ramo Agricultura, AMD.

13 Asunto Don José Antonio Alemán, una demanda, 1905; Don General Francisco Sierra, una demanda, 1904; Jueces de Agricultura, Ramo Agricultura, AMD.

14 Entre Casimiro Ramírez y Don Alejandro Mejía, 12 Feb. 1899, Juez de Agricultura, Ramo Agricultura, AMD.

15 Demanda verbal entre José Pavon y General Agustín Avilés, 1881, Juez de Agricultura, Libro de Condenas, AMD.

16 28 Mar. 1889, Correspondencia, Ramo Alcaldía Municipal, AMD.

17 Oral histories with Domingo Dávila and Isabel Rivera, Vera Cruz, Diriomo, 23 July 1995.

18 Oral histories with Gloria Tifer Figueroa and Cristina Tifer, Diriomo, 3 Aug. 1996.

19 Luis Cano contra Don Andrés Marcia, Libro de Condenas, 1894, Juez de Agricultura, Ramo de Agricultura, AMD.

20 Matrícula 346, 8 Jan. 1905, Operarios de los Señores Eisenstick y Bahlcke, Hacienda Alemania, Ramo Alcaldía Municipal, AMD.

21 Matrícula 287, 4 Feb. 1905, Operarios de los Señores Eisenstick y Bahlcke, Hacienda Alemania, Ramo Alcaldía Municipal, AMD.

22 "Los hacendados o empresarios tiene la obligación de celar y impedir que en su finca o labor se cometan desordenes y para ello tiene derecho de usar de todos los medios indespensables y disponibles . . ." Art. 15, Ley de Agricultura, 1862.

23 8 May 1900, Libro de Condenas, Juez de Agricultura, Ramo de Agricultura, AMD.

24 Oral histories with Néstor Sánchez, Feb. 1991, Teófilo Cano, Feb. 1991, July 1993, Aug. 1995, July 1998, Carmen Ramírez Pérez, Aug. 1993, Leticia Salazar Castillo, Jan. July 1998, Orlando Salazar Castillo, Jan. 1998, Emilio Vásquez, Jan. 1998, Diriomo.

25 Oral histories with Isabel Rivera and Domingo Dávila, July 1991 and Aug. 1994, Vera Cruz, Diriomo.

26 Demanda verbal entre Sr. Carlos Castillo y Don Andrés Marcia, 5 Jan. 1885, Ramo de Agricultura, AMD.

27 Ley de Trabajo, Art. 1, *La Gaceta* (Managua), 3 Oct. 1901.

28 The following is the labor contract of a female-headed household: "The widow Josefa Cano, jointly with her five children . . . swears to Don Agustín Avilés to serve on his haciendas Progreso or Cutierres on the Mombacho Volcano. The family will work as coffee pickers and be paid one 'real' for every 6 cartons of cof-

fee cherries [they pick], plus two meals per day. They are obligated to work as soon as they are needed, to remain working for the duration of the harvest and beyond until they have paid off their debt with labor. [Cano] received four pesos in advance. She swears to submit herself and her children to all of the practices and customs established by the patrón." Partida no. 325, Lista de Operarios 1879, Ramo Alcaldia Municipal, AMD.

29 Matrícula 573, 6 Jan. 1888, Libro de Operarios, Ramo Alcaldía Municipal, AMD.

30 Matrícula 357, 28 July 1879, Operarios de Alejandro Mejía, Libro de Operarios Comprometidos, Ramo Alcaldía Municipal, AMD.

31 Empadronamiento de Operarios, 14 Dec. 1896, Juez de Agricultura, Ramo Agricultura, AMD.

32 Margarita Aguilar contra Don Vicente Cuadra, 5 Feb. 1888, Juez de Agricultura, Rama Agricultura, AMD.

33 Benería and Roldán, *Crossroads of Class*, 1–16.

34 Estimate calculated by author from Libros de Operarios, 1881–1897, Ramo Alcaldía Municipal, AMD.

35 "Vicenta López lo comprometió su esposo Fernando Acevedo con 13 pesos deudando para cortar café a 2 medios por el real, cosecha próxima," 1882, Libro de Operarios Comprometidos, Operarios de Alejandro Mejía, Ramo Alcaldía Municipal AMD.

36 Oral history with Domingo Dávila, Vera Cruz, Diriomo, July 1991.

37 Oral history with Carmen Ramírez Pérez, Diriomo, Aug. 1993.

38 Besse, *Restructuring Patriarchy*; Vaughan, "Modernizing Patriarchy" and *Cultural Politics in Revolution*.

39 Polanyi, *The Great Transformation*, 45–58. For an analysis of the ways landlords in the highlands of Ecuador mastered the peasantry through *concertaje* (tied labor similar to debt peonage in Diriomo), see Guerrero, *La Semántica de la dominación*.

40 Richard Graham argues that patronage was an aspect of Brazilian capitalism; see *Patronage and Politics*.

Conclusion

1 Bauer, "Rural Workers in Spanish America."

2 Knight, "Mexican Peonage."

3 Quote from David McCreery, who makes a similar argument for Guatemala, *Rural Guatemala*, 223–28.

4 Polanyi, *The Great Transformation*, 73–80.

5 Brenner, "The Social Basis of Economic Development."

6 James C. Scott, *Weapons of the Weak*.

7 Gould, *To Die in This Way*; Charlip, *Cultivating Coffee*.

8 Wheelock, *Imperialismo y dictadura*; Vargas, *La revolución que inició el progreso*.

9 Charlip, *Cultivating Coffee*, 148.

10 Stern, *Secret History*, 19–20.

11 Comaroff, "Of Totemism and Ethnicity."

12 Vincent, *Structuring of Ethnicity*, 377.

13 27–29 Mar. 1911, Correspondencia, Ramo Alcaldía Municipal, AMD.

Epilogue

1 In "Ruling Memory," Anne Norton writes, "Nationalist movements are born with the knowledge of history as contested terrain, they recognize the writing of history and the constitution of memory as means to political power" (459).

2 Burke, *Reflections on the Revolution in France*, 99, cited in ibid.

3 Important Sandinista documents are "Programa Sandinista" (1969), "Dirección Nacional: Plataforma General" (1977), "FSLN, Sandinismo no es Democratismo" (1980), reprinted in Gilbert and Block, *Sandinismo*. See also Núñez Soto, *Transición y lucha*.

4 For an interesting analysis, see Robinson, "The New Right."

5 CIERA, *Marco jurídico de la reforma agraria en Nicaragua, 1979-1989*, 58–89.

6 MICOIN, *Sistemas de Comercialización*, vol. 1, D 1–28; Utting, *Economic Adjustment under the Sandinistas* and *Economic Reform*; Spoor, *State and Domestic Agricultural Markets*; Dore, "La Respuesta Campesina"; Biondi-Morra, *Revolución y política alimentaria*.

7 For elaboration of this argument, see Dore and Weeks, *The Red and the Black*. Portions of this chapter appear in different form in *The Red and the Black*.

8 For analysis of land distribution and landlessness before the Sandinista Revolution, see Weeks, *The Economies of Central America*, chap. 5.

9 Ibid., 113; Deere, Marchetti, and Reinhardt, "The Peasantry and the Development of Sandinista Agrarian Policy"; Deere, "Agrarian Reform."

10 Oral histories with Teófilo Cano, July 1998, Luis Salazar, Pedro Pablo Cano, Francisco Fuentes Cano, Zénon Pérez Malque, Leonora Cruz, July 1995, Francisco Campos Carcache and Doroteo Flores Pérez, July 1998, Diriomo. This interpretation is at variance with that developed by Vilas, *The Sandinista Revolution*, 62–65.

11 "Programa Sandinista" (1969) and "Dirección Nacional: Plataforma General" (1977), reprinted in Gilbert and Block, *Sandinismo: Key Documents*.

12 Enríquez, *Harvesting Change*, 121–46.

13 *Nicaraguan Perspectives*, no. 19 (fall–winter 1990): 3.

14 Asignación, Jaime Wheelock Róman, Ministro de Desarrollo Agropecuario y Reforma Agraria en uso de las facultades . . . resuelve: asignar un predio rústico a los siguientes compañeros . . . en el Municipio Diriomo, 9 July 1985, Departamento de Granada, AMD.

15 *Nicaraguan Perspectives*, no. 19 (fall–winter 1990): 3.

16 Robinson, *Transnational Conflicts*; de Groot and Spoor, *Ajuste Estructural y economia campesina*; Vilas, *Between Earthquakes and Volcanos*.

Glossary

adelanto cash advance on wages, usually repaid with labor

agricultor rich peasant or owner of medium property

aguardiente liquor, fermented sugar cane

alcade municipal, alcalde constitucional municipal mayor

alcalde indígena, alcalde natural, alcalde de vara leader of Indian community

alcaldía municipal municipal council

alguacil official of the Indian community

ayuda generic term for assistance planters gave peons

caballería the measure of large land areas; in original usage, the amount of land a horseman (a *caballero*) could traverse in one day; in Nicaragua, 105 acres

cabildo governing council, used for both municipal and Indian council

caja de comunidad funds belonging to Indian community

campesino peasant

caña de construcción type of bamboo used for buildings

canon de ley the fee the comunidad indígena, and later the municipality, charged for use of the community's corporate landholding

carbuya sisal

caserío rural hamlet

casta term applied in colonial-era and nineteenth-century Latin America to connote mixed-race peoples

casta indígena social strata of Indians

chaguite hay, animal fodder

choza rustic cottage

cofradía Indian association to administer common property, especially cattle, later with mixed Indian and ladino members

comandante top military leader, general

comarca political subdivision, rural hamlet

común del pueblo Indian common lands

comunero member of Indian community

comunidad indígena Indian community

corregidores colonial officials

denuncia land claim

derecho de posesión right of possession

desquitar to repay cash advances with labor

Diriomeña female inhabitant of Diriomo

Diriomeño male inhabitant of Diriomo

dueños/as owners

ejidos common lands administered by municipality

ejidos del común common lands administered by Indian community

empeñarse to pay off debt with labor, literally "to pawn labor"

encomenderos/as colonial Spanish settlers vested with authority over Indians

fanega grain measure, about 1.5 bushels

finca landed estate

FSLN Frente Sandinista de Liberación Nacional

guaro alcoholic beverage produced from sugar or grain

hacendado large land owner

hacienda large landed estate

hijos/as naturales illegitimate children

hombres de bien men of local elite

hombría de bien patriarchal generosity, manliness

huerta vegetable plot

indios principales senior males in Indian community; implies leadership role *jefe político* departmental or regional governor

jornalero poor male peasant who works for others, literally "day laborer"

juez de agricultura rural magistrate

junta municipal municipal council, municipal government

juzgado tribunal

ladino/a non-Indian, used in Nicaragua and the rest of Central America to indicate people broadly defined as not Indian

libreta de trabajadores workbook or passbook used to record peasants' labor on coffee fincas

limosna charity or alms

llaveros turnkey, keeper of the keys

mandón labor recruiter in Indian pueblos in colonial era

manzana measure of land: 1 manzana = 1.72 acres, or 0.7 hectares

matrícula labor contract

mayordomo foreman

medio a dry measure, a "boxful"

mejora(s) improvement(s) to land

mestizaje assimilation or race mixing; frequently implies social rather than biological processes

mestizo/a person of mixed Indian-Spanish descent

milpa subsistence plot of corn and beans

molendera grinder of corn

monte uncleared land

mozo peon, agricultural laborer

mulatto/a person of mixed Indian-African descent

municipalidad municipality

operario agricultural laborer

parcela small plot of land

parcelero subsistence producer

pasarle alimentos child support, literally to supply food *patria potestad* legal term for fathers' authority over daughters and sons in their household, later expanded to parents' authority

patrón/a boss, employer

peon agricultural laborer, frequently indebted

personería jurídica legal capacity

Plan de Arbitrios municipal taxes; in Diriomo included the municipality's annual plan

platanal banana orchard

postrera second annual harvest of beans and corn

potestad marital husbands' authority over the person and property of their wife

pueblo town, township

pueblo de indios Indian township

quebrador del trabajo lawbreaker

rastrojo field cleared for cultivation

raza term used in colonial-era and nineteenth-century Latin America to connote racial or ethnic status

real(es) coins, measure of money that fluctuated widely

repartimiento de mercancías forced sale of products in colonial era

sirvienta servant

socorro succor, generic term for planters' assistance to peons

terrateniente landowner, landlord; the word for "large planter" used in Spanish America throughout the colonial era and into the twentieth century, originally capturing the nature of the landed relationship between Crown and grantee: that landlords were tenants of the Crown

tierras baldías unclaimed land under state domain

tierras comunales common lands

trabajo al empeño working to repay debts

una solvencia paper demonstrating that a laborer is not indebted to a planter

usos y costumbres customs and traditions

usufruct use rights to land

zambo/a person of part-African descent

Bibliography

Archival Sources

Archivo General de Centro América, Guatemala City, Guatemala (AGCA)
Archivo General de Indias, Sevilla, Spain (AGI)
Archivo General de la Nación, Managua, Nicaragua (AGN)
Archivo Municipal de Diriomo, Nicaragua (AMD)
Archivo Municipal de la Prefectura de Granada, Nicaragua (AMPG)
Archivo Nacional de Nicaragua (ANN)

Government Documents and Reports

"El Censo Cafetalero de 1909/10." *Boletín de Estadística de la República de Nicaragua* 4, nos. 14–15 (1 Mar. 1911): 642–72.

Censo general de la República. Managua: Tipografía y Encuadernación Nacional, 1920.

Código Civil de la Republica de Nicaragua, 1867. Managua: Imprenta El Centro-Americano, 1871.

Decreto legislativo sobre comunidades indígenas y terrenos ejidales. Managua: República de Nicaragua, Tipografía Nacional, 1906.

Informe del Jefe Político de Managua, Memorias del Ministerio de Fomento, 1904. Managua: N.p., 1905.

Ministerio de Comercio Interior. *Sistemas de Comercialización: Productos Básicos de Consumo Popular*, 5 vols. Managua: MICOIN, 1983, vol. I.

Periodicals and Newspapers

El Comercio (Managua, 1899, 1902, 1904, 1908, 1913, 1919)
El Conservador (Granada, 1916)
El Correo de Nicaragua (Granada, 1914)
Diario de Granada (Granada, 1907–1909)
El Diario Nicaragüense (Granada, 1911–1913)
El Eco Liberal (Managua, 1909)
La Gaceta (Managua, 1894, 1898, 1901)

El Independiente (León, 1899)
El Periódico (Granada, 1911–1912)

Oral History Interviews Cited

Aguirre, Virgilio. Diriomo, July 1998.
Campos Carcache, Francisco. Diriomo, July 1998.
Campos Carcache, Noé. Diriomo, Feb. 1991.
Cano, Pedro Pablo. Diriomo, Mar. 1991, July 1995.
Cano, Teófilo. Vera Cruz, Diriomo, Jan., Feb., July 1991, July 1993, Feb. and Aug. 1995, July and Aug. 1998.
Cruz, Leonora. Diriomo, July 1995.
Dávila, Domingo. Vera Cruz, Diriomo, Jan., Feb., July 1991, July 1995.
Flores Pérez, Doroteo. Diriomo, Jan. and July 1991.
Fuentes Cano, Francisco. Diriomo, July 1995.
Mena López, Eusebio. Diriomo, July 1991.
Pérez Malque, Zénon. Diriomo, July 1995.
Ramírez Pérez, Carmen. Diriomo, Jan. and July 1991, Aug. 1992, Aug. 1993.
Rivera, Isabel. Vera Cruz, Diriomo, Feb. and July 1991, Aug. 1994, July 1995.
Rodríguez Ramírez, Enrique. Diriomo, July 1998.
Salazar, Luis. Diriomo, July 1995.
Salazar Castillo, Leticia. Diriomo, 8 July 1995, Jan. and July 1998.
Salazar Castillo, Orlando. Diriomo, Aug. 1995, Jan. and July 1998.
Sánchez, Néstor. Diriomo, Feb. 1991.
Tifer, Cristina. Diriomo, Aug. 1996.
Tifer Figueroa, Gloria. Diriomo, Feb. 1991, Aug. 1996.
Vasconcelos, José Esteban. Diriomo, July 1998.
Vásquez, Emilio. Mombacho, Diriomo, Feb. 1994, Jan. 1998.

Published Sources

Acuña Ortega, Víctor Hugo, and Iván Molina Jiménez. *El desarrollo económico y social de Costa Rica: De la colonia a la crisis de 1930*. San José, Costa Rica: Alma Mater, 1986.

———. *Historia económica y social de Costa Rica, 1750–1930*. San José, Costa Rica: Editorial Porvenir, 1991.

Adams, Richard N. "Ethnic Images and Strategies in 1944." In *Guatemalan Indians and the State*, ed. Carol Smith, 13–31. Austin: University of Texas Press, 1990.

Alonso, Ana María. "The Politics of Space, Time and Substance: State Formation, Nationalism and Ethnicity." *Annual Review of Anthropology* 23 (1994): 379–406.

Althusser, Louis, and Etienne Balibar. *Reading Capital*. Trans. Ben Brewster. London: New Left Books, 1970.

Alvarenga, Patricia. *Cultura y etica de la violencia: El Salvador 1880–1932*. San José, Costa Rica: Editorial Universitaria Centroamericana-EDUCA, 1996.

Anderson, Perry. *Arguments within English Marxism*. London: Verso, 1980.

Archer, Léonie, ed. *Slavery and Other Forms of Unfree Labour*. London: Routledge, 1988.

Arias, Arturo. "Changing Indian Identity: Guatemala's Violent Transition to Modernity." In *Guatemalan Indians and the State, 1540–1988*, ed. Carol A. Smith, 230–57. Austin: University of Texas Press, 1990.

Arrom, Silvia Marina. "Changes in Mexican Family Law in the Nineteenth Century: The Civil Codes of 1870 and 1884." *Journal of Family History* 10, no. 3 (1985): 305–17.

————. *The Women of Mexico City, 1790–1857*. Stanford: Stanford University Press, 1985.

Aston, T. H., and C. H. E. Philpin, eds. *The Brenner Debate*. Cambridge, England: Cambridge University Press, 1985.

Ayón, Tomás. *Historia de Nicaragua desde los tiempos más remotos hasta el año de 1852*. 3 vols. Granada: Tipografía de "El Centro-Americano," 1882.

Bales, Kevin. *Disposable People*. Berkeley: University of California Press, 1999.

Banaji, Jairus. "Modes of Production in a Materialist Conception of History." *Capital and Class* 3 (1977): 1–44.

Barahona, Amaru. *Estudio sobre la historia de Nicaragua: Del auge cafetalero al triunfo de la revolución*. Managua: Instituto Nacional de Investigaciones y Estudios Socioeconómicos, 1989.

————. "Intervención extranjera y dictadura." In *Economía y Sociedad en la Construcción del Estado en Nicaragua*, ed. Alberto Lanuza, Amaru Barahona, and Amalia Chamorro, 207–25. San José, Costa Rica: ICAP, 1983.

Bauer, Arnold J. *Chilean Rural Society from the Spanish Conquest to 1930*. Cambridge, England: Cambridge University Press, 1975.

————. "Reply." *Hispanic American Historical Review* 59 (1979): 478–89.

————. "Rural Workers in Spanish America: Problems of Peonage and Oppression." *Hispanic American Historical Review* 59 (1979): 34–63.

Baumeister, Eduardo. *Estructura y reforma agraria en Nicaragua, 1979–1989*. Managua: Centro de Estudios para el Desarrollo Rural, 1998.

————. "The Structure of Nicaraguan Agriculture and the Sandinista Agrarian Reform." In *Nicaragua: A Revolution under Siege*, ed. Richard Harris and Carlos M. Vilas, 10–35. London: Zed Press, 1985.

Benería, Lourdes, and Martha Roldán. *The Crossroads of Class and Gender: Industrial Homework, Subcontracting and Household Dynamics in Mexico City*. Chicago: University of Chicago Press, 1987.

Bennett, Judy. "Feminism and History." *Gender and History* 1, no. 3 (autumn 1989): 251–72.

Bergad, Laird W. *Coffee and the Growth of Agrarian Capitalism in Nineteenth-Century Puerto Rico*. Princeton, N.J.: Princeton University Press, 1983.

Berman, Marshall. *All That Is Solid Melts into Air: The Experience of Modernity*. New York: Penguin, 1982.

Bermann, Karl. *Under the Big Stick: Nicaragua and the United States Since 1848*. Boston: South End Press, 1986.

Besse, Susan. *Restructuring Patriarchy: The Modernization of Gender Inequality in Brazil, 1914–1940*. Chapel Hill: University of North Carolina Press, 1996.

Biondi-Morra, Brizio N. *Revolución y política alimentaria: Un análisis crítico de Nicaragua*. Mexico City: Siglo XXI, 1990.

Booth, John A. *The End and the Beginning: The Nicaraguan Revolution*. Boulder, Colo.: Westview Press, 1985.

Brass, Tom. "The Latin American Enganche System: Some Revisionist Reinterpretations Revisited." *Slavery and Abolition* 11, no. 1 (1990): 74–103.

———. "Unfree Labour and Capitalist Restructuring in the Agrarian Sector: Peru and India." *Journal of Peasant Studies* 14, no. 4 (1986): 50–77.

Brenner, Robert. "Agrarian Class Structure and Economic Development in Pre-Industrial Europe." *Past and Present* 70 (1976): 3–79.

———. "The Origins of Capitalist Development: A Critique of Neo-Smithian Marxism." *New Left Review* 104 (July–Aug. 1977): 25–92.

———. "The Social Basis of Economic Development." In *Analytical Marxism*, ed. John Roemer, 23–53. Cambridge, England: Cambridge University Press, 1986.

Buitrago, Edgardo. "El Municipio en Nicaragua." Unpublished ms. Aug. 1987.

Bulmer-Thomas, Victor. *The Political Economy of Central America Since 1920*. Cambridge, England: Cambridge University Press, 1987.

Burke, Edmund. *Reflections on the Revolution in France*. Indianapolis: Bobbs-Merrill, 1955.

Burns, E. Bradford. *Patriarch and Folk: The Emergence of Nicaragua, 1789–1858*. Cambridge, Mass.: Harvard University Press, 1991.

Byam, George. *Wild Life in the Interior of Central America*. London: Parker, 1849.

Byrd Simpson, Lesley. *Many Mexicos*. Berkeley: University of California Press, 1952.

Byres, Terence J. *Capitalism from Above and Capitalism from Below: An Essay in Comparative Political Economy*. Basingstoke, England: Macmillan, 1996.

Canning, Kathleen, and Sonya Rose, eds. *Gender, Citizenship and Subjectivities: A Theoretical Introduction*. Oxford: Blackwell, 2002.

Cardoso, Ciro F. S., and Héctor Pérez Brignoli. *Centro América y la economía occidental (1520–1930)*. San José: Universidad de la Costa Rica, 1977.

———. *Historia económica de América Latina: Economías de exportación y desarrollo capitalista*, vol. 2. Barcelona: Editorial Crítica, 1979.

Carmagnani, Marcello. *Estado y Sociedad en América Latina 1850–1930*. Barcelona: Editorial Crítica/Grijalbo, 1984.

Casanova Fuertes, Rafael. "Hacia una nueva valoración de las luchas políticas del periodo de la anarquía: El caso de los conflictos de 1845–1849." In *Encuentros con la historia*, ed. Margarita Vannini, 249–66. Managua: Instituto de Historia de Nicaragua, 1995.

———. "¿Heroes o Bandidos? Los Problemas de Interpretación de los Conflictos Políticos y Sociales entre 1845–1849 en Nicaragua." *Revista de Historia* (Nicaragua), no. 2 (1992–93): 13–26.

———. "Orden o anarquía: Los intentos de regulación proestatal en Nicaragua. Decada de 1840." In *Nicaragua en busca de su identidad*, ed. Frances Kinloch Tijerino, 277–94. Managua: Instituto de Historia de Nicaragua, 1995.

Caulfield, Sueann. *In Defense of Honor: Sexual Morality, Modernity, and Nation in Early-Twentieth Century Brazil*. Durham, N.C.: Duke University Press, 2000.

Centro de Investigación y Estudios de la Reforma Agraria. *Marco Jurídico de la Reforma Agraria en Nicaragua, 1979–1989*. Managua: CIERA, 1989.

———. *La Reforma Agraria en Nicaragua 1979–1989: Cifras y referencias documentales*. 9 vols. Managua: CIERA, 1989.

Chant, Sylvia. *Women and Survival in Mexican Cities: Perspectives on Gender, Labour Markets and Low Income Households*. Manchester, England: Manchester University Press, 1991.

———. *Women-Headed Households: Diversity and Dynamics in the Developing World*. Basingstoke, England: Macmillan, 1997.

Charlip, Julie A. *Cultivating Coffee: The Farmers of Carazo, Nicaragua, 1880–1930*. Athens: Ohio University Press, 2003.

Chassen-Lopez, Francine R. "'Cheaper Than Machines': Women and Agriculture in Porfirian Oaxaca, 1880–1911." In *Women of the Mexican Countryside, 1850–1990: Creating Spaces, Shaping Transitions*, ed. Heather Fowler-Salamini and Mary Kay Vaughan, 27–50. Tucson: University of Arizona Press, 1994.

Chayanov, A. V. *The Theory of Peasant Economy*. Manchester, England: Manchester University Press, 1966.

Clarence-Smith, William Gervase, and Steven Topik, eds. *The Global Coffee Economy in Africa, Asia, and Latin America, 1500–1989*. Cambridge, England: Cambridge University Press, 2003.

Comaroff, John. "Of Totemism and Ethnicity: Consciousness, Practice and the Signs of Inequality." *Ethnos*, no. 52 (1987): 301–23.

Connell, R. W. "The State, Gender and Sexual Politics: Theory and Appraisal." In *Power/Gender: Social Relations in Theory and Practice*, ed. H. Lorraine Radtke and Henderikus J. Stam, 136–73. London: Sage, 1994.

Cooper, Frederick. "Africa and the World Economy." In *Confronting Historical Paradigms: Peasants, Labor and the Capitalist World System in Africa and Latin America*, ed. Frederick Cooper, Allen Isaacman, Florencia Mallon, William Roseberry, and Steve Stern, 84–201. Madison: University of Wisconsin Press, 1993.

———. *From Slaves to Squatters: Plantation Labor and Agriculture in Zanzibar and Coastal Kenya, 1890–1925*. New Haven: Yale University Press, 1980.

Cooper, Frederick, Allen Isaacman, Florencia Mallon, William Roseberry, and Steve Stern, eds. *Confronting Historical Paradigms: Peasants, Labor and the Capitalist World System in Africa and Latin America*. Madison: University of Wisconsin Press, 1993.

Cooper, Frederick, and Ann Laura Stoler, eds. *Tensions of Empire: Colonial Cultures in a Bourgeois World*. Berkeley: University of California Press, 1997.

Coronel Urtecho, José. *Reflexiones sobre la Historia de Nicaragua alrededor de la Independencia*. León: Hospital San Juan de Dios, 1962.

Corrigan, Philip, and Derek Sayer. *The Great Arch: English State Formation as Cultural Revolution*. Oxford: Basil Blackwell, 1985.

Cuadra Downing, Orlando. *Bernabé Somoza (1815–1849): Vida y Muerte de un Hombre de Acción*. Managua: Imprenta Nacional, 1970.

Cubitt, Tessa, and Helen Greenslade. "Public and Private Spheres: The End of Dichotomy." In *Gender Politics in Latin America: Debates in Theory and Practice*, ed. Elizabeth Dore, 52–64. New York: Monthly Review Press, 1997.

Dean, Warren. *Rio Claro: A Brazilian Plantation System, 1820–1920*. Stanford: Stanford University Press, 1976.

Deere, Carmen Diana. "Agrarian Reform, Peasant Participation, and the Organization of Production in the Transition to Socialism." In *Transition and Development: Problems of Third World Socialism*, ed. Richard R. Fagen, Carmen Diana Deere, and José Luis Coraggio, 97–142. New York: Monthly Review Press/Center for the Study of the Americas, 1986.

———. *Household and Class Relations: Peasants and Landlords in Northern Peru*. Berkeley: University of California Press, 1990.

Deere, Carmen Diana, and Magdalena León. *Empowering Women: Land and Property Rights in Latin America*. Pittsburgh: University of Pittsburgh Press, 2001.

———. "Liberalism and Married Women's Property in Nineteenth-Century Latin America." *Hispanic American Historical Review* 85, no. 4 (2005): 627–78.

———, eds. *Rural Women and State Policy: Feminist Perspectives on Latin American Agricultural Development*. Boulder, Colo.: Westview Press, 1987.

Deere, Carmen Diana, Peter Marchetti, and Nola Reinhardt. "The Peasantry and the Development of Sandinista Agrarian Policy, 1979–1984." *Latin American Research Review* 20, no. 3 (1985): 75–109.

De Groot, Jan P. "Reforma Agraria en Nicaragua: Una actualización." In *Ajuste Estructural y Economía Campesina: Nicaragua, El Salvador, Centroamérica*, ed. Jan P. de Groot and Max Spoor, 106–8, tables 1 and 2. Managua: Escuela de Economía Agrícola (ESECA-UNAN), 1994.

De Groot, Jan P., and Max Spoor, eds. *Ajuste Estructural y Economía Campesina: Nicaragua, El Salvador, Centroamérica*. Managua: Escuela de Economía Agrícola (ESECA-UNAN), 1994.

de Janvry, Alain. *The Agrarian Question and Reformism in Latin America*. Baltimore: Johns Hopkins University Press, 1981.

de la Cadena, Marisol. *Indigenous Mestizos: The Politics of Race and Culture in Cuzco, Peru, 1919–1991.* Durham, N.C.: Duke University Press, 2000.

Dore, Elizabeth. "The Holy Family: Imagined Households in Latin American History." In *Gender Politics: Debates in Theory and Practice*, ed. Elizabeth Dore, 101–17. New York: Monthly Review Press, 1997.

———. "Introduction: Controversies in Gender Politics." In *Gender Politics: Debates in Theory and Practice*, ed. Elizabeth Dore, 9–18. New York: Monthly Review Press, 1997.

———. "Nicaragua: The Experience of the Mixed Economy." In *Latin American Political Economy: Financial Crisis and Political Change*, ed. Jonathan Hartlyn, 319–50. Boulder, Colo.: Westview Press, 1986.

———. "One Step Forward, Two Steps Back: Gender and the State in the Long Nineteenth Century." In *The Hidden Histories of Gender and the State in Latin America*, ed. Elizabeth Dore and Maxine Molyneux, 3–32. Durham, N.C.: Duke University Press, 2000.

———. "Patriarchy and Private Property in Nicaragua." In *Patriarchy and Economic Development*, ed. Valentine M. Moghadam, 56–79. Oxford: Clarendon Press, 1996.

———. "Patriarchy from Above, Patriarchy from Below: Debt Peonage on Nicaraguan Coffee Estates, 1860–1930." In *The Global Coffee Economy in Africa, Asia, and Latin America, 1500–1989*, ed. William Gervase Clarence-Smith and Steven Topik, 209–35. Cambridge, England: Cambridge University Press, 2003.

———. "La Producción Cafetalera Nicaraguense, 1860–1960: Transformaciones Estructurales." In *Tierra, café y sociedad: Ensayos sobre la historia agraria centroamericana*, ed. Héctor Pérez Brignoli and Mario Samper, 377–436. San José, Costa Rica: Facultad Latinoamericano de Ciencias Sociales (FLACSO), 1994.

———. "La Respuesta Campesina a las Políticas Agrarias y Comerciales en Nicaragua: 1979–1988." *Estudios Sociales Centroamericanos* 49 (Jan.–Apr. 1989): 25–43.

———. "The Somozas and the Legacy of Patriarchalism in Nicaragua: Diriomo, 1930–1990." Unpublished ms. 2005.

———. "Understanding Third World Capitalism." In *Anti-Capitalism: A Marxist Introduction*, ed. Alfredo Saad Fihlo, 164–75. London: Pluto Press, 2002.

———, ed. *Gender Politics in Latin America: Debates in Theory and Practice.* New York: Monthly Review Press, 1997.

Dore, Elizabeth, and Maxine Molyneux, eds. *The Hidden Histories of Gender and the State in Latin America.* Durham, N.C.: Duke University Press, 2000.

Dore, Elizabeth, and John Weeks. *The Red and the Black: The Sandinistas and the Nicaraguan Revolution.* Research Paper 28, University of London, Institute of Latin American Studies, 1992.

Dunkerley, James. *Power in the Isthmus: A Political History of Modern Central America.* London: Verso, 1988.

Edelman, Marc. "Don Chico y el Diablo: Dimensiones de Etnia, Clase y Genero en las Narrativas Campesinas Guanacastecas del Siglo XX." In *El Paso del Cometa: Es-*

tado, política social y culturas populares en Costa Rica (1800–1950), ed. Steven Palmer and Iván Molina Jiménez, 105–44. San José, Costa Rica: Editorial Porvenir, 1994.

Eisenstein, Zillah R., ed. *Capitalist Patriarchy and the Case for Socialist Feminism*. New York: Monthly Review Press, 1979.

Engels, Frederick. *The Origin of the Family, Private Property and the State*. New York: Lawrence and Wishart, 1972.

Enríquez, Laura J. *Harvesting Change: Labor and Agrarian Reform in Nicaragua, 1979–1990*. Chapel Hill: University of North Carolina Press, 1991.

Escobar Ohmstede, Antonio. *Historia de los pueblos indígenas de México: Las huastecas, 1750–1900*. Mexico City: CIESAS, 1998.

Escobar Ohmstede, Antonio, Romana Falcón, and Raymond Buve, eds. *Pueblos, comunidades y municipios frente a los proyectos modernizadores en América Latina, siglo XIX*. San Luis Potosí, Mexico: El Colegio de San Luis and Centro de Estudios y Documentación Latinoamericanos (CEDLA), 2002.

Etienne, Mona, and Eleanor Leacock, eds. *Women and Colonization: Anthropological Perspectives*. New York: Praeger, 1980.

Fagan, Richard, Carmen Diana Deere, and José Luis Coraggio, eds. *Transition and Development: Problems of Third World Socialism*. New York: Monthly Review Press, 1986.

Fernández, Ilva. "Nicaragua: Estructura Económica, Social y Política del Régimen de Zelaya." Tesis de Licenciatura, Escuela de Sociología, Universidad Centralamericana, Managua, 1978.

Field, Les W. *The Grimace of Macho Raton: Artisans, Identity and Nation in Late-Twentieth-Century Western Nicaragua*. Durham, N.C.: Duke University Press, 1999.

———. "Who Are the Indians? Reconceptualizing Indigenous Identity, Resistance and the Role of Social Science in Latin America." *Latin American Research Review* 29, no. 3 (1994): 237–48.

Findlay, Eileen. *Imposing Decency: The Politics of Sexuality and Race in Puerto Rico, 1870–1920*. Durham, N.C.: Duke University Press, 1999.

Fine, Ben, and Lawrence Harris. *Re-Reading Capital*. London: Macmillan, 1979.

Fine, Ben, and Alfredo Saad Fihlo. *Marx's Capital*. 2nd ed. London: Pluto Press, 2004.

Fisher, John. *The Economic Aspects of Spanish Imperialism in America, 1492–1810*. Liverpool, England: Liverpool University Press, 1997.

Foster-Carter, Aidan. "The Modes of Production Controversy." *New Left Review* 107 (Jan.–Feb. 1978): 47–78.

Fowler-Salamini, Heather. "Gender, Work and Coffee in Cordoba, Veracruz, 1850–1910." In *Women of the Mexican Countryside, 1850–1990: Creating Spaces, Shaping Transitions*, ed. Heather Fowler-Salamini and Mary Kay Vaughan, 51–73. Tucson: University of Arizona Press, 1994.

Freeland, Jane. *A Special Place in History: The Atlantic Coast in the Nicaraguan Revolution*. London: Nicaraguan Solidarity Campaign, 1988.

Frisch, Michael. "Oral History and Hard Times: A Review Essay." *Oral History Review* 7 (1979): 70–79.

Gámez, José Dolores. *Historia de Nicaragua desde los tiempos prehistóricos hasta 1860.* Managua: Tip. El Pais, 1889.

———. *Historia Moderna de Nicaragua: Complemento a Mí Historia de Nicaragua.* Managua: Banco de América, 1975. (Orig. pub. 1889.)

Gilbert, Dennis, and David Block, eds. *Sandinismo: Key Documents.* Working Papers, Department of Sociology, Cornell University, Ithaca, N.Y., 1990.

Gilroy, Paul. *Against Race: Imagining Political Culture beyond the Color Line.* Cambridge, Mass.: Harvard University Press, 2001.

Goldman, Wendy Z. *Women at the Gates: Gender and Industry in Stalin's Russia.* Cambridge, England: Cambridge University Press, 2002.

Gonzales, Michael J. *Plantation Agriculture and Social Control in Northern Peru, 1875–1933.* Austin: University of Texas Press, 1985.

González Montes, Soledad, and Vania Salles, eds. *Relaciones de Género y Transformaciones Agrarias.* Mexico City: El Colegio de México, 1995.

Goodman, David, and Michael Redclift. *From Peasant to Proletarian: Capitalist Development and Agrarian Transitions.* Oxford: Basil Blackwell, 1981.

Gould, Jeffrey L. "El café, el trabajo y la comunidad indígena de Matagalpa, 1880–1925." In *Tierra, café y sociedad: Ensayos sobre la historia agraria centroamericana,* ed. Héctor Pérez Brignoli and Mario Samper, 279–376. San José, Costa Rica: FLACSO, 1994.

———. *To Die in This Way: Nicaraguan Indians and the Myth of Mestizaje, 1880–1965.* Durham, N.C.: Duke University Press, 1998.

———. *To Lead as Equals: Rural Protest and Political Consciousness in Chinandega, Nicaragua, 1912–1979.* Chapel Hill: University of North Carolina Press, 1990.

Gould, Jeffrey L., and Aldo Lauria Santiago. "'They Call Us Thieves and Steal Our Wages': Toward a Reinterpretation of the Salvadoran Rural Mobilization, 1929–1931." *Hispanic American Historical Review* 84, no. 2 (May 2004): 191–237.

Graham, Richard. *Patronage and Politics in Nineteenth Century Brazil.* Stanford: Stanford University Press, 1990.

Gramsci, Antonio. *Prison Notebooks.* Vols. 1 and 2. Ed. and trans. Joseph A. Buttigieg. New York: Columbia University Press, 1996.

Grandin, Greg. *The Blood of Guatemala: A History of Race and Nation.* Durham, N.C.: Duke University Press, 2000.

Grele, Ronald J. *Envelopes of Sound: The Art of Oral History.* Westport, Conn.: Greenwood, 1975.

Gudmundson, Lowell. *Costa Rica before Coffee.* Baton Rouge: University of Louisiana Press, 1986.

———. "Lord and Peasant in the Making of Modern Central America." In *Agrarian Structure and Political Power,* ed. Evelyn Huber and Frank Safford, 151–76. Pittsburgh: University of Pittsburgh Press, 1995.

Guerrero, Andrés. *La semántica de la dominación: El concertaje de indios*. Quito: Libri Mundi, 1991.

Gunther Frank, André. *Capitalism and Underdevelopment in Latin America*. New York: Monthly Review Press, 1969.

———. *ReOrient: Global Economy in the Asian Age*. Berkeley: University of California Press, 1998.

Gutierrez, Iván. "La política de tierras de la reforma agraria Sandinista." In *El Debate sobre la Reforma Agraria en Nicaragua*, ed. Raúl Ruben and Jan P. de Groot, 113–28. Managua: INIES, 1989.

Gutmann, Matthew C. *The Meanings of Macho: Being a Man in Mexico*. Berkeley: University of California Press, 1996.

Guy, Donna J. "Lower-Class Families, Women and the Law in Nineteenth Century Argentina." *Journal of Family History* 10, no. 3 (1985): 318–31.

———. "Parents before Tribunals: The Legal Construction of Patriarchy in Argentina." In *The Hidden Histories of Gender and the State in Latin America*, ed. Elizabeth Dore and Maxine Molyneux, 172–93. Durham, N.C.: Duke University Press, 2000.

———. *Sex and Danger in Buenos Aires: Prostitution, Family and Nation in Argentina*. Lincoln: University of Nebraska Press, 1991.

Habermas, Jürgen. *The Structural Transformation of the Public Sphere: An Inquiry into a Category of Bourgeois Society*. Cambridge, England: Polity, 1989.

Hale, Charles A. *The Transformation of Liberalism in Late Nineteenth-Century Mexico*. Princeton, N.J.: Princeton University Press, 1989.

Hale, Charles R. *Resistance and Contradiction: Miskitu Indians and the Nicaraguan State, 1894–1987*. Stanford: Stanford University Press, 1994.

Hale, John. *Six Months' Residence and Travels in Central America through the Free States of Nicaragua, and Particularly Costa Rica*. New York: J. Hale, 1926.

Hall, Carolyn. *Costa Rica: Una interpretación geográfica con perspectiva histórica*. San José: Editorial Costa Rica, 1984.

Hall, Catherine. *White, Male and Middle Class*. Cambridge, England: Polity, 1992.

Harris, Richard L. "Marxism and the Agrarian Question in Latin America." *Latin American Perspectives*, 5, no. 4 (autumn 1978): 2–26.

Harstock, Nancy. *Money, Sex and Power: Toward a Feminist Historical Materialism*. Boston: Northeastern University Press, 1985.

Hartmann, Heidi. "The Unhappy Marriage of Marxism and Feminism: Towards a More Progressive Union." *Capital and Class* 8 (summer 1979): 1–34.

Hilton, Rodney, ed. *The Transition from Feudalism to Capitalism*. London: New Left Books, 1976.

Hobsbawm, Eric J. *The Age of Revolution 1789–1848*. New York: New American Library, 1962.

———. "Inventing Traditions." In *The Invention of Tradition*, ed. Eric Hobsbawm and Terence Ranger, 1–14. Cambridge, England: Cambridge University Press, 1983.

————. "Peasants and Politics." *Journal of Peasant Studies* 1, no. 1 (1973): 3–22.

Holmes, Douglas R. *Cultural Disenchantments: Worker Peasantries in Northeast Italy.* Princeton, N.J.: Princeton University Press, 1989.

Huber, Evelyne. Introduction to *Agrarian Structure and Political Power: Landlord and Peasant in the Making of Latin America*, ed. Evelyne Stephens and Frank Safford, 3–20. Pittsburgh: University of Pittsburgh Press, 1995.

Icaza, Jorge. *Huasipungo.* Barcelona: Plaza y Janés Eds., 1979. (Orig. pub. 1934.)

INRA-MERA. *Marco estratégico de la reforma agraria: Diagnóstico evaluación de la situación agraria y de la reforma agraria en Nicaragua*, vol. 2. Managua: Instituto Nacional de la Reforma Agraria (INRA), 1991.

Isaacman, Allen. *The Tradition of Resistance in Mozambique: Anti-Colonial Activity in the Zambesi Valley, 1850–1921.* Berkeley: University of California Press, 1976.

Jacobsen, Nils. *Mirages of Transition: The Peruvian Altiplano, 1780–1930.* Berkeley: University of California Press, 1993.

James, Daniel. "Listening in the Cold: The Practice of Oral History in an Argentine Meatpacking Community." In *Doña María's Story*, 119–56. Durham, N.C.: Duke University Press, 2000.

Kandiyoti, Deniz. "Bargaining with Patriarchy." *Gender and Society* 2, no. 3 (1988): 274–90.

————. "End of Empire: Islam, Nationalism and Women in Turkey." In *Women, Islam and the State*, ed. Deniz Kandiyoti, 22–47. London: Macmillan, 1991.

Katz, Friedrich. "Labor Conditions on Haciendas in Porfirian Mexico: Some Trends and Tendencies." *Hispanic American Historical Review* 54, no. 1 (1974): 1–47.

Kay, Cristóbal. *El sistema señorial europeo y la hacienda latinoamericana.* Mexico City: Serie Popular Era, 1980.

————. *Latin American Theories of Development and Underdevelopment.* London: Routledge, 1989.

Kelly, Joan. *Women, History, and Theory.* Chicago: University of Chicago Press, 1984.

Kinloch Tijerino, Frances, ed. *Nicaragua en busca de su identidad.* Managua: Instituto de Historia de Nicaragua, 1995.

————. *Nicaragua: Identidad y cultura política (1821–1858).* Managua: Banco Central de Nicaragua, 1999.

Klaren, Peter F. *Modernization, Dislocation, and Aprismo: Origins of the Peruvian Aprista Party, 1870–1932.* Austin: University of Texas Press, 1973.

Klubock, Thomas Miller. *Contested Communities: Class, Gender and Politics in Chile's El Teniente Copper Mine, 1904–1951.* Durham, N.C.: Duke University Press, 1998.

Knight, Alan. "Debt Bondage in Latin America." In *Slavery and Other Forms of Unfree Labour*, ed. Léonie Archer, 102–17. London: Routledge, 1988.

————. "Mexican Peonage: What Was It and Why Was It?" *Journal of Latin American Studies* 18 (1986): 41–74.

————. "Racism, Revolution and Indigenismo: Mexico, 1910–1940." In *The Idea of*

Race in Latin America, 1870–1940, ed. Richard Graham, 71–114. Austin: University of Texas Press, 1990.

Labanyi, Jo. *Gender and Modernization in the Spanish Realist Novel*. Oxford: Oxford University Press, 2000.

LaFeber, Walter. *Inevitable Revolutions: The United States in Central America*. New York: Norton, 1984.

Lal, Brij V., Doug Munro, and Edward D. Beechert, eds. *Plantation Workers: Resistance and Accommodation*. Honolulu: University of Hawaii Press, 1993.

Lamas, Marta. "Scenes from a Mexican Battlefield." NACLA: *Report on the Americas* 31, no. 4 (Jan.–Feb. 1998): 17–22.

Lanuza, Alberto. "Economía y sociedad en la construcción del estado nacional." In *Economía y Sociedad en la Construcción del Estado en Nicaragua*, ed. Alberto Lanuza, Amaru Barahona, and Amalia Chamorro, 7–139. San José, Costa Rica: ICAP, 1983.

———. "La formación del estado nacional en Nicaragua: Las bases económicas, comerciales y financieras entre 1821 y 1873." In *Economía y Sociedad en la Construcción del Estado en Nicaragua*, ed. Alberto Lanuza, Amaru Barahona, and Amalia Chamorro. San José, Costa Rica: ICAP, 1983.

Lanuza, Alberto, Amaru Barahona, and Amalia Chamorro, eds. *Economía y Sociedad en la Construcción del Estado en Nicaragua*. San José, Costa Rica: ICAP, 1983.

Lapavitsas, Costas. "Commodities versus Gifts: Why Commodities Represent More Than Market Relations." *Science and Society* 68, no. 1 (spring 2004): 33–56.

Larson, Brooke. *Colonialism and Agrarian Transformation in Bolivia: Cochabamba, 1550–1900*. 2nd, expanded ed. Durham, N.C.: Duke University Press, 1998.

———. *Trials of Nation Making: Liberalism, Race, and Ethnicity in the Andes, 1810–1910*. Cambridge, England: Cambridge University Press, 2004.

Lauria Santiago, Aldo. *An Agrarian Republic: Commercial Agriculture and the Politics of Peasant Communities*. Pittsburgh: University of Pittsburgh Press, 1999.

Lavrin, Asunción. *Women, Feminism and Social Change in Argentina, Chile and Uruguay, 1890–1940*. Lincoln: University of Nebraska Press, 1995.

———. "Women in Spanish American Colonial Society." In *Cambridge History of Latin America*, 2 vols., ed. Leslie Bethell, 2:314–36. Cambridge, England: Cambridge University Press, 1984.

Le Breton, Binka. *Trapped: Modern-day Slavery in the Brazilian Amazon*. London: Latin America Bureau, 2003.

Lenin, V. I. "A Characterization of Economic Romanticism," In *Collected Works*, 2: 129–226. Moscow: Progress Publishers, 1972.

———. "The Development of Capitalism in Russia." In *Collected Works*, 3:25–607. Moscow: Progress Publishers, 1972.

León, Magdalena, and Carmen Diana Deere, eds. *La mujer y la política agraria en américa latina*. Bogotá: Siglo XXI, 1986.

Lindo Fuentes, Héctor. *Weak Foundations: The Economy of El Salvador in the Nineteenth Century*. Berkeley: University of California Press, 1990.

Long, Norman, and Bryan Roberts. *Miners, Peasants and Entrepreneurs: Regional Developments in the Central Highlands of Peru.* Cambridge, England: Cambridge University Press, 1984.

Loveman, Brian. "Critique of Arnold J. Bauer's 'Rural Workers in Spanish America: Problems of Peonage and Oppression.'" *Hispanic American Historical Review* 59 (1979): 478–89.

Lynch, John. "The Origins of Spanish American Independence." In *The Independence of Latin America*, ed. Leslie Bethell, 1–48. Cambridge, England: Cambridge University Press, 1987.

———. *The Spanish American Revolutions 1808–1826*. New York: Norton, 1973.

McCreery, David. "Coffee and Indigenous Labor in Guatemala, 1880–1980." In *The Global Coffee Economy in Africa, Asia, and Latin America, 1500–1989*, ed. William Gervase Clarence-Smith and Steven Topik, 191–208. Cambridge, England: Cambridge University Press, 2003.

———. "An Odious Feudalism: *Mandamientos* and Commercial Agriculture in Guatemala, 1861–1920." *Latin American Perspectives* 13, no. 1 (winter 1986): 99–117.

———. *Rural Guatemala, 1760–1940*. Stanford: Stanford University Press, 1994.

McLeod, Murdo J. *Spanish Central America: A Socioeconomic History 1520–1720*. Berkeley: University of California Press, 1973.

Mallon, Florencia E. *The Defense of Community in Peru's Central Highlands: Peasant Struggle and Capitalist Transition, 1860–1940*. Princeton, N.J.: Princeton University Press, 1983.

———. "Exploring the Origins of Democratic Patriarchy in Mexico: Gender and Popular Resistance in the Puebla Highlands, 1850–1876." In *Women of the Mexican Countryside, 1850–1990: Creating Spaces, Shaping Transitions*, ed. Heather Fowler-Salamini and Mary Kay Vaughan, 3–26. Tucson: University of Arizona Press, 1994.

———. "Patriarchy in the Transition to Capitalism: Central Peru, 1830–1950." *Feminist Studies* 13, no. 2 (summer 1987): 379–407.

———. *Peasant and Nation: The Making of Post-Colonial Mexico and Peru*. Berkeley: University of California Press, 1995.

Markels, Julian. *The Marxian Imagination: Representing Class in Literature*. New York: Monthly Review Press, 2003.

Martínez Echazabal, Lourdes. "Mestizaje and the Discourse of National/Cultural Identity in Latin America, 1845–1959." *Latin American Perspectives* 25, no. 3 (May 1988): 21–42.

Martínez Peláez, Severo. *La patria del criollo*. San José, Costa Rica: Ed. Universitaria, 1979.

Marx, Karl. *Capital*. London: Lawrence and Wishart, 1971.

———. "The Eighteenth Brumaire of Louis Bonaparte." In *The Marx-Engels Reader*, ed. Robert C. Tucker. New York: Norton, 1978.

Mauss, Marcel. *The Gift: The Form and Reason for Exchange in Archaic Societies*. Trans. W. D. Halls. London: Routledge, 2000.

Meillassoux, Claude. "From Reproduction to Production." In *The Articulation of Modes of Production*, ed. H. Wolpe. London: Routledge and Kegan Paul, 1980.

———. *Maidens, Meal and Money: Capitalism and the Domestic Community*. Cambridge, England: Cambridge University Press, 1981.

Miles, Robert. *Capitalism and Unfree Labour: Anomaly or Necessity?* London: Tavistock, 1987.

Mintz, Sidney. *Caribbean Transformations*. Chicago: Aldine, 1974.

Molina Jiménez, Iván. *Costa Rica (1800–1850): El legado colonial y la génesis del capitalismo*. San José: Editorial Universidad de Costa Rica, 1991.

Molina Jiménez, Iván, and Steven Palmer. *The Costa Rica Reader: History, Culture, Politics*. Durham, N.C.: Duke University Press, 2004.

Molyneux, Maxine. "Twentieth-Century State Formations in Latin America." In *The Hidden Histories of Gender and the State in Latin America*, ed. Elizabeth Dore and Maxine Molyneux, 33–84. Durham, N.C.: Duke University Press, 2000.

———. *Women's Movements in International Perspective: Latin America and Beyond*. London: Institute of Latin American Studies and Palgrave, 2001.

Molyneux, Maxine, and Shahra Razavi. Introduction to *Gender Justice, Development, and Rights*, ed. Maxine Molyneux and Shahra Razavi. Oxford: Oxford University Press, 2002.

Montesinos, Sonia. *Madres y huachos*. Santiago, Chile: Centro de Estudios de la Mujer (CEM), 1991.

Montgomery, David. *Citizen Worker*. Cambridge, England: Cambridge University Press, 1993.

Moore, Barrington, Jr. *Social Origins of Dictatorship and Democracy*. Boston: Beacon Press, 1966.

Namier, Lewis. *Conflicts: Studies in Contemporary History*. London: Macmillan, 1942.

Nazzari, Muriel. *Disappearance of the Dowry: Families and Social Change in Sao Paulo*. Stanford: Stanford University Press, 1991.

Newson, Linda A. *Indian Survival in Colonial Nicaragua*. Norman: University of Oklahoma Press, 1987.

Norton, Anne. "Ruling Memory." *Political Theory* 21, no. 3 (Aug. 1993): 453–63.

Nugent, Daniel, and Ana María Alonso. "Multiple Selective Traditions in Agrarian Reform and Agrarian Struggle: Popular Culture and State Formation in the Ejido of Namiquipa, Chihuahua." In *Everyday Forms of State Formation: Revolution and the Negotiation of Rule in Modern Mexico*, ed. Gilbert M. Joseph and Daniel Nugent, 209–46. Durham, N.C.: Duke University Press, 1994.

Núñez Soto, Orlando. *Transición y lucha de clases en Nicaragua 1979–1986*. Mexico City: Siglo XXI, 1987.

Nussbaum, Martha. "Women's Capabilities and Social Justice." In *Gender Justice, Development, and Rights*, ed. Maxine Molyneux and Shahra Razavi, 45–77. Oxford: Oxford University Press, 2002.

Orwell, George. *Nineteen-Eighty Four*. Harmondsworth, England: Penguin, 1954. (Orig. pub. 1949.)

Paige, Jeffrey M. *Agrarian Revolution: Social Movements and Export Agriculture in the Underdeveloped World*. New York: Free Press, 1975.

———. *Coffee and Power: Revolution and the Rise of Democracy in Central America*. Cambridge, Mass.: Harvard University Press, 1997.

Passerini, Luisa. *Autobiography of a Generation: Italy, 1968*. Hanover, N.H.: Wesleyan University Press, 1966.

Patnaik, Utsa, and Manjari Dingwaney, eds. *Chains of Servitude: Bondage and Slavery in India*. Madras, India: Sangam Books, 1985.

Pearce, Jenny. *Under the Eagle: U.S. Intervention in Central America and the Caribbean*. Boston: South End Press, 1982.

Peña Torres, Ligia María. "Las cofradías indígenas en Nicaragua, siglo XVIII-1812." Master's thesis, Universidad Centroamericano, Managua, 1997.

Perelman, Michael. *The Invention of Capitalism: Classical Political Economy and the Secret History of Primitive Accumulation*. Durham, N.C.: Duke University Press, 2000.

Pérez Brignoli, Héctor. *A Brief History of Central America*. Berkeley: University of California Press, 1989.

Pérez Brignoli, Héctor, and Mario Samper, eds. *Tierra, café y sociedad: Ensayos sobre la historia agraria centroamericana*. San José, Costa Rica: FLACSO, 1994.

Pérez Rojas, Niurka. *El Hogar de Ana: Un estudio sobre la mujer rural nicaragüense*. La Habana: Editorial de Ciencias Sociales, 1986.

Phillips, Anne. *Divided Loyalties: Dilemmas of Sex and Class*. London: Virago, 1987.

———. *Which Equalities Matter?* Cambridge, England: Polity, 1999.

Polanyi, Karl. *The Great Transformation: The Political and Economic Origins of Our Time*. New York: Farrar and Rinehart, 1944; reprinted Boston: Beacon Press, 1957.

———. *The Great Transformation: The Political and Economic Origins of Our Time*. 2nd ed. Foreword by Joseph E. Stiglitz. Boston: Beacon Press, 2001.

Portelli, Alessandro. *The Death of Luigi Trastulli and Other Stories: Form and Meaning in Oral History*. Albany: State University of New York Press, 2001.

Quijano, Carlos. *Nicaragua: Ensayo sobre el imperialismo de los Estados Unidos (1909-1927)*. Managua: Editorial Vanguardia, 1987.

Ramachandran, V. K. *Wage Labour and Unfreedom in Agriculture: An Indian Case Study*. Oxford: Clarendon Press, 1990.

Robinson, William I. "The New Right and the End of National Liberation." NACLA *Report on the Americas* 37, no. 6 (May–June 2004): 15–20.

———. *Transnational Conflicts: Central America, Social Change and Globalization*. London: Verso, 2003.

Rodríguez Sáenz, Eugenia. "Civilizing Domestic Life in the Central Valley of Costa Rica, 1750–1850." In *The Hidden Histories of Gender and the State in Latin America*, ed. Elizabeth Dore and Maxine Molyneux, 85–107. Durham, N.C.: Duke University Press, 2000.

—————. *Hijas, novias y esposas: Familia, matrimonio y violencia doméstica en el Valle Central de Costa Rica (1750–1850)*. San José, Costa Rica: EUNA and Plumstock Mesoamerican Studies, 2000.

—————, ed. *Mujeres, Género e Historia en América Central durante los siglos XVIII, XIX y XX*. San José, Costa Rica: UNIFEM and Plumstock Mesoamerican Studies, 2002.

Romero Vargas, Germán. *Las Estructuras Sociales de Nicaragua en el Siglo XVIII*. Managua: Editorial Vanguardia, 1988.

Roper, Lyndal. *Oedipus and the Devil: Witchcraft, Sexuality and Religion in Early Modern Europe*. London: Routledge, 1994.

Rose, Sonya O. "Introduction to Dialogue: Women's History/Gender History. Is Feminist Inquiry Losing Its Critical Edge?" *Journal of Women's History* 5, no. 1 (spring 1993): 89–101.

—————. *Limited Livelihoods: Gender and Class in Nineteenth Century England*. Berkeley: University of California Press, 1992.

—————. *Which People's War? National Identity and Citizenship in Wartime Britain, 1939–1945*. Oxford: Oxford University Press, 2003.

Roseberry, William. "Beyond the Agrarian Question in Latin America." In *Confronting Historical Paradigms: Peasants, Labor and the Capitalist World System in Africa and Latin America*, ed. Frederick Cooper, Allen Isaacman, Florencia Mallon, William Roseberry, and Steve Stern, 318–68. Madison: University of Wisconsin Press, 1993.

—————. *Coffee and Capitalism in the Venezuelan Andes*. Austin: University of Texas Press, 1983.

—————. "La Falta de Brazos: Land and Labor in the Coffee Economies of Nineteenth-century Latin America." *Theory and Society* 20 (1991): 351–82.

—————. "An Introduction." In *Coffee, Society and Power in Latin America*, ed. William Roseberry, Lowell Gudmundson, and Mario Samper Kutschbach, 1–33. Baltimore: Johns Hopkins University Press, 1995.

Roseberry, William, Lowell Gudmundson, and Mario Samper Kutschbach, eds. *Coffee, Society, and Power in Latin America*. Baltimore: Johns Hopkins University Press, 1995.

Rosemblatt, Karin Alejandra. *Gendered Compromises: Political Cultures and the State in Chile, 1920–1950*. Chapel Hill: University of North Carolina Press, 2000.

Rosobo, Henrik. "State Formation and Property: Reflections on the Political Technologies of Space in Central America." *Journal of Historical Sociology* 10, no. 1 (Mar. 1997): 56–73.

Rubén, Raul, and Jan P. De Groot, eds. *El debate sobre la reforma agraria en Nicaragua*. Managua: Instituto Nicaragüense de Investigaciones Económicas y Sociales (INIES), 1989.

Salinas, Cecilia. *Las chilenas de la colonia: Virtud sumisa, amor rebelde*. Santiago, Chile: LOM Ediciones, 1994.

Samper, Mario. *Generations of Settlers: Rural Households and Markets on the Costa Rican Frontier*. Boulder, Colo.: Westview Press, 1990.

Sargent, Lydia, ed. *Women and Revolution: A Discussion of the Unhappy Marriage of Marxism and Feminism*. Boston: South End Press, 1981.

Scherzer, Carl. *Travels in the Free States of Central America*. London: Longman Brown, Green, 1857.

Scott, James C. *Domination and the Arts of Resistance: Hidden Transcripts*. New Haven: Yale University Press, 1990.

———. *The Moral Economy of the Peasant: Subsistence and Rebellion in Southeast Asia*. New Haven: Yale University Press, 1976.

———. *Weapons of the Weak: Everyday Forms of Peasant Resistance*. New Haven: Yale University Press, 1985.

Scott, Joan W. "Gender: A Useful Category of Historical Analysis." *American Historical Review* 15, no. 3 (1986): 1053–75.

———. *Gender and the Politics of History*. New York: Columbia University Press, 1988.

Seed, Patricia. *To Love, Honor and Obey in Colonial Mexico*. Stanford: Stanford University Press, 1988.

Spoor, Max. *The State and Domestic Agricultural Markets in Nicaragua*. New York: St. Martin's Press, 1995.

Stacey, Judith. *Patriarchy and Socialist Revolution in China*. Berkeley: University of California Press, 1983.

Stavenhagen, Rodolfo. "Seven Fallacies about Latin America." In *Latin America: Reform or Revolution?*, ed. James Petras and Maurice Zeitlin, 13–31. Greenwich, Conn.: Fawcett, 1968.

Stein, Stanley J. *Vassouras, a Brazilian Coffee County, 1850–1900: The Roles of Planter and Slave in a Plantation Society*. Princeton, N.J.: Princeton University Press, 1985. (Orig. pub. 1958.)

Stephen, Lynn. "The Creation and Re-Creation of Ethnicity: Lessons from the Zapotec and Mixtec of Oaxaca." *Latin American Perspectives* 23, no. 2 (spring 1996): 17–37.

———. *Zapata Lives! Histories and Cultural Politics in Southern Mexico*. Berkeley: University of California Press, 2002.

———. *Zapotec Women*. Austin: University of Texas Press, 1991.

Stern, Steve J. "Feudalism, Capitalism, and the World-System in the Perspective of Latin America and the Caribbean." *American Historical Review* 93 (Oct. 1988): 829–72.

———. *Peru's Indian Peoples and the Challenge of Spanish Conquest: Huamanga to 1640*. Madison: University of Wisconsin Press, 1982.

———. *The Secret History of Gender: Women, Men and Power in Late Colonial Mexico*. Chapel Hill: University of North Carolina Press, 1995.

Stolcke, Verena. *Coffee Planters, Workers and Wives: Class Conflict and Gender Relations on Sao Paulo Plantations*. London: Macmillan, 1988.

Stolcke, Verena, and Michael Hall. "The Introduction of Free Labour on São Paulo Coffee Plantations." *Journal of Peasant Studies* 10, nos. 2–3 (Jan.–Apr. 1983): 170–200.

Stoler, Ann Laura. *Capitalism and Confrontation in Sumatra's Plantation Belt, 1870–1979*. New Haven: Yale University Press, 1985.

———. *Capitalism and Confrontation in Sumatra's Plantation Belt, 1870–1979*. 2nd, expanded ed. New Haven: Yale University Press, 1995.

———. *Carnal Knowledge and Imperial Power: Race and the Intimate in Colonial Rule*. Berkeley: University of California Press, 2002.

———. *Race and the Education of Desire: Foucault's History of Sexuality and the Colonial Order of Things*. Durham, N.C.: Duke University Press, 1995.

Sunkel, Osvaldo, with Pedro Paz. *El subdesarrollo latinoamericano y la teoría del desarrollo*. Mexico City: Siglo XXI, 1981.

Szurchman, Mark. *Order, Family and Community in Buenos Aires, 1810–1860*. Stanford: Stanford University Press, 1988.

Teplitz, Benjamin. "The Political and Economic Foundations of Modernization in Nicaragua: The Administration of José Santos Zelaya, 1893–1909." Ph.D. diss., Howard University, 1973.

Thomas, Clive Y. *Dependence and Transformation: The Economics of the Transition to Socialism*. New York: Monthly Review Press, 1974.

Thompson, E. P. *Customs in Common*. London: Merlin Press, 1991.

———. "Patrician Society: Plebian Culture." *Journal of Social History* 7, no. 4 (1974): 382–405.

Thompson, Paul. *The Voice of the Past*. 2nd ed. Oxford: Oxford University Press, 2000.

Thomson, Guy P. C. "Agrarian Conflict in the Municipality of Cuetzalan (Sierra de Puebla): The Rise and Fall of 'Pala' Agustín Dieguillo, 1861–1894." *Hispanic American Historical Review* 71 (1991): 205–58.

———. *Puebla de Los Angeles: Industry and Society in a Mexican City 1700–1850*. Boulder, Colo.: Westview Press, 1989.

Thorner, Daniel, and Alice Thorner. "Employer-Labourer Relationships in Indian Agriculture in 1957." In *Land and Labour in India*, ed. Daniel Thorner and Alice Thorner. Bombay: Asia Publishing House, 1962.

Tinsman, Heidi. *Partners in Conflict: The Politics of Gender, Sexuality and Labor in the Chilean Agrarian Reform, 1950–1973*. Durham, N.C.: Duke University Press, 2002.

———. "Reviving Patriarchy," *Radical History Review* no. 71 (spring 1998): 182–95.

Tonkin, Elizabeth. *Narrating our Pasts: The Social Construction of Oral History*. Cambridge, England: Cambridge University Press, 1992.

Topik, Steven. "Coffee." In *The Second Conquest of Latin America: Coffee, Henequen and Oil during the Export Boom, 1850–1930*, ed. Steven Topik and Allen Wells, 37–84. Austin: University of Texas Press, 1998.

———. "Coffee Anyone? Recent Research on Latin American Coffee Societies." *Hispanic American Historical Review* 80 (2000): 225–66.

Torres Rivas, Edelberto. *Interpretación del desarrollo social centroamericano*. San José, Costa Rica: EDUCA, 1971.

Traven, B. *March to the Montería*. New York: Hill and Wang, 1971.

Tutino, John. *From Insurrection to Revolution in Mexico: Social Bases of Agrarian Violence, 1750–1940*. Princeton, N.J.: Princeton University Press, 1986.

Utting, Peter. *Economic Adjustment under the Sandinistas: Policy Reform, Food Security and Livelihood in Nicaragua*. Geneva, Switzerland: United Nations Research Institute for Social Development (UNRISD), 1991.

———. *Economic Reform and Third World Socialism*. London: Macmillan, 1992.

Valdés, Ximena. *Mujer, trabajo, y medio ambiente: Los nudos de la modernización agraria*. Santiago: CEM, 1992.

Valdés, Ximena, Loreto Rebolledo, and Angélica Willson, eds. *Masculino y feminino en la hacienda chilena del siglo XX*. Santiago, Chile: Fondart-CEDEM, 1995.

Van Young, Eric. *Hacienda and Market in Eighteenth-Century Mexico: The Rural Economy of the Guadalajara Region, 1675–1820*. Berkeley: University of California Press, 1981.

Vannini, Margarita, ed. *Encuentros con la historia*. Managua: Instituto de Historia de Nicaragua, 1995.

Vargas, Oscar René. *¿Adonde va Nicaragua? Perspectivas de una revolución latinoamericano*. Managua: Ediciones Nicarao, 1991.

———. *Elecciones presidenciales en Nicaragua, 1912–1932*. Managua: Fundación Manolo Morales, 1989.

———. *La intervención norteamericana y sus consecuencias: Nicaragua, 1910–1925*. Managua: CIRA, 1990.

———. *La revolución que inició el progreso, Nicaragua, 1893–1909*. Managua: ECOTEXTURA, 1990.

Varley, Ann. "Women and the Home in Mexican Family Law." In *The Hidden Histories of Gender and the State in Latin America*, ed. Elizabeth Dore and Maxine Molyneux, 238–61. Durham, N.C.: Duke University Press, 2000.

———. "Women Heading Households: Some More Equal Than Others?" *World Development* 24, no. 3 (1996): 505–20.

Vásquez, Juan Luis. "Luchas políticas y estado oligárquico." In *Economía y sociedad en la construcción del estado en Nicaragua*, ed. Alberto Lanuza, Amaru Barahona, and Amalia Chamorro, 139–206. San José, Costa Rica: ICAP, 1983.

Vásquez Pereira, José Luis. *La formación del estado en Nicaragua*. Managua: Fondo Editorial, 1992.

Vaughan, Mary Kay. *Cultural Politics in Revolution: Teachers, Peasants and Schools in Mexico (1930–1940)*. Tucson: University of Arizona Press, 1997.

———. "Modernizing Patriarchy: State Policies, Rural Households, and Women in Mexico, 1930–1940." In *The Hidden Histories of Gender and the State in Latin America*, ed. Elizabeth Dore and Maxine Molyneux, 194–214. Durham, N.C.: Duke University Press, 2000.

Vilas, Carlos M. *Between Earthquakes and Volcanos: Market, State and the Revolutions in Central America*. New York: Monthly Review Press, 1995.

———. "Nicaragua: A Revolution That Fell from the Grace of the People." In *Socialist Register*, ed. Ralph Miliband and Leo Panitch, 300–319. New York: Monthly Review Press, 1991.

———. *The Sandinista Revolution*. New York: Monthly Review Press, 1986.

Vincent, Joan. "The Structuring of Ethnicity." *Human Organization* 33, no. 4 (winter 1974): 375–79.

Vitale, Luis. "Latin America: Feudal or Capitalist." In *Latin America: Reform or Revolution?*, ed. James Petras and Maurice Zeitlin, 32–43. Greenwich, Conn.: Fawcett, 1968.

Wade, Peter. "La construcción de 'el negro' en América Latina." In *La Construcción de las Américas*, ed. Carlos Alberto Uribe, 141–58. Bogotá: Universidad de los Andes, 1993.

———. *Race and Ethnicity in Latin America*. London: Pluto Press, 1997.

———. "Race, Nature and Culture." *Man* 28, no. 1 (1993): 17–34.

Wallerstein, Immanuel. *The Modern World-System: Capitalist Agriculture and the Origins of the European World-Economy in the Sixteenth Century*. New York: Academic Press, 1974.

Walter, Knut. *The Regime of Anastasio Somoza, 1936–1956*. Chapel Hill: University of North Carolina Press, 1993.

Weber, Max. *Economy and Society*. Berkeley: University of California Press, 1968.

———. *The Theory of Economic and Social Organization*. New York: Free Press, 1947.

Weeks, John. *Capital and Exploitation*. Princeton, N.J.: Princeton University Press, 1981.

———. *The Economies of Central America*. New York: Holmes and Meier, 1985.

———. "Epochs of Capitalism and the Progressiveness of Capital's Expansion." *Science and Society* 49, no. 4 (winter 1985–86): 414–36.

———. "An Interpretation of the Central American Crisis." *Latin American Research Review* 21, no. 3 (1986): 31–53.

Weeks, John, and Elizabeth Dore. "International Exchange and the Causes of Backwardness." *Latin American Perspectives* 6, no. 2 (1979): 62–87.

Wells, Allen, and Gilbert M. Joseph. *Summer of Discontent, Seasons of Upheaval: Elite Politics and Rural Insurgency in Yucatán, 1876–1915*. Stanford: Stanford University Press, 1996.

Wheelock Román, Jaime. *Imperialismo y dictadura: Crisis de una formación social*. 1975; reprint Mexico City: Siglo XXI, 1979.

Williams, Brackette F. "A Class Act: Anthropology and the Race to Nation across Ethnic Terrain." *Annual Review of Anthropology* 18 (1989): 401–44.

Williams, Robert G. *States and Social Evolution: Coffee and the Rise of National Governments in Central America*. Chapel Hill: University of North Carolina Press, 1994.

Wolfe, Justin. "Rising from the Ashes: Community, Ethnicity, and Nation-State Formation in Nineteenth Century Nicaragua." Ph.D. diss., University of California at Los Angeles, 1999.

Wolpe, Harold, ed. *The Articulation of Modes of Production: Essays from "Economy and Society."* London: Routledge and Kegan Paul, 1980.

Wood, Ellen Meiksins. *The Origin of Capitalism.* New York: Monthly Review Press, 1999.

———. *The Origin of Capitalism: A Longer View.* London: Verso, 2002.

Yarrington, Doug. *A Coffee Frontier: Land, Society and Politics in Duaca, Venezuela, 1830–1936.* Pittsburgh: University of Pittsburgh Press, 1997.

———. "Public Land Settlement, Privatization and Peasant Protest in Duaca, Venezuela, 1870–1936." *Hispanic American Historical Review* 74, no. 1 (Dec. 1994): 33–61.

Zeitlin, Maurice. *The Civil Wars in Chile, or, The Bourgeois Revolutions That Never Were.* Princeton, N.J.: Princeton University Press, 1984.

Zúñiga Osorio, Luis. "Patria Potestad." Tesis para el doctor en derecho. Managua, 1935.

Index

Page numbers followed by the letter *p* refer to photographs. Page numbers followed by the letter *t* refer to tables.

Abrams, Elliott, 183 n.21
Acevedo, Felicia, 160
Acevedo, Fernando, 161–62
Adams, Richard, 31, 32
African descendants, 31
agrarian capitalism, 8, 20, 185 n.14; contradictory nature, 20; export crops, 71; Marxist theory, 24–26; rural proletariat, 7–8, 24, 173, 175–76. *See also* capitalist transitions; landholding; privatization of land
Agrarian Reform Laws of 1979, 6–8, 76, 92, 172–80
Aguilar, Enrique, 160
Aguilar, Margarita, 160–61
Aguirre, Marcos, 82–84, 87
alcaldes de vara, 138
alcaldes indígenas, 36, 58; appointment by ladino politicians, 45; collaboration in land privatization, 69, 73–74, 84, 95–96, 170–71, 196–97 n.52; conflict with comuneros, 14, 36–38, 50–52; double role, 33, 36–37, 50–52; rewards for collaboration, 84
Alfaro, Eufreciano, 65–66
Alfonso X, King of Castile, 190 n.5
Alvarado, Francisco, 42
Archivo Municipal de Diriomo (AMD), 9–10, 183 nn.25–26

Artaza, Doña Mariana de, 35–36
articulation of modes of production theory, 20
Avilés, Agustín: declarations of generosity, 154; labor bonding, 123–24, 203 n.45; labor contracts, 120–21, 133, 210 n.28; property claims, 85–86, 196 n.36
Ayala, Mercedes, 153
Ayón, Tomás, 46

Bahlcke, Sr., 203 n.38
Banco Nacional de Nicaragua, 197–98 n.66
Banegas, Gertrudis, 61
Básques, Francisco, 75
Bauer, Arnold, 145, 164–67
Bautista, Pedro, 36–37
Bermúdez, Josefana, 65–66
Bermúdez, Manuel, 41
Bodán, Juan, 86, 133
Borge, Celendino, 82–83, 154, 196 n.36
Bravo, M., 136–37
Brenner, Robert, 13, 24–25, 144, 164–67
Bula de la Santa Cruzada census of 1776, 39–40, 64, 188 n.31, 193 n.35
Burke, Edmund, 171
Burns, E. Bradford, 44, 46–47
Bush, George H. W., 176
Bush, George W., 183 n.21

caballerías, 194 n.6
cacao production, 42–43
Campos Carcache, Francisco, 183 n.24
Campos Carcache, Noé, 135
Cano, José, 45–46
Cano, José Ana, 138
Cano, Josefa, 210 n.28
Cano, Marcelino, 62–63
Cano, Pedro Pablo, 141*p*
Cano, Teófilo, 137–38, 140*p*, 142*p*, 175
capitalist transitions, 3–8, 15, 18–29, 145–47, 164–68, 182 n.8; agrarian forms, 7–8, 20, 24–26, 71, 173, 175–76, 185 n.14; articulation of modes of production theory, 20; Bauer-Knight thesis, 125, 145–46, 164–67; bourgeois revolution, 4–7; Brenner's analysis of coercion, 24–25, 144, 164–67; as cause of underdevelopment, 18–19; competitive markets, 6; contradictory definition of *freedom*, 22–23; debt peonage, 15, 143–47, 208 nn.124–25; dependency theory, 19; emergence of finance capital, 7; forced labor, 21, 110–14; free wage labor, 3, 6, 21–24; gendered aspects, 164; labor laws, 5; landlessness, 22–23, 165, 174; landlord-peasant relations, 24–26; money, 22; nature of markets, 20–24; peasant resistance, 25–26; Polanyi's observations of markets, 20–24, 94–95, 165–66; privatization of land, 94–96; Scott's theories of peasant resistance, 25–26, 167–68; state consolidation of agriculture, 147–48; theoretical views, 13, 18–29, 144–46, 164–68; world systems theory, 19. *See also* noncapitalist transitions
Carballo, Juana, 60–61
Carcache, Aristarco, 121
Carcache, Francisco, 144
Casanova, Rafael, 46–47

castas, 30, 39–40
Castillo, Feliz, 125, 160
Castillo, Julio, 152–53
Castillo, Margarita, 90*p*
Catholic Church: Bula de la Santa Cruzada census of 1776, 39–40, 64, 188 n.31, 193 n.35; class and gender hierarchies, 57, 62–63; landholding, 70; secularization of marriage, 55, 56–57, 63
census categories, 107–8
Centeno, Gregorio, 38–39
Centeno, Juana, 93–94
Central American Federation, 43
Centro de Investigaciones y Estudios de la Reforma Agraria (CIERA), 8
Chamorro, Dionesio, 75–76, 86, 197 n.61
Chamorro, Fruto, 64
Charlip, Julie, 168
child support cases, 65–67
Chuzcada hacienda, 162–63
citizenship, 59, 63–64, 192 n.20
Civil Code of 1867, 56–57, 102–3, 190–91 nn.5–6
Civil Code of 1904, 56–57, 191 n.6
class relations, 1; coercion of labor, 25–26, 95, 165; coffee-growing oligarchs, 9, 12–13; Comaroff's views of ethnicity and class, 32; debt peonage, 20–24, 113, 116–18, 127–29, 135–38; definition of class, 21; free wage labor, 3, 6, 21; gender analysis, 28; impact of coffee industry, 83; impact of liberalism, 97–104; patriarchal system, 149–63; polarization, 8; political elite, 2, 4–5, 14, 53–54, 165; privatization of land, 69; racial and ethnic basis, 30, 32; role of land ownership, 57, 59; rural proletariat, 7–8, 24, 173, 175–76; semiproletarians, 8; sexual violence, 62–63; social nature of markets, 20–24; stereotypes of peasants, 107–8,

117–19, 135–38; Stern's reciprocal pacts, 28–29, 169; surplus value, 21; theoretical views, 13, 17–20, 28–32; Thompson's moral economy of the poor, 28; transitions to capitalism, 18–20. *See also* debt peonage; patriarchal system

coffee fincas in Diriomo, 1–2, 9; avoidance of property fragmentation, 103–4; funding, 87; harvest festivals, 154; land title acquisitions, 86–87; productivity, 89, 198 n.69, 198 n.71; women ownership, 103–4. *See also* Mombacho Volcano region

coffee industry, 7, 91*p*, 182 n.8; appropriations of common lands, 75–77, 80–83; capitalist transition, 3–4, 147–48; census of 1909–1910, 89, 198 n.69, 198 n.71; emergence of migratory wage labor, 147–48; expanded role of patriarchal authority, 150–51, 161–63, 208 n.1; forced labor dependence, 110–11, 118–19, 120, 202 n.26; forced labor laws, 5, 111–20; funding and subsidies, 71, 87; noncapitalist analysis, 147–48, 164–68, 208 nn.124–25; patriarchy from above, 2, 15–17, 29, 149, 151–55, 165, 181 n.6; price crash of 1930, 5, 143, 147, 207 n.106; private property revolution, 69, 71–72, 194–95 n.16; productivity, 89; seasonal labor needs, 95, 198–99 n.78, 199 n.79; timing of harvest, 111–12, 126–27; trade and artisanal activities, 106–8, 200 n.23. *See also* debt peonage

cofradías, 41, 58

colonial period, 14, 18, 33–42; collapse of indigenous society, 34–36, 188 n.12; corporate land grants, 34–35, 70–72, 95–96, 194 nn.5–6; double role of local leaders, 33, 36–38; economic status, 41; expropriation of common

lands, 42–43, 188 n.31; labor requirements, 34–37, 42; legal system, 38–39, 55, 97–98; marriage rates, 64, 193 n.35; Masaya land dispute, 42–43, 188 n.31; origins of common land rights and indigenous autonomy, 34–35; patria potestad principles, 99, 100, 149–51, 199 n.4; patriarchal system, 54, 190 n.5; racial fluidity, 39–41, 188 n.21; rights and privileges of women, 55, 97–99; slavery, 34; Spanish indirect rule, 34–35, 37–39; terratenientes, 194 n.6; tribute requirements, 34–36, 187 n.9; tripartite racial system, 29–30, 33, 70

Comintern's two-stage revolution, 19

comunidad indígena of Diriomo, 9, 12, 184 n.31; canon de ley, 93; common land abolition, 72, 95, 170–71; common land expropriation, 69, 80–83, 88–89, 95–96; common land expropriation, early, 42–43, 45–52; common land jurisdiction, 57–64; common land usufruct rights, 93–94, 101–2; community unity activities, 76, 80–81, 133–34, 171, 195 n.30; conflict between leaders and comuneros, 84; control by local government, 58–59; denial of existence, 137–38; disputes with local government, 44–45; dissolution of political role, 69, 71, 72, 73, 95–96; Fiesta de la Virgen de la Candelaría, 45, 138, 139*p*; forced labor, 135; gender and poverty, 100–101; gender and property rights, 57–64, 97–104; Indians in census of 1883, 135, 136–37, 195 n.30; land rental, 41; population of 1776, 188 n.31; single motherhood, 64–67, 104–6; slash and burn agriculture, 89; uprisings of 1840s, 47–50

constitution of 1858, 71, 208 n.5

contra war of 1980s, 175–79; peasant participation, 8, 16; U.S. funding, 6, 8, 183 n.21

Corrigan, Philip, 54

Costa Rica, 30, 192 n.27

cotton cultivation, 147–48, 174

court testimony by peons and planters, 123–26, 129–34

creoles, 39–40

Cuadra, Francisco, 46

Cuadra, Gregorio, 84

Cuadra, Joaquín, 153, 195 n.24

Cuadra, Juan, 75–76

Cuadra, Vicente, 160

Dávila, Domingo, 139*p*, 162–63

debt peonage, 2, 3, 15, 17, 87, 110–48, 201 n.2; abolition in 1923, 120, 147, 167, 203 n.50; accommodations with patróns, 11, 112–13, 122–23, 144; additions to debts, 155–58; bonding methods, 123–24, 203 n.48; cash advances, 124–26; child peons, 65–66, 122, 125, 158–62, 165, 170; class basis, 20–24, 113, 116–18, 127–29, 135–38; coercion and consent, 10–11, 15, 23–26, 29, 95, 110–11, 113, 120–26, 132, 144–45, 163, 165–68; coffee industry's dependence on, 5, 110–11, 118–19, 202 n.26; community unity appeals, 133–34, 171; comparison to slavery, 113; contractual basis, 120–21, 135, 144, 151–52, 210 n.28; decline, 143–45, 147–48; enforcement, 112–13, 115–26, 131–32, 166–68, 204 n.59, 205 n.69; family obligations, 122, 124–25, 158–62, 170, 203 n.40, 210 n.28; feudal analysis, 145; funding methods, 116–17, 126; gendered analysis, 108, 122, 149–63; harvest festivals, 154; Knight's three categories of, 145–46, 165; legal system's role, 129–34,

169; middle peasants, 113, 125; money lending, 108; noncapitalist analysis, 110–14, 144–47, 208 nn.124–25; official race-blindness, 135; patriarchy from above, 149, 151–55, 165; patriarchy from below, 149, 158–62, 170; planters' pledges of protection, 121–22, 149–63, 167–68, 203 n.38; planters' uses of charity, 153–58; planters' violence, 156–58; poor peasants, 113, 124–25; potential for community violence, 127–29, 132, 204–5 n.66; punishment, 115–16, 131–32, 151, 169; race and ethnic relations, 113, 116, 134–43; regulatory legislation, 111–26, 129–34, 143–44, 201 n.9; resistance, 112, 126–29, 152–53, 167, 169; rich peasants, 125, 127, 129–31; rural magistrates, 114–15, 202 n.15; sexual violence, 158; taxation of peons as property, 94, 123; trabajo al empeño, 144; as transition to free wage labor, 110–14, 145–47, 164–65; wage rates, 125, 204 n.55; work passbooks, 113, 118, 119–20, 124, 131

Deere, Carmen Diana, 102–3

Defense of Community in Peru's Central Highlands, The (Mallon), 24

definitions: class, 21; ethnicity, 31; freedom, 22–23, 70; gender, 26–27; liberalism, 97–98; modes of production, 20, 184–85 n.8; race, 31; the state, 53–54

dependency theory, 19

Diriomo, 1, 14; Archivo Municipal de Diriomo (AMD), 9–10, 183 nn.25–26; denial of indigenous past, 138; indigenous past, 9, 12, 183 n.24, 184 n.31; *Pueblo de los Brujos* sign, 9, 138, 183 n.24. *See also* comunidad indígena of Diriomo; Mombacho Volcano region; municipal junta of Diriomo distribution of land in Diriomo, 88–92, 95–96; coffee estates on Mombacho, 89–92; commercial planters, 88–89; landless peasants, 88, 165, 174; middle peasants, 88; poor peasants, 88; rich peasants, 88–89; Sandinista Agrarian Reforms, 174–75, 178*p*

earthquake of 1931, 9

Echaverri, Doña Saula, 162–63

economic factors: banking, 87, 197–98 n.66; child support, 65–66, 193 nn.41–42; class stratification of land ownership, 57, 59; female heads-of-household, 104–7; feminization of privilege, 107; funding for coffee fincas, 71, 87; gender and poverty, 100–101; inheritance laws, 55–57, 99–104, 169, 199 n.6; landlessness, 88–89, 165, 174; liberal reforms, 70–72; marriage rates, 107; Marxist analysis, 6, 13, 19–24, 182 n.13; money lending, 108; nonmarket relations, 3; socialism, 7; state consolidation of agriculture, 147–48; trade and artisanal work, 106–8, 200 n.23. *See also* capitalist transitions; debt peonage; noncapitalist transitions

Eisenstuck, Sr., 203 n.38

ejidos del pueblo, 73, 87

elite classes. *See* class relations

El Progreso hacienda, 153–54

emancipated daughters, 99, 100, 150, 158

Engels, Friedrich, 105–6

Espinosa, Pablo, 46

ethnicity, 1, 11–13, 44; abolition of indigenous communities, 1–2, 9, 12–13, 170–71; Comaroff's views of, 32; debt peonage, 134–43; defining conditions of Indianness, 48, 52, 170–71; definition of, 31; distribution of land in Diriomo, 88–92; divide between Indians and ladinos, 44, 198 n.71; fluidity in postcolonial era, 59–60, 69, 92, 137, 170–71; Gilroy's views of self-identity, 31–32; Gould's views of Indian resistance to assimilation, 30–32; Indians' access to common land rights, 12–14, 31–32; mestizaje/forced assimilation, 11–13, 18, 30–32, 72, 137–38, 170–71; *mestizo* and *ladino* terminology, 13; planter class, 135–36; political power, 32, 54, 59–60; stereotypes of labor, 107–8, 117–19, 135–38; theoretical views, 13, 18, 29–32; Vincent's views of ethnic domination, 31–32; wealth, 59–60. *See also* debt peonage; indigenous groups

Fernández, Agapito, 153–54

Fernández, Francisco, 40

Fernández, Jacinto, 87, 197 n.65

Fernández, La Niña, 108

Fiesta de la Virgen de la Candelaría, 138, 139*p*

fincas. *See* coffee fincas

Flores, Valetín, 121

Flores Pérez, Doroteo, 140*p*

forced labor: coffee industry's dependence on, 110–11, 118–19; colonial era, 33–37, 95–96; enforcement methods, 112–13, 166–68; postcolonial period, 44–45, 50–51, 137, 196–97 n.52; regulatory laws, 111–20; as transition to free wage labor, 18–20, 110–14, 145–47. *See also* debt peonage

freedom, contradictory definition of, 22–23, 70

free wage labor, 3, 6, 18–24, 110–14, 145–47

Frente Sandinista de Liberación Nacional (FSLN), 6–8. *See also* Sandinista Revolution

Gámez, José Dolores, 46–47

gender relations, 1, 168–70, 191 n.17; capitalist transitions, 164; citizenship, 59, 63–64, 192 n.20; Civil Code of 1867, 56–57, 102–3, 190–91 nn.5–6; Civil Code of 1904, 56–57, 191 n.6; class relations, 28; debt peonage, 108, 149–63, 170; definition of gender, 26–27; double-sided nature of the patriarchal system, 26–29, 53–68, 98–99, 149–63; family basis of debt peonage, 122, 124–25, 158–62, 203 n.40, 210 n.28; family law, 64–67; female heads-of-households, 100–101, 104–7, 161, 169, 210 n.28; feminization of privilege, 106–7; gender blindness of labor laws, 159, 161; gender inequality of family law (patria potestad), 159, 161; inheritance and marital property laws, 55–57, 97–104, 169, 199 n.6; language conventions, 13; liberal reforms, 14–15, 97–109; in money lending activities, 108; moral codes of conduct, 14, 60–63; nonmarrying behavior, 105; patria potestad and potestad marital principles, 99, 100, 149–51, 158–59, 169, 199 n.4, 208 n.5; political power, 54, 58–59, 63–64, 191 n.19; property rights, 2, 15, 17, 57–64, 97–104, 169, 191 nn.14–15, 199 n.6; rights of married women, 56–57, 97–99, 158–62, 190–91 nn.8–9; rights of single mothers, 64–67, 104–7, 193 nn.41–42; role of Catholic Church, 56–57; secularization of marriage, 55, 56–57, 63; sexual violence, 61–63, 158; theoretical views, 13, 17–18, 26–29; in trade and artisanal work, 106–8, 200 n.23; usufruct rights, 55, 58, 101–2. *See also* patriarchal system

gender theory, 26–29; Joan Scott's analysis, 26–27; Stern's reciprocal pacts, 28–29, 169; Thompson's moral economy of the poor, 28; Weber's patrimonial networks, 28

geography of Nicaragua, 13

González Vílchez, Licenciado Alfredo, 183 n.25

Gould, Jeffrey, 11–13, 30–32, 120, 145, 168, 170, 208 n.129

Gramscian analysis of consent, 25–26

Granada: coffee estates on Mombacho Volcano, 75–76, 89–90, 91*p*, 92; coffee production, 89, 198 n.69, 198 n.71; colonial period, 35; Mombacho Volcano region property claims, 74, 75–76, 80–83, 171, 197 n.63, 197 n.65; murder of Santiago Rodríguez, 77, 85, 86; privatization of land, 69, 85–87, 194–95 n.16, 195 n.24; stereotypes of Diriomeños, 136. *See also* Mombacho Volcano region; oligarchy of Granada

Granera, Víctor, 124–25

Great Transformation, The (Polanyi), 22–24

Guatemala, 30

Hartmann, Heidi, 27

Hernández, Pedro, 38

historic overview, 1–2, 14, 181 n.2; bourgeois revolution, 4–7; colonial period, 14, 18, 29–30, 33–42, 188 n.12; comunidad indígena of Diriomo, 9, 12, 184 n.31; constitutions and charters, 50, 63; early expropriation of common lands, 42–50; independence, 43–44, 168; intraelite warfare of the postcolonial era, 44, 46, 48, 50, 74, 98, 189 n.42; local archives, 9–10; national politics, 4–5; postcolonial period, 14, 44–68; racial status under Spanish, 29–30, 33, 39–41; Spanish patriarchal system, 54, 190 n.5; uprisings of 1840s, 14, 46–50

Huasipungo (Icaza), 113

Icaza, Jorge, 113

Imperialismo y dictadura: Crisis de una formación social (Wheelock Román), 7–8, 24

indigenous groups, 14; acceptance of colonial rule, 38–39; biological breakdown of racial groups, 136–37; citizenship, 59, 63–64, 192 n.20; clothing, 138; cofradías, 41; common land abolition, 5, 9, 17, 72, 95, 170–71; common land jurisdiction, 57–64; common lands expropriations, 42–50; common land usufruct rights, 12–14, 31–35, 45–50, 55, 58, 74, 93–94, 101–2, 137; conflict between leaders and comuneros, 14, 36–38, 50–52, 84, 95–96; debt peonage, 134–43; defining conditions of Indianness, 48, 52, 95–96, 137, 170–71; double role of local leaders, 33, 36–37, 50–52; forced assimilation, 1–2, 5, 12–13, 18, 29–32, 72, 137–38; forced labor, 14, 33–37, 44–45, 135, 137, 196–97 n.52; gender and property rights, 57–64, 97–104, 191 nn.14–15; Gilroy's views of self-identity, 31–32; ladino political power over, 44–45, 53–54, 58–59; racial and ethnic fluidity, 39–41, 59, 69, 92, 137, 170–71; resistance to mestizaje, 11–13, 30–31; rustic enlightenment period, 44; Spanish tripartite racial system, 29–30, 33, 70; stereotypes, 107–8, 117–19, 135–38; uprisings of 1840s, 14, 46–50; use of the legal system, 38–39, 42–43, 60–63. *See also* alcaldes indígenas; comunidad indígena of Diriomo; ethnicity; privatization of land

Instituto de Estudios de Sandinismo, 8

jornaleros, 107–8

jueces de agricultura, 114–15, 202 n.15

Jungle Novels (Traven), 113, 201 n.6

junta municipal. *See* local government; municipal junta of Diriomo

justice system. *See* legal system

Kandiyoti, Deniz, 100

Kinloch Tijerino, Frances, 46–47

Knight, Alan, 125, 145–46, 165

labor relations: capitalist and non-capitalist appropriation, 21, 143–44; children, 65–66, 122, 125, 158–62, 165, 170; coffee industry needs, 110–11, 118–19, 120, 202 n.26; forced labor of colonial era, 33–37, 95–96; forced labor of postcolonial period, 44–45, 50–51, 110–14, 135, 137, 196–97 n.52; free wage labor, 3, 6, 21–24, 110–14, 164–65; gender analysis, 27, 149–63; gender blindness of labor laws, 159, 161; indigenous population's labor stereotypes, 107–8, 117–19; linkage of work with protection, 121–22, 149–63, 167–68, 203 n.38; modes of production, 20, 184–85 n.8; nature of markets, 21–24; peasants' prioritization of subsistence production, 25–26, 95, 111–12, 126–27, 159–60, 170, 198–99 nn.78–79; seasonal needs of coffee industry, 95, 198–99 nn.78–79; slavery, 34, 113; surplus value, 21; taxation, debt peons as property, 94, 123; transitions to capitalism, 18–20, 110–14, 145–47; wage labor, 147–48. *See also* debt peonage; peasantry

ladinos, 13, 168, 198 n.69; emergence as non-Indian grouping, 44; expropriations of Indian common land, 45–50; gender and property rights, 57–64; land rental from Indi-

ladinos (*continued*)
ans, 57; moral codes of conduct, 14,
60–63; political power, 44–45, 53–54,
66–67; regulation of gender norms,
63–67; sexual violence, 61–63
La Laguna del Apoyo, 57
landholding, 165; colonial corporate land grants, 70–72, 95–96, 194
nn.5–6; common lands of indigenous
groups, 12–14, 31–32, 34–35, 42–50,
170–71; early expropriation of common lands, 42–50, 188 n.31; ejidos, 73,
87; gender and property rights, 57–
64, 97–104; inheritance and marital
property laws, 55–57, 99–104, 169,
199 n.6; Masaya land dispute, 42–43,
188 n.31; mejoras (improvements), 57,
74, 192 n.21; in noncapitalist systems,
21–22; rentals of common lands, 57;
Sandinista land distribution, 6–7, 8,
16, 172–77, 178p, 179–80; stratification by wealth, 57; subsistence level,
88, 95, 198–99 n.78, 199 n.79; transitions to capitalism, 22–23; usufruct
rights, 45–46, 55, 58, 74, 93–94. *See
also* privatization of land
Larson, Brooke, 30
late capitalist development, 143–45,
147–48
legal system: bias toward planters, 153,
156; colonial period, 38–39, 55, 97–
98; enforcement of debt peonage,
112–13, 115–26, 129–34, 166–69; familial basis of debt peonage, 160–61;
land disputes, 42–43, 75, 77, 81–83;
moral codes of conduct, 14, 60–63;
parentage and single motherhood,
64–67, 104–7, 193 nn.41–42; peasants'
use of, 132–33; uxoricide, 56; women's
legal status, 55–57, 61
legislative regulation: Civil Code of
1867, 56–57, 102–3, 190–91 nn.5–6;

Civil Code of 1904, 56–57, 191 n.6;
debt peonage, 111–26, 129–34, 143–44,
169, 201 n.9; gender blindness of labor
laws, 159, 161; gender inequality of
family law (patria potestad), 159, 161;
inheritance and marital property laws,
55–57, 99–104, 169, 199 n.6; patria potestad and potestad marital principles,
99, 100, 149–51, 169, 199 n.4, 208 n.5;
privatization of land, 71; public vs.
private administration of justice, 151
León, Magdalena, 102–3
liberalism: administration of justice, 151;
assimilation of indigenous groups,
134; citizenship, 98; definitions, 97–
98; forced labor, 110, 133, 150–51; free
wage labor, 3, 6, 21–24, 70; gendered
contradictions, 97–109; individuation of women, 102; private property,
5, 70–72, 98; trade regulations, 98;
women's property rights, 97–104
local government, 44–45, 168; emergence of private property, 94–95;
enforcement of debt peonage, 116–
19; secularization of marriage, 55,
56–57, 63. *See also* municipal junta of
Diriomo; patriarchal system
local microhistories, 4
López, Diego, 40
López, Francisco, 51
López, Mercedes, 51
López, Procopio, 75
López, Santiago, 66
López, Simón, 37
López, Vicenta, 161–62

Malespin, Ynocente, 197 n.63
Mallon, Florencia, 24
Managua earthquake of 1931, 9
map of Nicaragua, xiv
March to the Montería (Traven), 113
Marcía, Andrés, 66, 130, 193 n.41

Marcía, José María, 160

Markels, Julian, 201 n.6

markets in noncapitalist and capitalist systems, 20–24, 94–95, 165–66

market societies. See capitalist transitions

marriage: common-law unions, 104–5; economic status, 107; husbands' control over wives, 99, 100, 149–51, 169, 199 n.4; joint property rights, 99, 102–3; legal rights of wives, 56–57, 99, 150, 160–62, 165, 190–91 nn.8–9; rates, 64, 100, 104, 107, 193 n.35, 200 n.24; secularization, 55, 56–57, 63

Marxian Imagination, The (Markels), 201 n.6

Marxist analysis, 13; agrarian capitalism, 24–26; Brenner's views of agrarian capitalist development, 24–25, 144, 164–67; class relations, 21; exploitation, 21; free wage labor, 21–24; history, 1, 181 n.2; labor power, 21; landlord-peasant relations, 24–26; modes of production, 20, 184–85 n.8; of patriarchy, 27–28; Polanyi's observations of markets, 20–24, 94–95, 165–66; rural proletariat, 7–8, 24, 173, 175–76; Sandinista's historical analysis, 172–74; Scott's theories of peasant resistance, 25–26, 167–68; surplus value, 21; transitions to capitalism, 6, 19–20, 182 n.13

Marzilla, Andrés de, 40

Masaya, 1, 42–43, 188 n.31

matrícula (debt peonage contract), 120–22

Mayorga, Solomon, 126–27

McCreery, David, 122, 168, 198 n.78

Mejía, Alejandro: declarations of generosity, 154; ethnicity, 90–92, 136, 138; treatment of debt peons, 129–30, 153–54, 156, 160

Meseta de los Pueblos, 1

mestizaje, 11–13, 18, 30–31, 72, 170–71

mestizos, 13, 30, 40, 136, 188 n.21

Mexico, 30, 43, 146

Ministry of Agriculture and Agrarian Reform (MIDINRA), 8

Ministry of Internal Commerce (MICOIN), 6

modernity, 5–6

modes of production, definition, 20, 184–85 n.8

molendera work, 107–8

Mombacho Volcano region, 9, 42, 57; coffee estates, 75–76, 89–90, 91*p*, 92, 194–95 n.16; coffee harvest timeframe, 111; coffee production, 89, 198 n.69, 198 n.71; debt peonage, 119–28, 202 n.26; private property claims, 74–76, 80–86, 171, 195 n.24, 197 nn.63, 65; riot of 1889, 127–29; Sandinista's land distribution, 174; women's land ownership, 103–4

money lending, 108

Montgomery, David, 201 n.10

Morales, Yndalecio, 80, 196 n.43

Morel, Bishop, 41

mulattos, 12, 40, 136

municipal junta of Diriomo, 44–45, 53–54, 58–59; appointment of alcalde indígena, 45; awards of derecho de posesión, 77, 94; census categories, 107–8; coffee production, 74; collaboration by the alcaldes indígenas, 69, 73–74, 84, 95–96, 196–97 n.52; community unity appeals, 76, 80–81, 133–34, 171, 195 n.30; distribution of land in early 1900s, 88–92; ejidos del pueblo, 87; enforcement of debt peonage, 120, 126–29, 144, 204 n.59, 205 n.69; ladino political power, 44–45; Mombacho Volcano land disputes, 75–76, 80–83, 85–87, 197 n.63, 197 n.65; moral codes of conduct, municipal junta of Diriomo (*continued*) 14, 60–63; owners of private property, 78–79, 197 n.57; parentage and single motherhood, 64–67, 104–7, 193 nn.41–42; Plan de Arbitrios of 1873, 78–79, 196 n.39; privatization of land, 69, 73–94; regulation of trade and artisanal work, 106–8, 200 n.23; rural magistrates' regulation of forced labor, 114–15, 202 n.15; secularization of marriage, 63; taboo on use of racial or ethnic descriptors, 135; taxes, 79, 93–94, 123; water rights, 79–80, 196 n.41

Muños, Hijinos, 124

Namier, Lewis, 57, 191 n.10

National Union of Farmers and Ranchers, 175

National War, 74, 75–76, 195 n.21

nation-state formation: abolition of communal landholding, 72; codification of political power, 63–64; secularization of marriage, 55, 56–57, 63; subsidies of coffee production, 71

Negroponte, John, 183 n.21

Newson, Linda, 36, 188 n.12

Nicaragua: Identidad y cultura política (Kinloch Tijerino), 46–47

Nicaraguan Census Bureau, 136–37

Niquinohomo, 1

noncapitalist transitions, 3–4; access to land, 21–22; coexistence with capitalism, 20; debt peonage, 144–47, 163, 208 nn.124–25; forced labor systems, 21, 110–14; land privatization, 94–96; societies with markets, 21–24, 165–66. *See also* patriarchal system

non-Indians, 12–13

nonmarket relations, 3. *See also* debt peonage; noncapitalist transitions; patriarchal system; Polanyi, Karl

Nororis, José Jesus, 125

Norton, Anne, 211 n.1

oligarchy of Granada, 168; coffee estates, 75–76, 80, 89–92; distribution of land in Diriomo, 88–92; intraelite conflict, 44, 46, 48, 50, 74, 98, 133, 189 n.42; land title acquisition, 86–87; money lending, 108; murder of Santiago Rodríguez, 77, 85, 86; privatization of common lands, 69, 72, 74–77, 80–83, 95–96; racial stereotypes of lower classes, 136; women land ownership, 103–4

oral history, 10–11

Origin of the Family, Private Property, and the State (Engels), 105–6

Ortega, Nilo, 79–80

Orwell, George, 8

paternity cases, 65–67, 193 nn.41–42

patria potestad and potestad marital principles, 99, 149–51, 158–59, 169, 199 n.4; gender inequality, 159, 161; property rights, 100; rights of sons, 150, 208 n.5

patriarchal system, 2–3, 14–17, 53–68; authority and protection dialectic, 54–55; benefits of patronage relations, 11, 112–13, 122–23, 144; child support, 65–66, 193 nn.41–42; Civil Code of 1867, 56–57, 102–3, 190–91 nn.5–6; Civil Code of 1904, 56–57, 191 n.6; clientelism of debt peonage system, 112–13; codification of political power, 63–64; coercion and consent, 10–11, 15, 23–26, 95, 165; colonial period, 54, 190 n.5; emancipated daughters, 99, 100, 150, 158; family law, 64–67; gender analysis, 15–16, 26–29, 53–68, 149–63, 168–70; historic basis, 54, 190 n.5; inheritance and marital property laws, 55–57, 99–104, 169, 199 n.6; lack of gender analysis, 27–28; moral codes of conduct, 14, 60–63; nonmarrying behavior, 105; patria potestad and potestad marital principles, 99, 100, 149–51, 158–59, 169, 199 n.4, 208 n.5; pledges of protection, 121–22, 149–63, 167–68, 203 n.38; property rights, 57–64, 191 nn.14–15; resistance to capitalism, 24–26; rights of married women, 55, 56–57, 97–99, 150, 190–91 nn.8–9; rights of single mothers, 64–67, 104–7, 193 nn.41–42; role in coffee industry, 150–51, 161–63, 208 n.1; secularization of marriage, 55, 56–57, 63; Stern's reciprocal pacts, 28–29, 169; theoretical views, 13, 18, 24–29; Thompson's moral economy of the poor, 28; Weber's patrimonial networks, 28; widow's rights, 55, 60, 99, 103–4, 105, 193 n.42. *See also* debt peonage; noncapitalist transitions; oligarchy of Granada

patriarchy from above, 2, 15–17, 29, 149, 151–55, 169, 181 n.6

patriarchy from below, 2, 15–17, 29, 149, 158–62, 170, 181 n.6

peasantry, 139–42, 143*p*; accommodation with authority, 11, 28, 112–13, 144; agrarian reforms, 8; alternative precapitalist framework, 26; civilian enforcement of debt peonage, 127; distribution of land in Diriomo, 88–90; funding of private property, 87; labor requirements, 5; landless peasants, 88, 165, 174; landlord-peasant relations, 24–26; middle peasants, 88, 113, 125; noncapitalist systems, 20; opposition to Sandinistas, 8, 16, 176; patriarchy from below, 2, 15–16, 17, 29, 149, 158–62, 170, 181 n.6; poor peasants, 88, 107–8, 113, 117–

19, 124–25, 135–38; prioritization of subsistence production, 25–26, 95, 111–12, 126–27, 159–60, 170, 198–99 nn.78–79; private property revolution, 72, 77–87, 96, 170–71, 197 n.64, 198 n.67; resistance to capitalism, 24–26; rich peasants, 88–89, 125, 127, 129–31; Sandinistas' Agrarian Reform, 172, 173*t*, 174–76, 177*t*, 178–80; stereotypes of peasants, 107–8, 117–19, 135–38; subsistence agriculture, 3, 88, 95, 107–8, 126–27, 159–60, 198–99 nn.78–79; use of legal system, 132–33; women land ownership, 103–4; work passbooks, 113, 118, 119–20, 124, 131. *See also* debt peonage; labor relations

peons. *See* debt peonage

Pérez, Francisco, 46, 80, 84, 196–97 n.52

Pérez, Mercedes, 129–30

Pérez, Teodoro, 51

Phillips, Anne, 103

planters: enforcement of debt peonage, 112–13, 115–26, 131–32, 166–68, 203 nn.45, 48, 205 n.69; patriarchy from above, 2, 15–17, 29, 149, 151–55, 169; pledges of protection, 121–22, 149–63, 167–68, 203 n.38; racial and ethnic issues, 135–36; sexual violence, 158; uses of charity, 153–58; uses of violence, 156–58. *See also* debt peonage; patriarchal system

Polanyi, Karl, 13, 18, 20–24, 165–66; noncapitalist and capitalist markets, 21–22, 94–95, 113; noncapitalist labor regimes, 144, 163, 166

political elite, 2, 4–5; codification of power, 63–64; "Freedom of property" banner, 5; intragroup warfare of the postcolonial era, 44, 46, 48, 50, 189 n.42; regulation of gender, 14

political history of Nicaragua, 4–5

political power, 165; class basis, 21, 53–54; dissolution of political role of comunidad indígena, 69, 71, 72; gendered structures, 27, 58–59, 63–64, 191 n.19; ladinos in local governments, 44–45, 53–54, 58–59, 63–64, 66; leadership of ethnic groups, 32; moral codes of conduct, 14, 60–63; privatization of land, 69, 73–87, 166, 196 n.36, 196 n.39, 197 n.57

postcolonial period, 44–68; constitutions and charters, 50, 63; double role of local leaders, 50–52; early expropriations of common lands, 45–52; gender and property rights, 57–64, 97–104, 191 nn.14–15; intraelite warfare, 38, 44, 46, 50, 74, 98, 189 n.42; jurisdiction of common lands, 57–64; labor requirements, 44–45, 50–51, 135, 196–97 n.52; ladino political power, 44–45, 50–52, 58–59; local governance authority and structures, 44–45, 50–51; rights and privileges of women, 55–57, 190–91 nn.8–9; uprisings of 1840s, 14, 46–50

potestad marital, 99

precapitalism. *See* noncapitalist transitions

privatization of land, 1–2, 5, 13, 14, 69–96, 165; boundary disputes, 85; claim procedures, 78; coexistence with communal property, 79–81, 93–94; coffee industry, 71–72, 194–95 n.16; collaboration of indigenous leaders, 69, 73–74, 84, 170–71, 196–97 n.52; colonial corporate land grants, 70–72, 95–96, 194 nn.5–6; common land abolition, 5, 9, 17, 72, 95, 170–71; common land auctions, 78; consolidation, 85–87; debt peonage, 110–11; Decree on Indigenous Communities and Ejidal Lands (1906), 72; derecho

de posesión, 77, 94; early activity, 74; ethnicity, 88–92; "Freedom of property" banner, 5; gender, 97–104, 169, 199 n.6; Indian land ownership, 31; land rights barters, 81; legal disputes, 75–77, 81–83; liberalism, 70–72; noncapitalist forms, 94–96, 166; peasantization, 96, 170–71, 197 n.64, 198 n.67; political power, 69, 73–87, 166, 196 n.36, 196 n.39, 197 n.57; poverty, 101–2; privatization fees, 78–79, 196 n.39; property taxes, 79, 93–94; regulatory legislation, 71; resistance activities, 77–78, 82–85; rights of way debates, 75; small landholders, 69, 86, 170; timeframe, 87–88; title acquisitions, 86–87; uprisings of 1840s, 14, 47–50. *See also* distribution of land in Diriomo

race and race relations, 44; African descent, 31; biological breakdown of groups, 136–37; colonial tripartite system, 29–30, 33, 70; debt peonage, 134–43; definition of race, 31; Gilroy's views of self-identity, 31–32; Gould's views of Indian resistance to assimilation, 30–32; Indian category, 33; landholding rights, 70; mestizaje/forced assimilation, 11–13, 18, 30–32, 72, 137–38; mixed race terms, 12, 13, 30, 39–40; planter class, 135–36; postcolonial repression of lower classes, 30; racial fluidity, 39–41, 137, 188 n.21; Wade's usage of race vs. ethnicity, 31. *See also* ethnicity

Ramírez, Casimiro, 154

Ramírez, Enrique, 11

Ramírez Pérez, Carmen, 138, 141*p*, 163

Reagan, Ronald, 6, 176–80, 183 n.21

research methods: archival research, 9–10, 113, 158, 162; comparison with other research, 16; microhistory, 10; oral histories, 137–38, 158, 162; oral history interview method, 10–11, 113–14

Reyes, Concepción, 132

Ríos, Tiburcio, 153

riot of 1889 in Diriomo, 127–29

Rodríguez, Santiago, 86

Rodríguez Ramírez, Enrique, 11, 140*p*

Romero Vargas, Germán, 38–39

rural police, 127

Salazar, Francisco, 90*p*

Salazar Castillo, Leticia, 143*p*

Salazar Castillo, Orlando, 156, 157*p*

Sandinista Revolution, 1, 6, 171–80; Agrarian Reforms, 6–7, 8, 16, 76, 92, 172–80; contra war, 6, 8, 16, 175–79, 183 n.21; electoral defeat in 1990, 16, 176–80; food production and distribution, 6; funding challenges, 179; historical analysis, 7–8, 168, 171–80, 211 n.1; land distribution, 6–8, 16, 76, 92, 172, 173*t*, 174–176, 177*t*, 178*p*, 179–80; Marxist analysis, 172–74; peasant opposition, 8, 16, 176; rural proletariat, 7, 173, 175–76; views of capitalism in Nicaragua, 172–74

Sandino, Augusto César, 1

Sayer, Derek, 54

Scott, James C., 13, 25–26, 28, 167–68

Scott, Joan, 13, 18, 26–27

Secret History of Gender, The (Stern), 11, 28–29

socialism. *See* Sandinista Revolution

societies with markets. *See* noncapitalist transitions; Polanyi, Karl

Somoza, Bernabé, 47–49

Somoza (Anastasio) regime, 6, 7, 172–73

state, definition, 53–54

state farms, 8, 16

Stern, Steve J., 11, 13, 18, 28–29, 38, 169

Stiglitz, Joseph E., 22–24

subsistence agriculture, 3, 88, 95, 107–8, 198–99 n.78, 199 n.79; clash with coffee harvest, 111–12, 126–27; male roles in, 159–60, 170; Sandinistas' discouragement of, 174

telegraph communication, 128–29

Telles, Julio, 152–53

terratenientes, 194 n.6

theoretical framework, 13, 17–32; articulation of modes of production theory, 20; Brenner's analysis of coercion, 24–25, 144, 164–67; capitalist transitions, 18–29, 144–46, 164–68; Comaroff's views of ethnicity and class, 32; dependency theory, 19; ethnicity and assimilation, 29–32; gender analysis, 26–29; Gilroy's views of self-identity, 31–32; Gould's views of Indian resistance to assimilation, 30–32; landlord-peasant relations, 24–26; Marxist analysis, 20–22; Polanyi's analysis of markets, 20–24, 94–95, 165–66; Scott's theories of peasant resistance, 25–26, 167–68; Vincent's views of ethnic domination, 31–32; world systems theory, 19

Thompson, E. P., 28

Tifer, Luis Felípe, 87, 133–34, 136, 197 n.65

Tisma dispute over common lands, 42–43

To Die in This Way: Nicaraguan Indians and the Myth of Mestizaje (Gould), 30–31, 170

Topik, Steven, 208 n.125

Traven, B., 113, 201 n.6

Trials of Nation Making (Larson), 30

Unión Nacional de Agricultores y Ganaderos (UNAG), 175

Unión Nacional Opositora (UNO), 179–80

United States: abolition of debt peonage in Nicaragua, 120, 147; funding of the *contras*, 6, 8, 175–78, 183 n.21; interventions in Nicaragua, 4, 72, 120, 147, 175–79, 195 n.21, 197–98 n.66; neocolonial relationships in Central America, 4; Nicaraguan elections of 1990, 179; support of Somoza regime, 172

Urtecho, Juan, 123

uxoricide, 56

Valle, José María, 47

Vallecío, Luiza, 66–67, 193 n.41

Vásquez, Emilio, 156, 157*p*

Vásquez, Olaya, 60–61

Vijil, Padre Agustín, 64

Vincent, Joan, 29–30, 171

Wade, Peter, 31

Walker, William, 195 n.21

Walter, Knut, 208 n.129

Weber, Max, 28

Wheelock Román, Jaime, 7–8, 24, 172–74

Which Equalities Matter? (Phillips), 103

women, 104–5; Civil Code of 1867, 56–57, 102–3, 190 nn.5–6; Civil Code of 1904, 56–57, 190 n.6; colonial-era rights and privileges, 55, 97–99; debt peonage, 122, 158–62, 165, 170, 203 n.40, 210 n.28; double morality standards, 14, 60–63; emancipated daughters, 99, 100, 150, 158; family basis of debt peonage, 158–62, 165, 210 n.28; feminization of privilege, 107; heads-of-households, 100–101, 104–7, 161, 169, 210 n.28; individuation, 102; inheritance and marital property rights, 55–57, 97–104, 169, 199 n.6; legal existence, 55; legal rights of wives, 56–57, 99, 150, 160–62, 165, 190–91 n.8, 191 n.9; marriage rates, 64, 100, 193 n.35, 200 n.24; money lending, 108; nonmarrying behavior, 64, 100, 104–7, 193 n.35; participation in commerce, 106–8, 165, 200 n.23; patria potestad and potestad marital principles, 99, 100, 149–51, 158–59, 169, 199 n.4; property rights, 2, 15, 17, 57–64, 97–104, 169, 199 n.6; rights and privileges, 55–57, 64–67, 98–99, 104–5, 190–91 n.8, 191 n.9, 193 nn.41–42; sexual violence, 61–63, 158; single motherhood, 64–67, 104–6, 193 nn.41–42; usufruct rights, 101–2; widow's rights, 55, 60, 99, 103–4, 105, 158, 162–63, 193 n.42

world systems theory, 19

zambos, 12, 136

Zambrano, Ramona, 203 n.38

Zelaya, José Santos, 7, 72, 133, 198 n.71; assimilation of indigenous people, 134; debt peonage system, 117–20; overthrow in 1909, 120

Elizabeth Dore is a Reader in Latin American History
at the University of Southampton.

Library of Congress Cataloging-in-Publication Data

Dore, Elizabeth.

Myths of modernity : peonage and patriarchy

in Nicaragua / Elizabeth Dore.

p. cm.

Includes bibliographical references and index.

ISBN 0-8223-3686-3 (cloth : alk. paper)

ISBN 0-8223-3674-X (pbk. : alk. paper)

1. Social stratification—Nicaragua—Diriomo (Municipio)

2. Peonage—Nicaragua—Diriomo (Municipio) 3. Patriarchy—

Nicaragua—Diriomo (Municipio) 4. Peasantry—Nicaragua—Diriomo

(Municipio) 5. Diriomo (Nicaragua : Municipio)—Ethnic relations.

6. Sex role—Nicaragua—Diriomo (Municipio) 7. Diriomo (Nicaragua :

Municipio)—Social conditions. 8. Diriomo (Nicaragua : Municipio)—History.

I. Title.   HN170.D57D67 2006

305.5'12'09728515—dc22   2005015955